MULTICULTURAL EDUCATION SERIES

James A. Banks, Series Editor

(continued)

DIVERSITY AND EQUITY IN SCIENCE EDUCATION

RESEARCH, POLICY, AND PRACTICE

Okhee Lee
Cory A. Buxton

Teachers College
Columbia University
New York and London

Published by Teachers College Press, 1234 Amsterdam Avenue, New York, NY 10027

Library of Congress Cataloging-in-Publication Data

Lee, Okhee, 1959–
  Diversity and equity in science education : research, policy, and practice / Okhee Lee, Cory A. Buxton.
      p. cm. — (Multicultural education series.)
  Includes bibliographical references and index.
  ISBN 978-0-8077-5068-1 (pbk. : alk. paper) —ISBN 978-0-8077-5069-8 (hardcover : alk. paper) 1. Science—Study and teaching—United States. 2. Multicultural education—United States. I. Buxton, Cory A. II. Title.
  LB1585.3.L439 2010
  507.1073—dc22

                                                                    2009054156

ISBN 978-0-8077-5068-1 (paperback)
ISBN 978-0-8077-5069-8 (hardcover)

Printed on acid-free paper
Manufactured in the United States of America

17 16 15 14 13 12 11 10   8 7 6 5 4 3 2 1

Contents

PART IV: CALL FOR ACTION

Series Foreword

The nation's deepening ethnic texture, interracial tension and conflict, and the increasing percentage of students who speak a first language other than English (Suárez-Orozco, Suárez-Orozco, & Todorova, 2008) make multicultural education imperative. The U.S. Census (2008) projects that ethnic minorities will increase from one-third of the nation's population in 2006 to 50% in 2042 (Roberts, 2008). Ethnic minorities made up 100 million of the total U.S. population of just over 300 million in 2006.

American classrooms are experiencing the largest influx of immigrant students since the beginning of the 20th century. About a million immigrants are making the United States their home each year (Martin & Midgley, 1999). Between 1997 and 2006, 9,105,162 immigrants entered the United States (U.S. Department of Homeland Security, 2007). Only 15% came from nations in Europe. Most came from nations in Asia, from Mexico, and from nations in Latin America, Central America, and the Caribbean (U.S. Department of Homeland Security, 2007). A large but undetermined number of undocumented immigrants also enter the United States each year. In 2007, The *New York Times* estimated that there were 12 million illegal immigrants in the United States ("Immigration Sabotage," 2007). The influence of an increasingly ethnically diverse population on U.S. schools, colleges, and universities is and will continue to be enormous.

Schools in the United States are characterized by rich ethnic, cultural, linguistic, and religious diversity. United States schools are more diverse today than they have been since the early 1900s when a flood of immigrants entered the U.S. from Southern, Central, and Eastern Europe. In the 34-year period between 1973 and 2007, the percentage of students of color in U.S. public schools increased from 22 to 55% (Dillon, 2006; National Center for Education Statistics, 2008). If current trends continue, students of color will equal or exceed the percentage of White students in U.S. public schools within one or two decades. In 2004, students of color exceeded the number of White students in six states: California, Hawaii, Louisiana, Mississippi, New Mexico, and Texas.

Language and religious diversity is also increasing in the U.S. student population. In 2000, about 20% of the school-age population spoke a language at home other than English (U.S. Census Bureau, 2003). The Progressive Policy Institute

(2008) estimated that 50 million Americans (out of 300 million) spoke a language at home other than English in 2008. Harvard professor Diana L. Eck (2001) calls the United States the "most religiously diverse nation on earth" (p. 4). Islam is now the fastest-growing religion in the United States as well as in several European nations such as France, the United Kingdom, and The Netherlands (Banks, 2009; Cesari, 2004). Most teachers now in the classroom and in teacher education programs are likely to have students from diverse ethnic, racial, linguistic, and religious groups in their classrooms during their careers. This is true for both inner-city and suburban teachers in the United States as well as in many other Western nations (Banks, 2009).

An important goal of multicultural education is to improve race relations and to help all students acquire the knowledge, attitudes, and skills needed to participate in cross-cultural interactions and in personal, social, and civic action that will help make the United States more democratic and just. Multicultural education is consequently as important for middle-class White suburban students as it is for students of color who live in the inner city. Multicultural education fosters the public good and the overarching goals of the commonwealth.

The major purpose of the *Multicultural Education Series* is to provide pre-service educators, practicing educators, graduate students, scholars, and policy makers with an interrelated and comprehensive set of books that summarizes and analyzes important research, theory, and practice related to the education of ethnic, racial, cultural, and linguistic groups in the United States and the education of mainstream students about diversity. The books in the *Series* provide research, theoretical, and practical knowledge about the behaviors and learning characteristics of students of color, language-minority students, and low-income students. They also provide knowledge about ways to improve academic achievement and race relations in educational settings.

The definition of multicultural education in the *Handbook of Research on Multicultural Education* (Banks & Banks, 2004) is used in the *Series:* Multicultural education is "a field of study designed to increase educational equity for all students that incorporates, for this purpose, content, concepts, principles, theories, and paradigms from history, the social and behavioral sciences, and particularly from ethnic studies and women's studies" (p. xii). In the *Series*, as in the *Handbook*, multicultural education is considered a *metadiscipline.*

The dimensions of multicultural education, developed by Banks (2004) and described in the *Handbook of Research on Multicultural Education*, provide the conceptual framework for the development of the publications in the *Series*. They are: *content integration, the knowledge construction process, prejudice reduction, an equity pedagogy,* and *an empowering school culture and social structure.* To implement multicultural education effectively, teachers and administrators must attend to each of the five dimensions. They should use content from diverse groups when teaching concepts and skills, help students to understand how knowledge in the

various disciplines is constructed, help students to develop positive intergroup attitudes and behaviors, and modify their teaching strategies so that students from
different racial, cultural, linguistic, and social class groups will experience equal
educational opportunities. The total environment and culture of the school must
also be transformed so that students from diverse groups will experience equal
status in the culture and life of the school.

Although the five dimensions of multicultural education are highly interrelated, each requires deliberate attention and focus. Each publication in the series focuses on one or more of the dimensions, although each book deals with all
of them to some extent because of the highly interrelated characteristics of the
dimensions.

A high level of scientific literacy is essential for productive work and to be an
effective citizen in our globalized world society. Lee and Buxton make it explicit
why scientific literacy is imperative in this well-researched and informative book.
They describe how scientific knowledge is needed for citizens to understand and
take effective actions on issues such as the reduction of greenhouse gases and the
obesity epidemic in the United States.

Serious problems exist in the achievement of U.S. students in science. They
perform less well on international achievement tests in science than students
in most other developed nations. A serious gap also exists between the science
achievement of White mainstream students, some groups of Asian American students, and students from other racial and ethnic groups. Low-income students
and students who are English language learners are also underachieving in science. This significant, timely, and useful book provides researchers, policy makers, teachers, curriculum specialists, administrators, and other educators with the
knowledge, understandings, and empirical knowledge needed to reform science
teaching and learning so that students from diverse racial, ethnic, cultural, and
linguistic groups will have an equal opportunity to learn science and to become
scientifically literate citizens.

Lee and Buxton present an ingenious way to conceptualize and think about
achievement in science. They maintain that educators need to think of achievement in science as broader than scores on standardized tests. They identify two
significant indicators of achievement in science—whether students develop identities as science learners and acquire individual agency. On nearly every page on
this skillfully crafted and erudite book, the authors describe empirically supported
ways to reform science teaching and learning that will help students from marginalized and underachieving groups attain identities as science learners and develop
agency.

A predominant theme in this book is that effective and culturally responsive science teaching must draw upon and use the knowledge about science that
students bring to school from their families and communities. Lee and Buxton
describe imaginative ways in which teachers can help students bridge the cultural

divide between home and school knowledge. They also discuss continuities and discontinuities between science in the homes of students from marginalized groups and school science. When home knowledge is inconsistent with the scientific knowledge taught in school, the authors encourage teachers to show respect and recognition for students' cultural knowledge and to use it to help students understand school science.

This notable book has several distinguishing characteristics that make it a unique contribution to the literature on science education and multicultural teaching and learning. It applies the theory of culturally responsive teaching to an academic school subject that students from many marginalized and vulnerable groups find alienating; it explicates ways in which science is a socially and culturally constructed discipline; and it challenges scientific universalism and describes how multicultural perspectives in science can enrich science as well as science teaching. The authors have accomplished a rare feat that promises to give this book a long shelf life—they have written a volume replete with citations of research studies and empirical insights that is compelling, practical, lucid, and engaging.

James A. Banks

REFERENCES

Banks, J. A. (2004). Multicultural education: Historical development, dimensions, and practice. In J. A. Banks & C. A. M. Banks (Eds.), *Handbook of research on multicultural education* (2nd ed., pp. 3–29). San Francisco: Jossey-Bass.

Banks, J. A. (Ed.). (2009). *The Routledge international companion to multicultural education.* New York and London: Routledge.

Banks, J. A., & Banks, C. A. M. (Eds.) (2004). *Handbook of research on multicultural education* (2nd ed.). San Francisco: Jossey-Bass.

Cesari, J. (2004). *When Islam and democracy meet: Muslims in Europe and the United States.* New York: Palgrave Macmillan.

Dillon, S. (2006, August 27). In schools across U.S., the melting pot overflows. *The New York Times,* vol. CLV [155] (no. 53,684), pp. A7 & 16.

Eck, D. L. (2001). *A new religious America: How a "Christian country" has become the world's most religiously diverse nation.* New York: HarperSanFrancisco.

Immigration Sabotage [Editorial]. (2007, June 4). *New York Times,* p. A22.

Martin, P., & Midgley, E. (1999). Immigration to the United States. *Population Bulletin,* 54 (2), pp. 1–44. Washington, DC: Population Reference Bureau.

Minkenberg, M. (2008). Religious legacies and the politics of multiculturalism: A comparative analysis of integration policies in Western democracies. In A. C. d'Appollonia & S. Reich (Eds.), *Immigration, integration, and security: America and Europe in comparative perspective* (pp. 44–66). Pittsburgh, PA: University of Pittsburgh Press.

National Center for Education Statistics. (2008). *The condition of education 2008*. Washington, DC: U.S. Department of Education. Retrieved August 26, 2009, from http://nces.ed.gov/pubsearch/pubsinfo.asp?pubid=2008031

Progressive Policy Institute. (2008). *50 million Americans speak languages other than English at home*. Retrieved September 2, 2008 from http://www.ppionline.org/ppi_ci.cfm?knl gAreaID=108&subsecID=900003&contentID=254619

Roberts, S. (2008, August 14). A generation away, minorities may become the majority in U.S. *The New York Times*, vol. CLVII [175] (no. 54,402), pp. A1 & A18.

Suárez-Orozco, C., Suárez-Orozco, M. M., & Todorova, I. (2008). *Learning a new land: Immigrant students in American society*. Cambridge: Harvard University Press.

U.S. Census Bureau (2003, October). *Language use and English-speaking ability: 2000*. Retrieved September 2, 2008, from http://www.census.gov/prod/2003pubs/c2kbr-29.pdf

U.S. Census Bureau (2008, August 14). *Statistical abstract of the United States*. Retrieved August 20, 2008 from http://www.census.gov/prod/2006pubs/07statab/pop.pdf

United States Department of Homeland Security (2007). *Yearbook of immigration statistics, 2006*. Washington, DC: Office of Immigration Statistics, Author. Retrieved August 11, 2009, from http://www.dhs.gov/files/statistics/publications/yearbook.shtm

Acknowledgments

We would like to dedicate this book to Okhee's late husband, Michael Salwen, who is remembered with love and respect. We would also like to dedicate the book to Cory's wife, Jean-Marie, and three children, Jonah, Remy, and Lindy. Jean-Marie was always there to listen patiently, and Jonah, Remy, and Lindy were constant reminders that all children need and deserve well-prepared teachers and engaging science-learning opportunities.

We would like to acknowledge the people who have helped in the creation and production of the book. James Banks, who gave us the opportunity to prepare this volume, provided support and guidance throughout the process. Our sincere thanks also go to our editors at Teachers College Press who worked on this project, including Brian Ellerbeck and Aureliano Vázquez Jr., as well as to marketing specialist Beverly Rivero.

We learned a great deal through the writing of this book and hope that it will be of value to you, the reader. It is only through thoughtful collaboration that educators will find ways to meet the science-learning needs of all our children.

Okhee Lee
Cory Buxton

Introduction

The imperative that all students achieve high academic standards has been fundamental to the sweeping wave of educational reforms of the last decade. In the area of science education, this challenge has become both more urgent and complex as a result of four primary factors: 1) the growing diversity of the U.S. student population; 2) persistent achievement gaps among demographic subgroups; 3) the increasing demands of high-stakes testing and accountability for all students according to the No Child Left Behind (NCLB) Act of 2001, and 4) the necessity of a functional, applied understanding of science and scientific practice to make informed decisions in today's technologically and scientifically driven world.

First, the school-aged population in the United States continues to grow more racially, ethnically, socioeconomically, and linguistically diverse (National Center for Education Statistics [NCES], 2008; U.S. Census Bureau, 2005). The 2007 racial and ethnic makeup of students in U.S. schools was 55% White, 21% Hispanic, 17% Black, 5% Asian/Pacific Islander, and 1% American Indian/Alaska Native (NCES, 2008). This represents the lowest percentage of White students and the highest percentage of Hispanic students in U.S. schools to date, an ongoing demographic shift that is likely to continue for the foreseeable future. In terms of socioeconomic status (SES), in 2007, 42% of the nation's K–12 students received free or reduced-price lunch (NCES, 2008), indicating students coming from homes where the family income is less than $38,200 for a family of four during the 2007–2008 school year (NCES, 2008). Free and reduced-price lunch data over the past decade indicate a rising trend that is likely to continue given both demographic and economic trends.

Another rising trend among demographic subgroups is the steady increase in English language learning (ELL) students who can now be found in virtually every school in the nation. Currently, more than 20% of U.S. residents speak a language other than English at home. Over 5.5 million, or 11%, of public school students are categorized as ELL students (NCES, 2006a). There are nearly 9 million Hispanic students in U.S. schools, of which approximately 4.4 million are Spanish-speaking ELL students (U.S. Department of Education [USDOE], 2007). While Spanish speakers make up approximately 80% of the U.S. ELL student population, there are over 400 different languages spoken by U.S. students.

1

Increasing concentrations of ELL students have spread into geographic regions of the U.S. that lack a history of educating linguistically diverse populations. Most notably, the 12-state Southeastern region has seen the largest percentage increase of ELL students in the last decade (National Clearinghouse for English Language Acquisition, 2007). In Georgia, for example, the number of students classified as ELL students jumped from approximately 16,000 in 1995 to approximately 56,000 in 2005, a near quadrupling in only a decade (National Council of La Raza, 2008). Similarly, in North Carolina, the number of ELL students increased from 18,000 to 83,000 in the same time period. Despite such demographic shifts, major urban school districts continue to educate the vast majority of ELL students. A study by the Urban Institute found that 70% of ELL students are educated in 10% of U.S. schools and that these schools are predominantly located in large urban school districts (Cohen, Deterding, & Clewell, 2005). Thus, the challenge of preparing teachers to meet the academic needs of ELL students is both a new challenge in response to shifting demographics in some parts of the nation and a renewal of old and entrenched challenges in major urban settings.

Second, U.S. students have a less than glowing academic track record when compared to their international peers. The National Center for Education and the Economy (2006) analyzed results of the Program for International Student Assessment (PISA), Trends in International Mathematics and Science Study (TIMSS), and Progress in International Reading Literacy Study (PIRLS) for the years 1995–2003. American students failed to score in the top 10 on any of these three assessments. Furthermore, while there have been some signs of improvement on the National Assessment of Educational Progress (NAEP) science scores over the past decade, especially at fourth grade, the results are less than stellar (NCES, 2006b). On the 2005 NAEP science, over 30% of fourth graders, over 40% of eighth graders, and over 45% of 12th graders failed to attain the basic achievement level. For ELL students, the picture presented on NAEP science is likewise troubling. While the science achievement gaps between ELL and non-ELL students have diminished somewhat from 1996 to 2005 for both fourth and eighth graders, the achievement level results for ELL students were still bleak (NCES, 2006b). On 2005 NAEP science results, only 28% of fourth-grade ELL students achieved at the basic level or higher with only 4% scoring at the proficient level, as compared to 71% of fourth-grade non-ELL students achieving at the basic level or higher with 31% scoring at the proficient level.

Third, there is a growing role of science in accountability systems. NCLB requires that by the 2007–2008 school year each state must have in place science assessments to be administered at least once during grades three through five, grades six through nine, and grades 10 through12 (NCLB, §1111). Nearly all states are now in compliance with this mandate, administering science assessments and reporting assessment results for formative purposes. Although NCLB does not currently mandate the inclusion of science in the calculation of annual yearly progress

(AYP), the compulsory nature of science assessments seems to foreshadow such future inclusion. The ultimate role that science will play in accountability systems in the near future hinges on decisions to be made in the reauthorization of NCLB (Penfield & Lee, in press).

Finally, the challenge of high academic standards in science for all students is intertwined with the increasing importance of knowledge about science and technology in today's world. While science achievement gaps persist across student demographic subgroups, science and technology knowledge is becoming ever more important for all citizens. In addition to the growing number of professions that require a working familiarity with scientific concepts and high-tech tools, the future of our society may well hang in the balance of decisions made on the basis of general scientific literacy as well as specialized scientific knowledge. Systematic reduction of greenhouse gasses, controlling the spread of pandemic viral infection, and combating the obesity epidemic in the U.S. are just three examples of critical social issues that can only be addressed by a scientifically literate public. Science education standards documents (American Association for the Advancement of Science [AAAS], 1989, 1993; National Research Council [NRC], 1996, 2000) represent the science education community's best efforts to define what constitutes science learning and achievement (NRC, 2007; also see the summary in Lee & Paik, 2000; Raizen, 1998). Although these documents have been critiqued for not adequately addressing the learning needs of the broad range of students in the U.S. schools (Eisenhart, Finkel & Marion, 1996; Rodriguez, 1997), they can at least serve as a touchstone and marker of achievement as defined by the predominant community of scientists and science educators.

The four major factors described above are nested within the context of a broader range of education reforms focused on *all* students with the dual aims of promoting high academic achievement and ensuring educational equity in science (AAAS, 1989, 1993; NRC, 1996, 2000, 2007). Science educators agree that systemic reforms are needed to support the academic achievement of those students who are currently performing poorly in school science. This need is especially urgent, given the current climate of standards-based instruction, high-stakes testing, and accountability policies. Children of color, children from low-SES backgrounds, and children who are learning English as a new language are all disproportionately likely to be academically "at risk" according to these assessments. A vision of reform aiming at academic achievement for all students requires the integration of disciplinary knowledge with knowledge of student diversity.

With ELL students, content area instruction, such as science, should provide a meaningful learning environment for English language and literacy development. At the same time, improving English skills should provide the medium for understanding academic content (Lee & Fradd, 1998; Rosebery, Warren, & Conant, 1992; Teachers of English to Speakers of Other Languages [TESOL], 1997, 2006). In reality, however, ELL students frequently confront the demands of academic learning through a yet unmastered language *without* the instructional support they need. As a result, ELL students often fall behind their English-speaking peers in content area learning. Thus, instructional interventions that promote academic learning with ELL students are urgently needed, especially given the context of high-stakes testing and accountability policies facing today's schools, teachers, and students.

Traditionally, the research conducted on disciplinary knowledge and student diversity has been treated as separate fields of study. In the case of science education, the reform documents give a central place to the notion of "science for all," claiming that standards provide the potential to simultaneously promote equity and excellence (AAAS, 1989, 1993; NRC, 1996). Despite this promise, the science reform documents provide neither a coherent conception of equity nor concrete strategies for achieving it (Eisenhart et al., 1996; Lee, 1999a; S. Lynch, 2000; Rodriguez, 1997). On the other hand, the research on multicultural education focuses on the need to consider cultural and linguistic diversity as key components of creating equitable learning environments (Banks, 1993a, 1993b), but this literature generally does not consider the specific demands placed on learners in each of the academic disciplines. Finally, research on the unique learning needs of ELL students has focused primarily on developing English language and literacy with little attention to discipline-specific differences (August & Hakuta, 1997; August & Shanahan, 2006). One central premise of this book is that the integration of *discipline-specific* and *diversity-oriented* approaches to teaching and learning is essential to achieve the goal of science for all students.

Poor science performance of U.S. students overall and persistent science achievement gaps among demographic subgroups in the United States highlight the need for a greater awareness of the sociocultural contexts of teaching and learning. Teachers, administrators, policy makers, and the public need more explicit awareness of students' cultural, linguistic, and socioeconomic circumstances as these are related to science learning opportunities and outcomes. Both the scientific and science education communities claim an awareness of and a desire to rectify inequities of representation in science-related fields. However, because the historical development of science paints a universal truth that is culture- and value-free, the implicit and explicit expectation is that individuals studying science will assimilate to the established culture of the discipline. It goes against this tradition to consider how an individual might bring unique cultural and linguistic resources to the science classroom or the science laboratory that could influence science and science learning for the better. Despite philosophical arguments to this effect from feminist and multicultural scholars, in practice, it is rarely considered how an individual's cultural and linguistic resources might be aligned with the values and practices of science, or how such an alignment might enhance science outcomes in school and beyond.

Although classroom practices, local institutional conditions, and broader policy contexts affect all students, they are more likely to negatively impact non-mainstream students. Many teachers lack the knowledge of effective classroom practices with culturally and linguistically diverse students. This includes both general practices, such as how to strive for cultural congruence, as well as content-specific practices, such as how to structure inquiry-based science with ELL students. School-level policies and other institutional conditions also tend to disadvantage non-mainstream students. For example, beginning teachers are given classes full of students with the highest learning needs. Similarly, inner-city schools are more likely to hire uncertified and underprepared teachers and to ask teachers to teach out of their certification areas (Marx & Harris, 2006; Tuerk, 2005). In addition, resources are scarcer and teacher attrition is higher in inner-city schools. Limited resources often force trade-offs on issues, such as reducing class size versus providing more enriching resources (e.g., lab equipment) and experiences (i.e., field trips). Broader policy contexts are also detrimental to non-mainstream students. For example, high-stakes testing has resulted in an increase of teaching to the tests, but such changes in pedagogy are much more prominent for students who are deemed to be at risk of failing those tests (McNeil, 2000). Schools often view non-mainstream students as synonymous with at risk when they engage in such policy calculations.

PURPOSE OF THE BOOK

The poor performance of U.S. students on international and national science assessments has received much public attention in recent years. In addition, the achievement gaps in science across demographic subgroups and the underrepresentation of individuals from non-mainstream groups in science-related fields have been longstanding national concerns. If we start from the assumption that high academic achievement is possible for all children, then gaps in science outcomes among racial, ethnic, cultural, linguistic, or SES groups can be interpreted as a product of 1) the learning opportunities available to different groups of students and 2) the degree to which circumstances permit students to take advantage of those opportunities. These assumptions lead to questions such as: What constitutes equitable learning opportunities? In what ways might equitable learning opportunities vary for different student groups? and How can such opportunities be fostered in the context of limited resources and conflicting educational priorities?

All students come to school with previously constructed knowledge, grounded in their home language and cultural values. *Equitable learning opportunities* occur when school science: 1) explicitly and implicitly values and respects the experiences that all students bring from their home and community environments, 2) articulates this cultural and linguistic knowledge with disciplinary knowledge, and 3) offers sufficient educational resources to support science learning in all schools and classrooms. When provided with equitable learning opportunities, non-mainstream students are capable of attaining high levels of science achievement, adopting science learner identities, demonstrating individual and collective agency, and becoming bicultural and bilingual border-crossers by linking their own cultural and linguistic communities and the science learning community.

This book addresses the roots of the problem of gaps in science outcomes by offering a comprehensive, state-of-the-field analysis of current trends in the research, practice, and policy of science education with non-mainstream students. Many of the research studies described in this book provide promising results for effective science education with non-mainstream students. With regard to student diversity, the book focuses on issues of race, ethnicity, social class, culture, and language. Special attention is given to the unique learning needs of ELL students who need to acquire English language and literacy while simultaneously learning academic subjects such as science.

This book makes connections across theory, research, and practice for improving the science outcomes, broadly defined, of diverse student groups in elementary and secondary science classrooms. While many of the same and related challenges continue for non-mainstream students at the post-secondary level, we limit the scope of work addressed here to the K–12 education system. Research from a range of theoretical and methodological perspectives is brought to bear on the question of how and why our nation's schools continue to fall short of providing equitable learning opportunities for all students. Drawing from this research literature, we describe effective practices for narrowing achievement gaps among diverse student groups in elementary and secondary science classrooms.

The book addresses the relationship between student outcomes and factors influencing those outcomes as they relate to issues of student diversity and equity. There is a pressing need to challenge the conception of student outcomes as the single measure results of standardized tests. To this end, we include a range of student outcomes including course-taking patterns, school retention or dropout, learning with understanding, identity as science learners, cultural and linguistic identity, and individual agency, in addition to achievement on standardized tests. Factors influencing these outcomes include science instructional practices, curriculum materials including computer technology, assessment, teacher education, school organization, state and district policies, and home and community connections to school science. Each of these factors is given a dedicated chapter in the main body of the book.

The structure of each chapter consists of three components. First, key issues regarding how the factor in question influences student outcomes are described based on theory and research. The book focuses primarily on research programs conducted in the U.S. and published as peer-reviewed journal articles that provide clear statements of research questions, clear descriptions of research methods, convincing links between the evidence presented and the research questions, and valid conclusions based on the results (Shavelson & Towne, 2002). Second, illustrative examples of effective practices related to that factor are provided based on the work of specific research programs. A goal of this book is to tell stories about these research programs, to connect these stories together, and to highlight common themes, rather than to simply describe a series of studies and their conclusions. Finally, to make research findings relevant to practice, each chapter concludes with a set of activities and discussion questions that apply these findings to the classroom context.

We have tried to minimize ideological bias by including research drawing on multiple theoretical perspectives and their accompanying methodological orientations. A major goal of the book is to highlight theory-practice interactions and to point the ways toward practical means of narrowing or eliminating gaps, both in opportunity to learn and in outcomes. We do not attempt to provide a complete literature review on each of these topics, but rather to highlight specific research programs that seem to provide fruitful directions for improving both our understanding and practice.

In addition to its focus on the links between research and practice, the book addresses ways in which evolving educational policies have affected both research and practice in classrooms and schools. In several chapters, the role of high-stakes testing and accountability in the context of NCLB policy is addressed (for examples, Chapters 2, 5, 6, 8). The book concludes with a chapter of recommendations for practitioners, teacher educators, and policy makers.

ORGANIZATION OF THE BOOK

The book consists of four parts, each with multiple chapters. Part I describes the conceptual and policy issues that influence science education as generally experienced by non-mainstream students. The discussion starts with science achievement (i.e., measured outcomes) and student diversity as two key constructs. Based on this discussion, desired science outcomes for non-mainstream students are defined (Chapter 1). Then, conceptual and policy issues are described, including the theoretical perspectives that guide the research programs discussed throughout the book, the epistemological debate over definitions of science and school science, high-stakes testing and accountability policies in science education, language policies with ELL students, and issues of urban schooling (Chapter 2).

Part II focuses on the characteristics of both students and science learning environments that have been associated with gaps in science outcomes among diverse student groups. Student learning occurs in the context of classroom practices—how students learn science, what materials are used, what content is taught, how the content is taught, and how students' mastery of the content is assessed. This part is organized into the following: student characteristics and science learning (Chapter 3), science instruction (Chapter 4), science curriculum including computer technology (Chapter 5), and science assessment (Chapter 6). Within each chapter, studies addressing bilingual or ELL students are discussed as separate subsections.

Part III addresses school- and home-based factors that can serve both to support and to hinder science education as related to gaps in science outcomes among diverse student groups. Classroom practices occur in connection to broader contextual issues of teacher education programs, educational policies, and the ways in which families and communities are situated in relation to school science. Teachers face the challenge of making academic content accessible and meaningful for students from diverse backgrounds, which has made teacher education a major focus of science reform initiatives. Although educational policies and practices influence all students, these impacts are often more consequential for non-mainstream students who are less likely to live in homes that provide the sort of academic supports that schools often take for granted. Thus, establishing connections between home, community, and school science is critically important for non-mainstream students. Part III consists of the following: science teacher education (Chapter 7), school organization and educational policy (Chapter 8), and home and community connections to school science (Chapter 9). Again, within each chapter, studies addressing bilingual or ELL students are discussed separately.

Part IV of the book consists of conclusions from the research literature and a call to action that highlights the need for education reform to better meet the science learning needs of non-mainstream students. Part IV summarizes key features of the literature with regard to theoretical perspectives and methodological orientations, key findings about factors related to science outcomes of non-mainstream students, and suggestions for an ongoing research agenda (Chapter 10). The final chapter offers implications for classroom practices and educational policies, laying out a series of concrete steps that can be taken by teachers, schools, and districts to improve the science learning opportunities for all students, but particularly for non-mainstream students including ELL students (Chapter 11).

PART I

Context for Diversity and Equity in Science Education

Widespread scientific and technological literacy will be critical to the economic well-being of the nation and the personal well-being of its citizens in the 21st century. Persistent science achievement gaps, however, imply that non-mainstream students will be increasingly disadvantaged in both job markets and civic decision-making. While achievement gaps in school science are generally comparable to those in other subject areas, science has not received as much attention as have the core subjects of reading, writing, and mathematics. Unlike literacy and numeracy, science has not traditionally been regarded as a basic skill. The profile of science education, however, has recently been raised by economic realities pointing to the need for increased science knowledge combined with the inclusion of science in NCLB, which began in 2007. States must now administer science assessments at least once during grades 3 through 5, grades 6 through 9, and grades 10 through 12. This policy change forces states, districts, and schools to allocate additional resources to science instruction. This presents significant challenges to underresourced school systems as they consider how to divert a portion of already limited funding and resources to science instruction while maintaining funding for developing basic literacy and numeracy. The reality is that non-mainstream students are more likely to attend schools facing these budget constraints, highlighting the challenge of ensuring that all students receive equitable opportunities to learn science.

CHAPTER 1

An Overview of Student Diversity and Science Outcomes

We consider student diversity in terms of race, ethnicity, culture, language, and social class. We attend to the academic needs of immigrant and U.S.-born racial and ethnic minority students, and especially to the needs of many of these students to acquire the standard language and shared culture of "mainstream" American society. Most of these students are non-White and many come from low-income families.

Increasing numbers of non-mainstream students in U.S. classrooms have caused concerns to school personnel and the broader public. Continued achievement gaps on standardized assessment measures between non-mainstream students and their mainstream peers have led to further concerns among policy makers as well. Beyond such narrow single-measure test scores, there are multiple ways to consider achievement and meaningful learning outcomes, including learning with understanding, enrolling in honors or Advanced Placement science courses, majoring in science-related fields in college, and choosing science-related careers. More abstract but also meaningful science outcomes include positive identity as well as increased agency as a science learner. As we discuss gaps among demographic subgroups, we will consider these broader definitions of science outcomes, as well as the more typical view of gaps based on standardized test scores.

STUDENT DIVERSITY

It should be clearly understood that the demographic subgroups typically used to categorize people are not fixed natural characteristics, but rather social constructions. Human beings are all one species, whatever apparent physical differences, and as such, it is often more meaningful to focus on our similarities than differences. Still, these demographic classifications can be useful in identifying patterns and trends, as long as we remember not to place too much significance on differences that are in some ways artificial creations. The identities that individuals create for themselves are unique and flexible constructions, but are also partially defined and constrained by the interplay of race, ethnicity, culture, language, social class, and gender.

Demographic Designations. We describe the definitions of demographic categories that we will use throughout this book. While we have consulted with existing literature (American Anthropological Association, 1998), these are working definitions that express our own thinking about student diversity.

While it is nearly universally accepted in modern social sciences that human "races" are cultural categories rather than biological ones (American Anthropological Association, 1998), racial differences are still widely recognized as meaningful. Race is often defined as a human population considered distinct based on physical characteristics. Skin color is generally the most obvious marker of racial distinction. Still, different societies may use different rules for defining race. In Haiti, for example, a light-skinned mulatto may be considered White, especially if she or he comes from the upper class, while in the United States, this same individual would likely be considered Black. Despite a history in the United States where any amount of Black ancestry defines one as racially Black, *multiracial* identity is becoming more widely accepted as a racial category.

Ethnicity is generally used to represent membership in a social group with a shared history, sense of identity, geography, and cultural roots. Shared ethnicity frequently occurs across racial differences. Ethnicity is often associated with one's country of origin, itself a constructed category, rather than a naturally occurring category. To take one example, consider Brazilians as an ethnic group. Most Brazilians represent various blends of races and yet collectively share an ethnic identity rooted in language and culture. It is also worth noting that many White Americans do not consider themselves as having an ethnicity, relating ethnicity to "other" or foreign individuals. It is likely, however, that both the ethnic background(s) of one's forefathers (Italian, Irish, and so forth) as well as ethnic constructions of being "American" play important roles in how one interprets and interacts with the world. Helping all children lay claim to their ethnic identities may help our society put all of these demographic designations in perspective in the future.

Culture, which is often but not always closely tied to race and ethnicity, serves as a framework for how we interpret and interact with other individuals and with the broader world around us. More than just one's propensity for certain types of food, clothing, music, or spirituality, culture generally refers to the values and worldviews shared by the members of a social group. Culture provides agreed-upon meanings of what is important and what is not, what should be preserved and what should not, and what should be shared and what should not. It is often easier to begin to understand the cultural norms of other groups by first trying to closely examine one's own cultural norms, which are generally implicit and taken for granted.

Language is usually defined as a symbol system used by people for the purpose of shared communication. This system may be spoken, written, gestural, and so forth, and is generally used within a shared culture. Along with reasoning and tool use, language is considered to be one of the core defining characteristics of the human species. Despite their vast differences, all languages have the same basic communicative purposes of sharing thoughts, needs, and feelings with others.

Social class is often defined to be a person's rank within a social hierarchy. As with the other demographic constructs discussed here, social class is by no means an objective category, but rather a socially agreed-upon construct. High, middle, or low social class membership is a result of social perception and treatment that is granted accordingly. Class-related norms play out in terms of behavioral expectations, attitudes, and lifestyles. While most accurately a function of one's power, in Western society as well as much of the rest of the world, social class has become synonymous with material wealth. The term socioeconomic status (SES) is widely used as a synonym for social class, and highlights the link between class and material wealth. In discussing educational outcomes, SES of students is often of primary relevance. In schools and in educational research, students' eligibility for free or reduced price lunch is often used as a marker for SES because the lunch data are readily available to researchers.

While gender and sex are often thought of as synonymous and representative of a clear biological distinction, social scientists usually make a distinction between the two. Sex generally refers to the biological aspects of being male or female, while gender generally refers to the behavioral, social, and psychological characteristics of men and women or boys and girls. Thus, while sex is biological, gender is a social construct. While sex is generally fixed (at least in human beings), gender is more fluid and is largely the result of socialized behavior patterns. For the purposes of demographic distinctions and how terms are used in relation to educational data, however, gender is almost always used to represent the biological dichotomy between males and females; in other words, it is collapsed with sex.

We stress again that these constructs of demographic designations are not static. In much current sociology, race and ethnicity are treated as one construct (race/ethnicity). In current anthropology, language and culture are often treated together (*languaculture* by Agar, 1996; *dialectal relationship between indigenous language and culture* by McKinley, 2005, 2007). Similarly, social class is sometimes treated as a culture (*class cultures* by Bourdieu, 1984) or as a dialect (*social class dialects* by Labov, 1966). Despite the fact that all of these demographic variables—race, ethnicity, culture, language, social class, and gender—are clearly fluid social constructions, the distinctions continue to have significance when we consider issues of diversity and equity. Governmental bureaucracies, including education systems, continue to treat these constructions as discrete, self-evident designations. As a result, children continue to be categorized using these designations, although they may be categorized differently in different places. To make sense of questions involving student diversity and learning outcomes, we must keep in mind the subtleties in these demographic categories while also understanding the broad ways in which bureaucracies tend to treat these distinctions. To this end, throughout the book, we will follow the categories we have outlined above, rather than the more modern mergers.

Keeping these demographic categories as distinct does not mean that they should be thought of separately at the level of the individual. In practice, they always exist in combination. One is never just Black, or Puerto Rican, or Spanish-English bilingual, or working-class, or female, but rather a Black, Puerto Rican, Spanish-English bilingual, working-class female. This reality raises the methodological challenge of how to separate out the influences of different variables when studying patterns in learning outcomes. There are also conceptual reasons why it might not always make sense to try to separate these demographic distinctions. For example, language is an important element of how race, ethnicity, social class, and especially culture are defined. Racial and linguistic identities may vary within a given family or across the lifespan of an individual.

Additionally, with the passage of time, and with the changing demographic makeup of the population in the United States, social and political connotations of different terms have shifted. This sometimes causes difficulties when considering and comparing studies of student outcomes across time periods. However, such challenges are unavoidable given the socially constructed nature of demographic distinctions. Indeed, such "messiness" is a necessary part of the evolution of how educational research and evaluation considers the learning outcomes of students living in an ever more demographically varied society.

Terminology Related to Student Diversity. Throughout this book, the terms *mainstream* and *non-mainstream* are used with reference to students' racial, ethnic, cultural, linguistic, and social class backgrounds. By mainstream we do not refer to numerical majority, but rather to social prestige and institutionalized privilege. In school settings, mainstream students (i.e., those who are White, from middle- or high-income families, and native speakers of standard English) have certain inherent advantages over non-mainstream students (i.e., students of color, students from low-income families, and students learning English as a new language). Compared to their non-mainstream peers, mainstream students are more likely to encounter ways of talking, thinking, and interacting in school that are continuous with the skills and expectations they bring from home. This continuity between home and school creates numerous and substantial academic advantages for mainstream students that are often reflected in broader outcome measures. Even in those cases where mainstream students are the numerical minority, the same privileging of academic backgrounds exists.

This kind of group-level phenomenon, of course, may not apply in all settings and for all individuals. Academic disadvantages caused by non-mainstream status may be offset by a range of factors, such as proficiency levels in home language and English, immigration history, parents' educational levels, and community attitudes toward education, among other factors. Recognizing overall differences between groups does not justify limiting expectations of individual students, but does provide an important framework for interpreting observed patterns that occur with differing frequencies among different groups (Gutierrez & Rogoff, 2003).

We use the broader terms *diverse student groups* and *students from diverse backgrounds* to refer to all students, mainstream and non-mainstream. We include mainstream students in these terms to highlight that all students are culturally and linguistically diverse and that White, middle-class, speakers of standard English should not be set up as the norm against which all other groups are measured. In fact, culture and language play as large a role in the educational experience of mainstream students as in that of non-mainstream students. We do not use *student diversity* or *diverse students* as a synonym for non-mainstream students, as is often done in education discourse. In many cases to say that a school is becoming increasingly diverse is simply untrue. In fact, in many school districts, the past decade has witnessed resegregation of schools primarily along racial lines (Orfield, 2002).

When speaking of language, we use the terms *first language*, *home language*, *native language*, and *mother tongue* interchangeably in this book because their use is not consistent in the research literature. For some families, the home language may not actually be the first language, such as French-speaking Haitian families and children in U.S. schools who come to consider English to be their first language despite having another mother tongue.

Other terminology is used as it appears in original studies that are discussed throughout the book. Different researchers often use the same terms in different ways or invent new terms to describe nuances that they wish to highlight. Unless necessary to avoid undue confusion, we attempt to honor other researchers' choices of terminology.

SCIENCE OUTCOMES

The results of national and international science assessments, described below, indicate the need for a two-pronged approach to enhancing student science outcomes. Achievement gaps must be closed between mainstream and non-mainstream students. At the same time, improved science outcomes for all students should be fostered. While much has been done to document both the persistent gaps and the overall lackluster performance of U.S. students, less has been done to adequately explain such performance patterns or to design and test interventions in closing the gaps. Further, as noted earlier, inadequate attention has been given to science outcomes that extend beyond test performance. More robust measures of science outcomes should include science course-taking patterns in high school, science majors in college, college degrees granted in the STEM (science, technology, engineering, and mathematics) fields, and entrance into and retention in STEM occupations.

Methodological Limitations in Measuring Achievement Gaps. A
clear understanding of science achievement gaps should take into account certain methodological limitations in how these gaps are measured and reported.
Achievement is typically measured by standardized tests administered to national
and international student samples. A strength of these measures is that they provide access to large data sets that allow for the use of powerful statistical analyses.
A limitation of these measures is that they provide only a general picture of how
demographic variables relate to achievement results. For example, while these
measures might allow for analysis of test performance as a function of ethnicity,
Hispanic is likely to be treated as a single category, masking potentially important differences in performance among Mexican Americans, Puerto Ricans, and
Cubans of varied races, social classes, and home languages. Such overgeneraliza-
tion hinders more nuanced understanding of achievement gaps, thereby limiting
the potential effectiveness of interventions aimed at reducing these gaps. It also
has the potential to reinforce stereotypes, both positive and negative, of certain
demographic groups (Rodriguez, 1998a). For example, the *model minority* stereotype of Asian American students, as strong performers in mathematics and science, may well be supported by generalized test data for the racial category of
Asian American. However, such a result masks great disparities within this group,
such as for Southeast Asian refugees with little schooling and limited literacy development in their home countries. These students are less likely to have their
needs met in equitable ways if teachers presume that they naturally learn science
and mathematics with little trouble. Similarly, high-achieving Hispanic or African
American students may be disadvantaged by teachers or counselors who underestimate them and set low expectations of their academic success.

Until recently, ELL students were systematically excluded from large-scale
assessment, resulting in limited knowledge about their performance. While the
2000 NAEP report card was the first since the NAEP's inception in 1969 to analyze assessment accommodations in science, the results did not disaggregate the
accommodations given to limited English proficient students from those given to
students with disabilities (O'Sullivan, Lauko, Grigg, Qian, & Zhang, 2003).

Gaps in Science Achievement. Overall, U.S. students have not ranked
favorably on international measures of science achievement. In the largest study of
its kind, results from the 1995 TIMSS indicated that U.S. students did not perform
favorably compared to those in other developed nations (NCES, 1996; Schmidt,
McKnight, & Raizen, 1997). While U.S. fourth grade students scored within the
cluster of top-performing nations, eighth grade students scored only slightly above
the international average, and 12th-grade students scored among the lowest-
performing nations. In other words, the longer students studied science in U.S.
schools, the farther they dropped in international comparison.

The 1999 TIMSS-Repeat (TIMSS-R) was meant to provide a more detailed comparison of science performance, but involved only eighth-grade students. Again, U.S. eighth-grade students ranked slightly above the international average, placing 18th out of 34 nations (NCES, 2000). The students showed no significant change in science performance between 1995 and 1999, despite a good deal of work to implement systemic science education reforms during this time period. Additionally, when the TIMSS-R data were disaggregated according to the 14 U.S. school districts that participated, striking differences were seen. Several of the more economically privileged suburban districts scored on par with the highest-achieving nations such as Singapore and Japan, whereas the lower-SES urban school districts performed significantly below the international average, on par with Turkey and Tunisia.

The third administration of the TIMSS was conducted in 2003 and showed positive trends for U.S. students in science. The U.S. fourth-grade students continued to score towards the top of the international comparison. For the first time, eighth-grade students also scored above the international average. Equally importantly, the achievement gap between White and Black eighth-grade students closed significantly, as did the gap between girls and boys. The gap between White and Hispanic students, however, remained approximately the same as in 1999 (NCES, 2004).

The most recent administration of the TIMSS was conducted in 2007 and showed no significant changes for U.S. fourth and eighth graders in science performance when compared to the 2003 results. Thus, while achievement gaps narrowed between U.S. students and students in the highest-performing nations since the first TIMSS study in 1995, TIMSS data show that there are still troubling achievement gaps between lower- and higher-SES school districts and across racial groups within the U.S. student population.

The other major international assessment that measures science learning is the Program for International Student Assessment (PISA), which is administered to 15-year-olds. PISA was administered to students in 43 countries in 2000, 2003, 2006, and 2009. PISA assesses students in reading, mathematical, and scientific literacy and strives to assess not only basic content knowledge but also problem solving and relevant life skills related to the disciplines. While the TIMSS results for fourth and eighth graders have been promising over this same time period, the PISA results for 15-year-olds are somewhat less so. When it comes to applying science in meaningful ways, such as using scientific evidence, identifying scientific issues, and explaining phenomena scientifically, U.S. students performed in the bottom half of the international comparison in 2000, 2003, and 2006 and did not show significant improvements across the three administrations (no data are available yet for the 2009 administration). The only demographic subgroup data reported on the PISA are for gender. In the United States, males slightly outperformed females on the mean science score, but by a lower amount than the international average (NCES, 2006b). In other words, gaps by gender were not as prominent in the U.S. as in other nations participating in the PISA.

At the national level, NAEP provides assessment of U.S. students' science performance over time. Average scores for students of every age level (9-year-olds, 13-year-olds, and 17-year-olds) and across racial groups have increased slightly between 1977 and 1999 (Campbell, Hombo, & Mazzeo, 2000). At the same time, achievement gaps across racial groups gradually narrowed, as scores for African American and Hispanic students improved at a slightly faster rate than the scores of White non-Hispanic students. Nevertheless, Black and Hispanic students' scores remained well below those of White students at each grade level.

Focusing only on more recent NAEP data from the assessments in 1996, 2000, and 2005, trends are quite similar to those seen in the TIMSS data for U.S. students. Fourth-grade students have continued to make steady progress in science in terms of both overall achievement and closing of achievement gaps. The 2005 fourth-grade data show improvement over both the 1996 and 2000 data and narrowing of both the White-Black and the White-Hispanic achievement gaps. Scores for eighth-grade students remained approximately flat across the three tests (1996, 2000, and 2005), showing no significant changes in either overall achievement or achievement gaps for the White-Black or White-Hispanic groups. Scores for 12th-grade students in 2005 actually decreased slightly when compared to both the 1996 and 2000 achievement levels. The White-Black achievement gap increased between 2000 and 2005, while the White-Hispanic achievement gap has remained the same.

Overall achievement gaps across racial groups remain so large that the final 12th-grade NAEP science achievement levels of male and female African American students and female Hispanic students still fell well below the initial eighth-grade achievement levels of Whites and Asian Americans (Muller, Stage, & Kinzie, 2001; NCES, 2005). In other words, White and Asian American eighth-grade students' science achievement was higher than that of 12th-grade African American and female Hispanic students.

Over the same time period of 1996, 2000, and 2005, NAEP results indicate that students who were eligible for the free or reduced price lunch program performed well below those who were not eligible at each of the three age groups (NCES, 2005; O'Sullivan et al., 2003). While these data on science achievement gaps are striking, it is difficult to pinpoint the factors accounting for these gaps because, as we noted earlier, standardized achievement tests such as the NAEP do not analyze or report interactions between variables, such as race and SES. Because students of color are disproportionately represented in free or reduced price lunch programs, achievement gaps across racial and SES groups become confounded.

Gaps in High School Science Course Enrollment, College Major, and Career Choice. Besides achievement data, other indicators of science outcomes include science course enrollment, college major selection, and career choice.

While this book intentionally limits its scope to K–12 science education, the decision and the ability to major in a STEM field in college or to pursue a STEM career is largely influenced by science and mathematics learning experiences throughout elementary and secondary school. Overall, non-mainstream students have made substantial gains in science and engineering fields from high school and beyond, but gaps persist (Chipman & Thomas, 1987; NSF, 2002, 2009; Oakes, 1990). In order to place the following demographic data in perspective, it is useful to remember that the 2007 racial and ethnic makeup of students in U.S. schools was 55% White, 21% Hispanic, 17% Black, 5% Asian/Pacific Islander, and 1% American Indian/Alaska Native (NCES, 2008).

High school science course-taking patterns, in both 1990 and 1998, indicate that most students, regardless of racial group, had taken 2 years of science, including general science and biology, whereas relatively few had taken AP/honors biology or an engineering course (NSF, 2002, pp. 6, 104). Racial differences are prominent for enrollment in high school chemistry and physics. In 1990, smaller percentages of Black, Hispanic, and American Indian high school graduates took chemistry and physics, compared to White and Asian American graduates. By 1998, the percentages for Black, Hispanic, and American Indian high school graduates had increased, but the percentages of White and Asian American graduates had also increased as well, maintaining this course-taking gap.

In higher education, non-mainstream students have made gains with regard to both absolute numbers and percentages of bachelor's, master's, and doctoral degrees awarded in STEM fields throughout the 1990s and 2000s (NSF, 2009). However, gaps in STEM degrees granted between mainstream and non-mainstream students persist. Overall, Whites predominate in STEM degrees earned and Asians/Pacific Islanders are overrepresented, whereas Blacks, Hispanics, and American Indians continue to be underrepresented (NSF, 2009). Additionally, the higher the degree, the greater this underrepresentation. For example, in 2006, Blacks, Hispanics, and American Indians/Alaska Natives earned a total of 17% of bachelor's degrees in science and engineering, 12% of the master's degrees, and 10% of the doctoral degrees. While each of these percentages is an increase compared to a decade earlier, they indicate persistent gaps when compared to the increasing population of non-mainstream students in our schools. For women there is a similar pattern of lower representation at successively higher levels of education. In 2006, women earned half of the bachelor's degrees in science and engineering, 45% of the master's degrees, and 38% of the doctoral degrees (NSF, 2009).

Conception of Science Outcomes. Science education reform highlights several key components of science learning that tend to be underemphasized in standardized tests such as TIMSS and NAEP. Students need to have deep and complex understandings of science concepts, be able to make connections among

science concepts, and be able to apply science concepts in explaining natural phenomena or real world situations (AAAS, 1989, 1993; NRC, 1996, 2000, 2007).
Scientific understanding also involves applying science concepts in previously un-
encountered situations and being able to solve nonroutine problems (Romberg,
Carpenter, & Dremock, 2005).

No science learning outcome has been given more attention in the science
reform literature than the ability to perform science inquiry (NRC, 2000). Science inquiry is defined as the ability to generate questions about natural phenomena, design investigations, collect data from a variety of sources, develop
explanations from the data, draw and defend conclusions, and communicate
findings using multiple formats. These skills are difficult to assess on standardized tests.

Science education standards treat scientific understanding and inquiry as
closely intertwined. By definition, "inquiry refers to the activities of students in
which they develop knowledge and understanding of scientific ideas, as well as an
understanding of how scientists study the natural world" (NRC, 1996, p. 23). This
suggests that inquiry is central to science learning; and science inquiry is a main
tool to ensure that scientific understanding has occurred.

In addition to scientific understanding and inquiry, science reform also emphasizes *talking science*, whereby "teachers structure and facilitate ongoing formal
and informal discussion based on a shared understanding of rules of scientific
discourse. A fundamental aspect of a community of learners is communication"
(NRC, 1996, p. 50). In science, this communication often takes the form of *scientific argumentation*, which is defined as the coordination of evidence and theory
to support or refute an explanation, model, or prediction (Osborne, Erduran, &
Simon, 2004). Argumentation is different from simply arguing that one's belief or
finding is correct; rather, it involves the reasoned connection between evidence
and claims (Toulmin, 1958).

The scientific worldview, often considered to be the cornerstone of Western
modern science, is only one of a number of possible epistemologies or philoso-
phies for understanding the natural world around us. The cultivation of scientific habits of mind entails adopting this scientific worldview, at least when one
is practicing or trying to understand science. It is possible to hold more than
one worldview or epistemology, depending on the context. For example, most
people, when enjoying art in a museum, are unlikely to use a scientific framework
to understand what they are experiencing. Instead, they probably use aesthetic
or perhaps historic ways of knowing to make sense of the art they are observing. When learning science, however, students must learn to adopt the scientific
worldview if they are to be successful, even if this worldview is different from
what they typically experience at home or in their community. Most cultural traditions embrace some values and attitudes that are associated with science, such

as wonder, curiosity, interest, diligence, persistence, openness to new ideas, imagination, and respect toward nature. Other values and attitudes are particularly characteristic of Western modern science; for example, questioning fundamental beliefs, thinking critically and independently, making arguments based on logic rather than personal or institutional authority, openly critiquing the arguments of others, and tolerating ambiguity. In these ways, science as a way of knowing, "distinguishes itself from other ways of knowing and from other bodies of knowledge" (NRC, 1996, p. 201).

Although the standards documents generally define science as a Western modern construction (AAAS, 1989, p. 136; NRC, 1996, pp. 201, 204), alternative views of science have been advocated by scholars in fields such as multiculturalism, feminism, sociology and philosophy of science, and critical theory (Atwater & Riley, 1993; Calabrese Barton, 1998a; Eisenhart, Finkel, & Marion, 1996; Hodson, 1993; Lee, 1999a; Rodriguez, 1997; Stanley & Brickhouse, 1994, 2001). These critiques focus on the issue of power and the marginalization of non-mainstream groups, and challenge whether the scientific worldview is as objective and value-free as it is generally portrayed to be.

For students from non-mainstream backgrounds, coming to adopt the scientific worldview may be seen as a form of biliteracy and biculturalism, in which they value both the scientific worldview and other worldviews from their home culture as determined by the context. Thus, desired learning outcomes include becoming bicultural, bilingual, and biliterate with regard to the home language and culture, on the one hand, and Western modern science, on the other. We will return to this question of scientific worldview and the impact it has on the science education of both mainstream and non-mainstream students at various times throughout the book.

SUMMARY

In this chapter we have considered various perspectives on student diversity, science outcomes, and science itself. While healthy debates about the most constructive ways to address these issues are ongoing, participants in these debates generally agree that non-mainstream students have not been effectively served by school science as it has traditionally been taught. The main body of this book offers a map for better understanding of the state of science education research as it relates to student diversity. We consider the areas of learning, instruction, curriculum, assessment, teacher education, school organization, educational policies, and school science in connection to students' home and community. Each of these topics raises unique questions and challenges with regard to the goal of providing equitable learning opportunities in science for all students.

ACTIVITIES FOR CHAPTER 1

1. The study of multicultural education has given rise to a number of debates over meanings and practices that will serve to create equitable learning environments. For each of the following pairs of terms, do the following:
   A. Consider your own ideas about the distinctions between the two.
   B. Find out how the terms have been described and debated in popular education writing.
   C. Describe in a few sentences which of the two better represents your own ideas on the topic and why.
      i. Equality versus equity
      ii. Color blind versus color sensitive
      iii. Tracking versus mainstreaming
      iv. Science as *culture free* versus science as *culture laden*
      v. English-only versus bilingual education
2. Visit several of the Web sites below to learn more about 1) changing demographics and 2) achievement gaps in science both nationally and in your state.
   A. Compare your state to the national data. What can you conclude?
   B. Imagine that you were asked to give a presentation to faculty in your school about trends in demographics and science achievement in your state. What are some of the most important points you would want to make?
      i. Public Elementary and Secondary School Student Enrollment and Staff, 2006–2007, http://nces.ed.gov/pubsearch/pubsinfo.asp?pubid=2009305
      ii. National Assessment of Educational Progress (NAEP), http://nces.ed.gov/nationsreportcard/science/
      iii. Third International Mathematics and Science Study (TIMSS), http://nces.ed.gov/timss/
      iv. Program for International Student Assessment (PISA), www.pisa.oecd.org/
      v. U.S. Department of Education—Testing Limited English Proficient Students, http://www.ed.gov/nclb/accountability/schools/factsheet-english.html
      vi. PBS—Race—The Power of an Illusion, http://www.pbs.org/race/000_About/002_04-experts-03-02.htm

CHAPTER 2

Conceptual Grounding and Policy Context

In this chapter we discuss several key conceptual and policy considerations that serve to organize the remainder of the book. First, theoretical perspectives guiding research studies reviewed in this book are discussed. Rather than interpreting issues of science education from one particular theoretical perspective, this book includes research originating from multiple theoretical perspectives. Second, the epistemological debate over definitions of science and school science (i.e., what counts as science and school science) is discussed with a focus on universal versus multicultural views of science. Third, we provide an overview of the policy context of high-stakes testing and accountability in science education. Fourth, policies for English to Speakers of Other Languages (ESOL), bilingual education, and home language are discussed. Finally, we consider issues of urban schooling.

THEORETICAL PERSPECTIVES GUIDING THIS BOOK

Learning is influenced by a range of cultural, linguistic, and social factors. Learning is enhanced—indeed, it is made possible—when it occurs in contexts that are culturally, linguistically, and cognitively meaningful and relevant to the learner. When schooling fails to adequately account for students' linguistic and cultural resources, it ignores or even negates some of the key tools that students can use to construct their understandings of the world. While connecting new knowledge to prior knowledge is a fundamental part of learning for all students, the linguistic and cultural resources that mainstream students bring to school are more likely to be closely aligned with typical classroom practices. Non-mainstream students often find themselves disadvantaged by a school culture that seems to devalue the linguistic and cultural resources that are valued in their home and community (Banks & McGee Banks, 1995). Effective science instruction incorporates students' prior cultural and linguistic knowledge and draws connections to the science disciplines.

The research studies, professional development activities, and classroom interventions that are discussed in this book highlight the intersection between science education and students' race, ethnicity, culture, language, and/or social class. Science educators have applied a range of theoretical perspectives to their research and practice in teaching science to non-mainstream students. These have included multicultural perspectives on the epistemology of science (Brickhouse,

1994; Snively & Corsiglia, 2001), cognitive science perspectives on scientific reasoning and argumentation of non-mainstream students (Rosebery, Warren, & Conant, 1992; Warren, Ballenger, Ogonowski, Rosebery, & Hudicourt-Barnes, 2001), cross-cultural perspectives on worldviews (Aikenhead & Jegede, 1999; Cobern, 1991, 1996), culturally relevant pedagogy in science classrooms (i.e., instructional congruence by Lee, 2002, 2004), contextually authentic science learning (Buxton, 2006), social constructivist perspectives on multicultural science education (Atwater, 1993, 1996), broader sociocultural perspectives on communities of science practice (Lemke, 2001; O'Loughlin, 1992), postmodern perspectives on grand narratives in science (Norman, 1998; Haraway, 1990, 1991), critical theory perspectives on power and positioning (Calabrese Barton, 1998a, 1998b; Rodriguez, 1998b; Seiler, 2001; Tobin, Seiler, & Smith, 1999), social justice perspectives on science as a civil right (Tate, 2001), and integration of science with English language and literacy for ELL students (Lee, 2005).

Rather than interpreting issues of science teaching and learning from any one particular theoretical perspective that we may personally tend to favor, we have tried to faithfully represent each study on its own terms that are grounded in the theoretical perspective of its authors. At times we also point out critiques of research programs that have been leveled by detractors. Despite their theoretical variety, the works described in this book share a common vision of increasing our understanding of the racial, ethnic, cultural, linguistic, and SES contexts in science education, as well as attempting to address resulting inequities and ways to remedy these inequalities.

VIEWS OF SCIENCE: IS SCIENCE INDEPENDENT OF CULTURE?

While often overlooked as a topic of discussion in science classrooms, there has been lively philosophical debate in the scholarly literature about epistemological questions in science, such as what counts as science, what questions are worth asking, and what methods are acceptable for answering those questions. Much of this debate has its origins in the feminist philosophy of science from the late 1980s and early 1990s. Writers such as Longino (1990), Harding (1991), and Fox Keller (1985) challenged the taken-for-granted norms of science practice, or what has come to be known as *universalist science*. Universalist science is the view that because the natural world follows a consistent set of rules, and because science is the quest to understand and explain those rules, then science must be practiced in the same way no matter where or by whom it is done. There is no place in universalist science for one's race, ethnicity, culture, language, gender, or other external factors to influence science practice. When applied to science education, this definition of universalist science becomes "a *de facto* 'gate-keeping' device for determining what can be included in a school science curriculum and what cannot" (Snively & Corsiglia, 2001, p. 6) and, by extension, who is most likely to be successful in science and who is not (Brickhouse, 1994; Southerland, 2000; Stanley & Brickhouse, 1994, 2001).

Some science educators have supported a universalist view of science (e.g., Loving, 1997; Matthews, 1998), a view that has largely been upheld in the national science standards documents. *Science for All Americans* (AAAS, 1989), which was the precursor to the *National Science Education Standards* (NRC, 1996), argued that science has typically been equated with "a tradition of thought that happened to develop in Europe during the last 500 years" (p. 145) and that "science assumes that the universe is, as its name implies, a vast single system in which the basic rules are everywhere the same. Knowledge gained from studying one part of the universe is applicable to other parts" (pp. 3–4).

Along with the continued prominence of universalist science in schools, a growing body of work, built on the feminist science studies, has proposed various multiculturalist views of science and science education (Buxton, 2001a; Snively & Corsiglia, 2001; Siegel, 2002; Stanley & Brickhouse, 1994). The centerpiece of multiculturalist science involves the critique of science as universal and culture-free and claims that such a standpoint fails to consider the role that humans play as we study and interact with the natural world (Atwater, 1996; Eisenhart et al., 1996; Rodriguez, 1997). While the natural world may exist as a physical and objective reality "out there," it is impossible for humans to study the natural world without bringing our own subjective selves, languages, cultures, beliefs, and values to that study. A scientist is not simply an instrument in the study of the natural world. He or she decides, within the confines and structures of a science discipline, which is itself constrained by a history of past human decisions, what questions to ask and how to go about answering them. The system is full of cultural, historical, and value judgments ranging from what questions are likely to receive research funding at a given point in time to who are the strongest personalities in the disciplinary professional organizations at a given point in time. From this perspective, science is a socially and culturally constructed discipline. Thus, multiculturalist critiques of science question the necessity of the dominance of Western modern science and advocate the inclusion of non-Western, indigenous traditions of understanding the natural world.

This literature also calls into question the assumption that Western science is a uniquely Western construct (Teresi, 2003). For example, there is a rich and well-documented indigenous knowledge in ecology that has sustained indigenous populations over many centuries and has gradually become more widely accepted by Western modern science (Chinn, 2007; McKinley, 2004; Ogunniyi, 2007a, 2007b; Riggs, 2005; Snively & Corsiglia, 2001). Other ethnoscientific traditions in fields as varied as agriculture, botany, medicine, astronomy, navigation, climatology, and architecture have contributed over time to Western modern science in ways that often go unrecognized (e.g., Hodson, 1993; Krugly-Smolska, 1996; Teresi, 2003). This multiculturalist perspective on science argues that a broader view of what counts as science and who does science is not a threat, but can actually serve to advance and strengthen Western modern science.

The argument for a multiculturalist broadening of the definition of science is largely based on the sense that there are continuities between the practices of Western modern science and the practices that evolve from indigenous ways of knowing the natural world. At the same time, there are ways in which the world-views associated with diverse linguistic and cultural groups may be discontinuous with the worldview of Western modern science (e.g., Cobern, 1991; Kawasaki, 1996; Ogawa, 1995). The question of continuous and discontinuous worldviews is described in the next chapter. We should note that within mainstream culture there are also worldviews that are largely discontinuous with Western modern science. While questions such as the relationship between science and religion in modern America are beyond the scope of this book, we would not wish to present the false perception that the worldview of Western modern science and main-stream culture are seamless in their overlap. The "culture wars" that have often pitted aspects of science, such as evolution and natural selection, against aspects of religious thought have been driven by powerful elements of mainstream culture.

Beyond epistemological reasons for considering the contributions of multi-culturalist science to Western modern science, arguments for including multicul-turalist perspectives in science have been made on the grounds of moral justice (Irzik & Irzik, 2002; Siegel, 1997) and antiracism (Carter, 2004; Hodson, 1999; Hodson & Dennick, 1994). If a core value of multiculturalism is a commitment to treat members of all cultures justly and with respect, then it is unjust to dis-count the belief systems held by others, even when it is unclear how these beliefs can contribute to the work at hand—in this case, the advancement of scientific understanding. From an antiracist perspective, spreading an awareness of the con-tributions of indigenous and non-Western ways of knowing to Western modern science may help to combat racist attitudes and practices that disadvantage and discriminate against people of color, resulting in an unequal distribution of oppor-tunity, wealth, and power. This antiracist position goes beyond a simple celebra-tion of diversity to include explicit treatment of racism.

Multiculturalist science perspectives have been applied to science in a variety of ways that cover a spectrum from critical to moderate approaches. Critical ap-proaches focus on portraying the nature and practice of science as the purview of middle-class White males, and the value that might come from transforming science to include multiple voices and epistemologies that are characteristic of female and non-Western groups (Buxton, 2001b; Calabrese Barton, 1998a, 1998b; Rodriguez, 1997). Moderate approaches highlight the value of integrating the beliefs and worldviews of non-Western groups into science, while emphasizing the explanatory and predictive power of Western modern science as currently constructed (Aikenhead & Jegede, 1999; Lee, 1999a; Loving, 1997).

Despite the variety of emphases, multiculturalist perspectives on science are consistent in their concern that scientific universalism discounts and devalues the important role that people bring to science. When people bring a broad range of ideas, which are informed by diverse cultures, languages, and worldviews, to the questions of how the natural world works, science can only be enriched. When people are asked to leave their cultures, languages, and ways of knowing behind in order to study the natural world, then science is impoverished. School science has remained largely immune from these philosophical debates, however, and continues to draw largely upon scientific universalism in teaching the scientific worldview (Stanley & Brickhouse, 1994, 2001).

Recent scholarship on the debate between universalism and multiculturalism has advanced a framework to overcome the points of contention between the two. Van Eijck and Roth (2007) abandon the notion of truth and, instead, adopt a contemporary worldview that 1) entails both the cultural and material aspects of human reality, 2) concerns the usefulness of knowledge, and 3) highlights the dynamic and plural nature of products of human being and human understanding. Drawing on narratives of both scientists and aboriginal people explaining the natural phenomenon of a salmon run, they illustrate that traditional indigenous ecological knowledge and scientific knowledge are incommensurable and irreducible to each other. The two views, while both concerned with the salmon run, are fundamentally interested in unrelated questions for unrelated purposes. The views are not at odds because the resulting knowledge is gained for different reasons.

Taking a different perspective, Chinn (2007) and Ogunniyi (2007a) reported that after professional development opportunities, teachers from various Asian countries (in Chinn's study) and South African countries (in Ogunniyi's study) developed a better understanding of indigenous ecological knowledge in their local contexts. The teachers also changed their own views from considering science and indigenous ecological knowledge as polar opposites to considering the two thought systems as compatible and complementary. These results illustrate an alternative to the work of Van Eijck and Roth (2007) with regard to the compatibility or incompatibility between science and indigenous ecological knowledge.

While recognizing the existence of multiple views of science in the science education community, this book generally uses the term *school science* to refer to the teaching of science as it is implicitly and explicitly defined in the science standards documents, i.e., as the systematic search for empirical explanations of natural phenomena while engaging in the practices of science (AAAS, 1989, 1993; NRC, 1996, 2000, 2007; see the summary in Lee & Paik, 2000; Raizen, 1998). From this perspective, the goal of school science is to guide students in developing an understanding of key science concepts, engaging in science inquiry and reasoning, participating in scientific discourse, and cultivating scientific habits of mind, including scientific values and attitudes as well as the Western scientific worldview. Multiculturalist perspectives are raised as a counterpoint to this mainstream view, but we must acknowledge that scientific universalism remains the norm in school science.

HIGH-STAKES TESTING AND ACCOUNTABILITY POLICIES

The implementation of content standards and curriculum frameworks at the national, state, and district levels has created guidelines and mandates for curriculum and instruction at the classroom level (Cohen & Hill, 2000; Knapp, 1997; McLaughlin, Shepard, & O'Day, 1995; Smith & O'Day, 1991). Science has been no exception, with curriculum frameworks and pacing guidelines becoming more prescriptive in recent years. Although one of the initial goals of the standards movement is to provide more content focus, science content standards have been criticized for being a mile wide and an inch deep (i.e., covering too many topics in not enough depth).

While the science standards documents began to pull classroom practice in some new directions, it is the subsequent implementation of high-stakes testing and accountability policies that has caused the most radical changes in classroom practice. High-stakes testing has realigned curriculum and instruction in different ways across each of the content areas. Initially, the focus of testing fell on language arts and mathematics, resulting in decreased attention to science, social studies, and other untested subjects (Lee & Luykx, 2005; Marx & Harris, 2006). Diamond and Spillane (2004) found that teachers in both high- and low-performing schools emphasized language arts and mathematics in response to high-stakes testing and accountability policies. Science was taught when time allowed, if at all, typically after testing was completed for the year. Similarly, the National Institute of Child Health and Human Development (2005) reported that a substantial amount of instructional time in third-grade classrooms was spent on literacy (56%) and mathematics (29%), and very little time was spent on science (6%). More recently, as science has become part of accountability policies, a renewed attention to science education has followed.

The passing of NCLB ushered in a new era of high-stakes testing and accountability policies. Under NCLB, districts and schools are accountable for making an adequate level of achievement gain each year. In the lingo of NCLB, the adequate level of gain is referred to as *annual yearly progress* (AYP). The theory behind NCLB assumes that states, districts, and schools will allocate resources to best facilitate the attainment of AYP, which is determined by achievement test scores in reading and mathematics (for now), graduation rates (for secondary schools), and at least one other academic indicator as determined by each state (e.g., writing or science) or other indicators (e.g., dropout rate, number of students going to college). Thus, decisions concerning resources and practices are determined largely by test scores on state assessments. To accomplish this action plan, NCLB introduced a three-stage process of accountability: 1) states define what constitutes AYP according to the above guidelines, 2) states measure achievement to determine whether AYP is met, and 3) sanctions are imposed on districts and schools if AYP is not maintained.

Although NCLB is most often associated with this accountability system, there is a second property of NCLB that has also been a focus of attention in the educational community. NCLB mandates that each state report AYP disaggregated for the following student populations: 1) students of particular racial/ethnic groups as determined by the state (e.g., African American/Black, Hispanic/Latino, Asian/Pacific Islander, etc.); 2) students with limited English proficiency (LEP); 3) students with disabilities; and 4) students who are economically disadvantaged. Mandating this disaggregated reporting of AYP results in three potentially desirable outcomes: 1) each of the groups is publicly monitored to examine achievement and progress; 2) resources are allocated differentially to these groups to enhance the likelihood that they meet AYP; and 3) if AYP is not met for these groups in schools receiving Title I funding, students are provided with additional resources, such as supplemental educational resources (e.g., tutoring) and the right to transfer to another public school. Schools, districts, and states cannot hide historically underperforming demographic groups, since NCLB forces the state to publicly monitor these groups and to be accountable for their performance. In the end, lack of AYP by these groups is the responsibility of the state, district, and school, rather than the federal government. On the undesirable side, however, all of the added attention to testing does not necessarily result in improved teaching. Similarly, calling more public attention to the failures of schools to adequately meet the needs of students from certain demographic subgroups does little to ensure that those students will receive instruction that is more engaging, more intellectually challenging, or more culturally or socially relevant.

In addition, while NCLB mandates reporting of AYP for reading and mathematics, the same is not currently true for science. With respect to science, NCLB only required that by the 2007–2008 school year each state would have in place science assessments to be administered and reported for formative purposes at least once during grades three through five, grades six through nine, and grades 10 through 12 (NCLB, §1111). Some states include high-stakes science testing in state accountability systems. Furthermore, a state can voluntarily include science in its AYP reporting by designating science as one other academic indicator.

NCLB in science education involves multiple steps for implementation in each state's assessment system: first, develop the assessment; second, administer the assessment; third, report the assessment results for formative purposes; fourth, decide whether to include the assessment results as part of state accountability;

and finally, decide whether to include science in AYP calculation. The extent to which each state has met the NCLB requirements pertaining to science assessment is unclear. What is known is that, with the exception of a few states that are currently developing or pilot-testing science assessments, all states currently administer science assessments (R. Blank of the Council of Chief State School Officers, personal communication, August 29, 2008). What is not known is how many states report science assessment results or include these results as part of state accountability. In addition, while no accessible documentation exists concerning which states are including science assessments in AYP calculation, a Web-based search of current AYP indicators did not uncover any state that included science assessments in AYP calculation to date.

Although NCLB does not currently mandate that science be included in the calculation of AYP, the mandate of compulsory science assessments indicates a growing role of science in school accountability and foreshadows the potential future inclusion of science in AYP calculation. Indeed, the American Competitiveness Initiative proposed the future inclusion of science in calculating AYP (Domestic Policy Council, Office of Science and Technology Policy, 2006). The ultimate role that science will play in the accountability systems in the near future hinges on decisions to be made in the reauthorization of NCLB.

Given that NCLB is inadequately funded, it does not provide schools with the resources necessary to meet the accountability standards it imposes. The consequences of policy changes will likely be greater for students at underfunded inner-city schools (McNeil, 2000) and ELL students (Abedi, 2004; Abedi, Hofstetter, & Lord, 2004) than for their mainstream counterparts. Science instruction for students in inner-city schools, who are disproportionately low-income or ELL students, is often deemphasized relative to the urgent task of developing English proficiency as well as basic skills in literacy and numeracy (Lee & Luykx, 2005). If high-quality instructional materials that meet current science education standards are difficult to find (NSF, 1996; Kesidou & Roseman, 2002), materials that also take into account the cultural and linguistic diversity of today's classrooms are even scarcer (NSF, 1998).

Assessments of science achievement necessitate consideration of fairness to different student groups (Penfield & Lee, in press). How can valid and equitable assessments be ensured for all students? With ELL students, assessments should distinguish among academic achievement, English proficiency, and general literacy (Solano-Flores, 2008; Solano-Flores & Trumbull, 2003). Although large-scale assessments may include various accommodation strategies, they are rarely administered in languages other than English (Abedi, 2004; Abedi, Hofstetter, & Lord, 2004). Even when assessments are administered in a student's home language, ensuring the comparability of assessment instruments between two languages is complicated. Such assessment policies can drive curriculum in directions that lead to inequitable outcomes.

Standards-based instruction and accountability policies reinforce the mainstream view that linguistic and cultural minorities are expected to assimilate to the dominant language and culture (see the critiques in Lee & Luykx, 2005). In science, this includes the implicit acceptance of scientific universalism and the disregard of the multiculturalist perspectives on science, discussed earlier in this chapter. State science standards and benchmarks usually make no mention of students' home language and culture and, thus, there is no expectation to infuse home language and culture into accountability measures. These policies give rise to ideological and conceptual challenges, since there are few incentives to incorporate multiculturalist science in the climate of one-size-fits-all assessment. Such policy demands are felt more strongly in urban schools where the threat of accountability-related sanctions is more serious.

ESOL, BILINGUAL EDUCATION, AND HOME LANGUAGE POLICIES

Content area assessment and measures of AYP for ELL students cannot be separated from the language programs that serve these students. The nature of language programs has been an ongoing topic of debate among politicians, the public, and the educational community (García & Curry Rodríguez, 2000; Wiley & Wright, 2004). Policies mandating the types of language programs that ELL students have access to largely determine how subject area content, such as science, is taught to these students. If a state supports bilingual education, then it is likely that at least some portion of science instruction is conducted in the student's home language while they are developing academic language proficiency in English (Kelly & Breton, 2001; Rosebery et al., 1992). In states that follow an English only policy for ELL students, then all science instruction takes place in their second language and science knowledge has to be developed concurrently with academic English (Gutierrez, Asato, Pacheco, Moll, Olson, Horng, Ruiz, Garcia, & McCarty, 2002).

There are numerous challenges to both of these approaches. Bilingual programs have been critiqued for the lack of rigorous content area instruction they sometimes provide for ELL students, especially when bilingual teachers lack the necessary content area training in subjects such as science and mathematics. English-only programs have been critiqued for failing to take advantage of the rich linguistic and cultural resources that ELL students bring to the science classroom, but which are effectively shut out when home language is ignored, or worse yet, penalized. Additionally, pull-out models of ESOL instruction remove students from content area instruction such as science, while they work on developing social and communicative English skills at the expense of content knowledge and academic language development. Push-in models, where an ESOL teacher works with ELL students within the content area classroom, may better allow these students to engage in content knowledge and academic language development, but create significant staffing and budgeting challenges. Finally, ELL students are often assessed as English-proficient based on their social and communicative skills, resulting in the removal of ESOL services and support well before students have mastered academic English. All of these policies tend to restrict the science learning opportunities available to ELL students.

Teachers who are willing (and allowed) to make use of students' home language and culture in science instruction face additional challenges. Curriculum materials and other science trade books in languages other than English are limited. Many of these resources are translations of English-language materials that lag behind the current generation of English-language curriculum and may not be fully aligned with the demands of accountability policy. In addition, the more innovative curriculum materials, such as those developed in the science education research community, are less likely to be translated into languages other than English than some of the mass-produced curricular materials.

Research on science instruction with ELL students highlights the role of hands-on, inquiry-based science in enabling these students to develop scientific understanding and academic English proficiency simultaneously (Amaral, Garrison, & Klentschy, 2002; Lee & Fradd, 1998). In reality, however, ELL students rarely experience hands-on, inquiry-based science. There are many reasons for this, including the limited number of teachers who have the required knowledge and experience in both ESOL and inquiry-based science instruction, pull-out programs that remove ELL students from content area instruction, limited instructional time for science because of the urgency of developing basic literacy and numeracy, lack of science instructional materials that are both content- and language-appropriate, and inadequate science supplies for hands-on inquiry. Each of these topics is taken up in more detail later in the book.

URBAN SCHOOLING

Even when non-mainstream students have access to teachers with adequate knowledge of science content and appropriate instructional strategies, both students and teachers also need access to the resources required to practice inquiry-based science. Compared to their peers in suburban schools, students and teachers in urban schools often face additional challenges, including a general lack of resources and funding, lack of appropriate science instructional materials and supplies including technology, overcrowding and management issues, and emotional concerns related to conditions of poverty in students' homes (Knapp & Plecki, 2001; Spillane, Diamond, Walker, Halverson, & Jita, 2001).

Another set of issues, common in urban settings, involves the inequitable distribution of highly qualified teachers across schools and districts. While all students need access to highly qualified teachers, schools serving non-mainstream students need the best teachers to help students overcome achievement gaps (Marx & Harris, 2006). However, the neediest students in urban or low-performing schools often have the least prepared teachers, who are frequently teaching out of their content areas or without teacher certification. Using NCLB criteria for defining highly qualified teachers, Tuerk (2005) examined the distribution of teachers in Virginia in 2002. The results indicated that students who attended high-poverty schools were more likely to be taught by teachers who do not meet the criteria of highly qualified teachers.

Still another set of challenges to innovative science education in urban settings involves issues of mobility. Urban schools experience high rates of teacher mobility (moving about within the education system) and attrition (leaving the education system) (Loeb, Darling-Hammond, & Luczak, 2005). Mobility is a limiting factor because even the best curriculum materials and instructional strategies can only be as effective as their implementation. Innovative curriculum materials require extensive professional development. If teachers move from grade to grade, school to school, or district to district, they are less likely to be able to take advantage of systematic professional development that could help them make better use of innovative curriculum. The same can be said of teacher attrition. As teachers leave the profession altogether, they are frequently replaced by inexperienced teachers who must be trained anew.

Student mobility and attrition (dropout) can be seen in much the same way because a cycling of students through classrooms can negatively influence innovative science curriculum and instruction. High rates of student mobility are commonly observed in urban, economically disadvantaged areas (Engec, 2006; Kerbow, 1996; Mehana & Reynolds, 2004; Rumberger, 2003; Temple & Reynolds, 1999). In the current context of high-stakes testing, some science programs are designed to spiral students through several years of coordinated topics. Students coming and going within and beyond a given school or district means that these students are bound to miss large chunks of the curriculum and lack continuity in curriculum exposure. Student mobility also poses an obstacle to implementing and evaluating the effects of an educational intervention because high mobility rates influence student exposure to the intervention, which, in turn, influences achievement. This can lead to two undesirable outcomes: 1) mobile students may not receive the full benefit of the intervention resulting in lower achievement, and 2) evaluations of the intervention's influence on student achievement may underestimate the effect of the intervention.

Because rates of both teacher and student mobility are often highest among children of economically disadvantaged households in urban areas, these undesirable outcomes may be most common in schools that are often targeted by interventions. High mobility rates complicate an educational intervention, compromise fidelity of implementation, disrupt students' learning progression and achievement outcomes, and underestimate the potential (true) effect of the intervention. As a result, high mobility rates can counteract best efforts at implementing and evaluating school-based reforms. Educational researchers, curriculum developers, and policy makers alike must consider teacher and student mobility issues in designing, implementing, and evaluating educational interventions in urban settings in order to reach those students who need such interventions the most.

SUMMARY

The topics of varying theoretical perspectives, definitions of science and school science, high-stakes testing and accountability policies in science education, language policies for ELL students, and the challenges facing urban schools are all issues that will arise repeatedly throughout the remainder of this book. Teaching science to non-mainstream students is a complex proposition that must take into account many features of learners, teachers, schools, and policies. Research studies that focus on ways to improve science teaching for non-mainstream students must similarly take each of these features into account, making such research challenging and sometimes problematic. It is to the credit of the researchers whose work is described here that the field has made much progress over the past 2 decades.

ACTIVITIES FOR CHAPTER 2

1. Multicultural views of scientific discovery are often difficult for people to conceptualize because most of us have been taught only a universalist view of Western modern science.
   A. With a partner, pick one of the following topics and search for resources that provide relevant information about the topic. Possible topics include:
      i. Navigation techniques developed by people of the Pacific Islands
      ii. Astronomy and calendars developed by the Mayans
      iii. Crop development and controlled breeding of potatoes developed by the Incas
      iv. Mathematics and architecture developed by the Egyptians
      v. Earthquake detection and prediction by the Chinese
      vi. Medicinal value of plants and herbal medicine developed by indigenous people in tropical regions around the world
      vii. Ecological monitoring of animal populations and environmental conservation practices developed by First Nations people in Canada
      viii. Other examples you can find on your own

    B. Prepare a 5–10 minute oral presentation for your class on: 1) the science-related work done on your topic, 2) the reasons behind this scientific work, and 3) how this work might be similar to or different from how and why Western modern science might study the same topic.

2. Are students and teachers better off when science is part of state accountability measures or when it is not? Do the following tasks:

    A. Make a list of five reasons why it might be better for science to be part of accountability. Make a list of five reasons why it might be better if it is not.

    B. Share your list with a partner and discuss both of your lists. How are they similar and different?

    C. Merge your two lists into one list that includes the best of both of your ideas.

    D. Join with another pair of students and repeat this process—compare and contrast your two lists and then merge the lists into one list of your best ideas.

    E. Each group of four students shares their combined list with the rest of the class.

3. Many Americans have strong opinions about bilingual education and English-only policies, yet relatively few Americans have lived or traveled for extended periods of time in other countries where English is not commonly spoken. Imagine that you will be working in another country for a year, and in your job you will be working mostly with people who do not speak English. You receive ongoing job training to help you in your new position. Think about yourself as a learner.

    A. Would you rather receive all of the training only in English? All of the training only in the language of the people with whom you'll be working? Some combination of the two?

    B. Write a detailed description of how you would like to receive the training and why.

    C. How is this hypothetical situation both similar to and different from the experience of ELL students who arrive in U.S. schools?

PART II

Classroom Practices

In an attempt to address the gaps in science outcomes that are outlined in Chapter 2, the second part of this book focuses on the characteristics of both students and science learning environments that have been linked to those gaps. Students' science learning occurs primarily in the context of classroom practices—how students learn science, how science content is taught, what curriculum materials are used and what science content is taught, and how students' mastery of science content is assessed. Chapters in this part present research and classroom practices in the following areas: science learning and student diversity (Chapter 3), science instruction (Chapter 4), science curriculum including computer technology (Chapter 5), and science assessment (Chapter 6). Special attention is given to the unique needs of ELL students in the science classroom.

Science Learning and Student Diversity

In recent years, science learning has been studied using a wide range of theoretical perspectives and research methods. Some studies examine student characteristics and beliefs related to science learning, others focus on learning processes in the context of science instruction, and yet others focus on learning outcomes. This chapter describes the following topics as they have been grounded in particular theoretical or conceptual perspectives: 1) student characteristics related to science achievement and career choices from educational psychology perspectives, 2) scientific reasoning and argumentation from learning sciences perspectives, 3) students' cultural beliefs and practices related to science learning from cross-cultural and multicultural perspectives, 4) the sociopolitical process of learning from critical theory and postmodern perspectives, and 5) identity, discourse, and third (or hybrid) space as they apply to science learning.

FACTORS RELATED TO SCIENCE ACHIEVEMENT AND CAREER CHOICE

In a literature review that has guided much of the subsequent work on this topic, Oakes (1990) outlined a wide range of cognitive and affective attributes, school experiences, and societal influences that have been linked to differences in students' science achievement, persistence, and career choices. She highlighted how these factors play out differentially among racial/ethnic and gender groups. The studies described below examined various combinations of student characteristics and school experiences. These studies relied upon national databases such as the National Assessment of Educational Progress (NAEP), the National Educational Longitudinal Study (NELS), High School and Beyond, and the Scholastic Achievement Test (SAT).

Science Achievement. A set of key studies carried out by multiple research groups examined science achievement using NELS data disaggregated by race/ethnicity, SES, and gender in secondary school. Hamilton, Nussbaum, Kupermintz, Kerkhoven, and Snow (1995) examined both student and teacher factors related to science achievement scores of over 5,000 students in eighth grade and then 2 years later in 10th grade. This data set was expanded further when Nussbaum, Hamilton, and Snow (1997) gathered additional NELS data on nearly 3,900 of the initial 5,000 students when they reached 12th grade. Analysis showed a variety of effects across identified science factors, such as spatial-mechanical reasoning, quantitative science, and scientific reasoning. At both the 10th and 12th grades, race/ethnicity and gender were the greatest predictors of spatial-mechanical reasoning ability. In 10th grade, Black and Hispanic students performed lower than White students, but there was no difference between Asian and White students. In 12th grade, Black and Asian students performed lower than White students, but there was no difference between Hispanic and White students. In both grades, females performed lower than males. The effects of SES also differed between the two grade levels. In 10th grade, low-SES students performed lower than middle-SES students, but in 12th grade there was no difference between low- and middle-SES students. Thus, at each grade level, different patterns of student factors were associated with science achievement. The results of this series of large-scale studies suggest that achievement tests are multidimensional and that analyses based solely on total scores can obscure meaningful patterns in the data. Instead, the addition of psychologically meaningful subscores can enhance test validity. More important for students and teachers, these subscores point to patterns of strength and weakness that may guide and improve classroom practices.

Muller, Stage, and Kinzie (2001) used the same longitudinal NELS data (8th, 10th, and 12th grades) to examine student and school factors related to science achievement. Particularly, they looked at the demographic subgroups of race/ethnicity, SES, and gender. The results indicated that across all racial/ethnic and gender subgroups, students' SES and sixth- through eighth-grade science report card grades were positively related to students' eighth-grade standardized science performance. At the high school level, the total number of Carnegie units in science was the only consistent predictor of science growth rates across all racial/ethnic and gender subgroups. However, the relationships between student and school factors and science growth rates differed greatly across demographic subgroups. The results indicated that requiring all students to take 4 years of high-quality science coursework would be the most effective way to reduce science achievement gaps in high school.

Peng and Hill (1994) also used the NELS data to analyze science achievement of about 6,500 African American, Hispanic, and Native American/Native Alaskan students. The students were classified into four achievement levels based on their science and mathematics test scores in the eighth grade. Peng and Hill examined the influence of three sets of factors, including student characteristics, school context, and family resources and activities. They differentiated high- and low-achieving minority students in science and mathematics. They were able to identify both student and school factors that were related to science achievement, regardless of the students' cultural and ethnic backgrounds. Students taking college preparatory courses were more likely to be in the high-achieving group, suggesting the value of all students receiving more rigorous academic training.

Students who were less actively involved in class and less likely to complete homework were more likely to be in the low-achieving group, suggesting the need to find ways to more fully engage all students in science learning activities.

Science Careers. Another set of studies examined factors related to students' choice of science majors or science-related careers and whether these factors varied based on students' race/ethnicity and gender. Maple and Stage (1991) used the High School and Beyond data to study a national sample of close to 2,500 Black and White students. They analyzed the data using a wide range of students' background characteristics (seven variables) and high school experiences (six variables). They used these variables to explore the rates at which students chose a mathematics or science major in college. Across racial/ethnic and gender subgroups, significant predictors of choosing a mathematics or science major included the expressed interest in a mathematical or scientific field of study in the first 2 years of high school, the number of mathematics and science courses completed in high school, and parental involvement in their children's education during the high school years. There were also many differences, however, across the demographic subgroups and interactions between race/ethnicity and gender. The model explained nearly twice as much variance for the Black male, Black female, and White male subgroups compared with the White female subgroup. This finding indicates that different subgroups follow different paths in arriving at the selection of a mathematics or science major.

Similarly, Hill, Pettus, and Hedin (1990) surveyed students about their perceptions of seven factors that could influence science career choices: teacher/counselor encouragement, participation in science-related hobbies and activities, academic self-image, science-related career interest, parental encouragement and support, perceived relevance of mathematics and science, and mathematics and science-related abilities such as critical thinking. The study used a series of three surveys with over 500 middle and high school students in Virginia. The analysis focused on the effects of race/ethnicity, gender, and personal acquaintance with a scientist. The results indicated that whereas Black students expressed a significantly higher science career preference than their White counterparts, Black students also expressed significantly lower perceptions of their science-related ability. The results also indicated that across both race/ethnicity and gender, having personal contact with a scientist was a major factor affecting student preferences for science-related careers. The findings suggest the importance of science role models, and particularly those from one's own race and gender, in promoting the idea of choosing a science career.

Grandy (1998) used data from a longitudinal survey of high-achieving minority SAT takers to determine the effects of students' background and school variables on their persistence in science over a 5-year period. Data collection occurred at three points in time during the 5-year period. The first round of data collection in 1985 involved high school students who had scored at least 550 on the SAT mathematics section (which placed them among the top 29% of scores at that time) and who indicated a plan to major in a science-related field in college. The second round of data collection took place 2 years after these students graduated from high school, by means of a lengthy questionnaire that was sent to all the students from the first pool. The third round of data collection occurred in 1990, 5 years after the students graduated from high school. Students who had completed the questionnaire in the second round of data collections were either contacted by phone or sent a short questionnaire. Eventually, the number of students for whom all the three rounds of data were available totaled over 2,500 (43% of the original sample). This final sample included students who persisted in science-related fields, as well as those students who switched majors or did not complete college. The results of this long-term study indicated two key predictors of student persistence in science from high school through college. The first involved maintaining a commitment to science (defined in terms of the extent to which students both enjoyed and felt committed to their chosen major field) that persisted during the sophomore year of college (the time of the second round of data collection). The second predictor involved the perceived availability of minority support systems (defined in terms of access to minority or female role models and advisors, advice and support from more advanced students of their own racial/ethnic group, and a dedicated minority relations staff at their college). The availability of role models and advisors of the same racial/ethnic background was shown to be especially important to building enthusiasm for science during the first 2 years of college.

Overall, when considering factors that influence students' science achievement, static demographic variables such as race/ethnicity, SES, and gender seem to play a role. They do not determine performance, however, and other factors predict performance as well. Students who are actively engaged in learning science and challenged with rigorous science coursework are likely to be high achievers regardless of demographic variables. Despite the small number of studies looking at racial/ethnic, SES, and gender differences on factors related to science achievement and choice of science-related careers, these studies were large in scale and provided consistent patterns.

First, three sets of factors seem to play key roles in students choosing science-related careers: 1) reasoning and critical thinking ability; 2) prior academic training and achievement in science, such as science grades and coursetaking; and 3) the presence of support systems, including role models and mentors of similar racial/ethnic and gender backgrounds (Grandy, 1998; Hill et al., 1990; Peng & Hill, 1994; Muller et al., 2001). Each of these factors can and should be promoted rigorously in schools to provide equitable science learning opportunities for all students. As was pointed out in Chapter 2, however, these opportunities are not equitably distributed, and non-mainstream students are likely to have fewer high school science course enrollment options and less access to role models of science college students or scientists from similar racial/ethnic backgrounds.

Second, although some factors seem to be consistently significant across racial/ ethnic, SES, and gender subgroups, other factors play differential roles with specific subgroups (Hamilton et al., 1995; Maple & Stage, 1991; Muller et al., 2001; Nussbaum et al., 1997). In addition, while little is known about the variance in science outcomes by race/ethnicity, SES, and gender, even less is known about non-mainstream students specifically. These findings caution against assuming that factors influencing mainstream students' science achievement apply to non-mainstream students and argue for more research involving non-mainstream students.

Finally, results consistently highlight the need for data to be disaggregated by demographic subgroups. Disaggregated results can help researchers develop more valid and reliable predictors and models of science outcomes tailored to specific subgroups (Hamilton et al., 1995; Nussbaum et al., 1997). Disaggregated data are also essential for policy makers and practitioners who are making decisions to effect changes in science outcomes across subgroups. Making such decisions based on collapsed data that do not adequately consider the unique needs of students from diverse demographic subgroups runs the risk of further disadvantaging the very students that such interventions are at least nominally proposed to help.

SCIENTIFIC REASONING AND ARGUMENTATION

Access to rigorous and engaging science teaching that promotes scientific reasoning and argumentation has emerged as a key factor in promoting science learning of all students. While this factor can be directly enhanced through improved instructional practices, these studies also show that non-mainstream students tend to have less access to such instruction than their mainstream peers. To better provide learning opportunities that support the development of reasoning skills to a wider range of students, teachers need to understand the place of scientific reasoning and argumentation in science learning.

Literature on Scientific Reasoning and Argumentation. Research on reasoning has its foundation in the highly controlled experimental studies of classical developmental and cognitive psychology. Building on the work of Piaget (Inhelder & Piaget, 1964; Piaget, 1973), reasoning has been conceived as the required thinking skills for conducting scientific inquiry through experimentation (Keil & Wilson, 2000), evaluating evidence (Klahr, 2000), and engaging in argumentation in the service of promoting scientific understanding (Kuhn, 1991).

Historically, two main approaches have been used to study and interpret reasoning, sometimes referred to as *experimentation strategy* and *conceptual change*

(Schauble, 1996). The first approach, experimentation strategy, has used a domain-general focus on reasoning and problem-solving strategies applicable to a range of science and everyday tasks (Kuhn, White, Klahr, & Carver, 1995; Metz, 1991). The focus has been on studying the strategies that individuals develop for generating and interpreting evidence. These strategies include hypothesis generation, control of variables, and evaluation of evidence. This research has used *knowledge-lean tasks* designed to isolate general skills and strategies in the absence of required domain-specific knowledge. The second approach, conceptual change, has used a domain-specific focus on the development of conceptual knowledge within particular scientific domains (Carey, 1987; Keil & Wilson, 2000; Smith, Maclin, Houghton, & Hennessey, 2000). This research has used *knowledge-rich tasks* designed to examine the content and structure of students' domain-specific reasoning and problem solving.

Research from developmental and cognitive psychology provides several important lessons when attempting to support the reasoning development of all students and especially non-mainstream students. First, this research indicates that a focus on generic process skills (e.g., observation, description, prediction, inference) and direct instruction of science content is a weak way to promote reasoning as compared to knowledge-rich activities within a particular domain (Zimmerman, 2000). Knowledge-lean activities, however, remain typical in the experience of many students and are especially common in science instruction with non-mainstream students.

Second, teachers should be aware that it is a significant challenge for students to recraft their prior ideas and conceptions to align with more scientifically acceptable explanations of the natural world. This challenge highlights the importance of identifying students' prior knowledge on science topics (diSessa & Sherin, 1998). Accessing prior knowledge, including connections to students' home language and culture, is essential for students to create frameworks upon which they can build new understandings.

In addition to these developmental and cognitive psychology perspectives, other literature rooted in the sociology of science and cultural psychology argues that the ways of knowing and talking characteristic of children from outside the cultural and linguistic mainstream may be more generally continuous with those characteristic of scientific communities than is generally recognized. This research primarily employs discourse analysis of students' oral and written communication as they interact with teachers or peers during scientific inquiry tasks.

Based on detailed analyses of the everyday practice and talk of scientists, research in the sociology of science defines science and scientific practices more broadly than traditional definitions that emphasize experimentation and theory-building (Latour & Woolgar, 1986; M. Lynch, 1985). This view of scientific practices is embedded within the personal, social, and historical contexts of scientific communities. It also highlights the creative and interpersonal aspects of scientific practice, such as the role of imagination, conjecture, the beliefs and desires of individual scientists, and the emergent rather than predetermined nature of scientific investigation and discovery.

Scientific Reasoning and Argumentation of Non-Mainstream Students.

Following a programmatic line of research since the mid-1980s, the Chèche Konnen team, led by Ann Rosebery and Beth Warren, has conducted case studies of low-income students from African American, Haitian, and Latino backgrounds in both bilingual and monolingual classrooms. This research considers children's experimental reasoning in ways that differ substantially from the cognitive development tradition. As described above, most studies in the cognitive development tradition approach experimentation as a process of logical inference through which children identify variables and uncover relationships already designed into the experimental setup. In contrast, the Chèche Konnen research uses fairly open-ended tasks in which experimentation is approached as an exploratory process of constructing meanings from emerging variables (Warren, Ballenger, et al., 2001). The research addresses questions such as: What do children do as they engage in experimental tasks? What resources—linguistic, conceptual, material, and imaginative—do they draw on as they develop and evaluate experimental tasks? How does children's scientific reasoning correspond to the nature of experimentation as practiced by scientists?

The results indicated that non-mainstream students were capable of conducting scientific inquiry and using scientific reasoning through open science inquiry or "doing science." For example, Rosebery, Warren, and Conant (1992) examined the effects of doing science on non-mainstream students' use of scientific reasoning. The study involved students in one middle school and one high school classroom, and was based on interviews with 16 students at the beginning and end of instruction. At the start of the school year, students showed almost no evidence of understanding hypothesis testing through experimentation. They relied on personal experience as evidence for a particular belief. During the school year, they engaged in inquiry tasks, such as analyzing the water quality of school water fountains and the ecology of a local pond. At the end of the school year, they could generate hypotheses that were explanatory and testable. They understood that hypothesis testing through experimentation provided more reliable evidence than unstructured observation.

The research also considers students' everyday experiences and ways of knowing and talking. When views of both science practices and children's sense-making are broadened and treated flexibly, conclusions can be drawn about the degree of convergence between the two. Rosebery, Warren, and colleagues on the Chèche Konnen Project have examined relationships between scientific practices and the everyday sense-making of children from diverse cultures and languages (Ballenger, 1997; Hudicourt-Barnes, 2003; Rosebery, Warren, & Conant, 1992;

Warren, Ballenger et al., 2001; Warren & Rosebery, 1996; Warren, Rosebery, & Conant, 1994). This work has predominantly focused on continuities between the forms of reasoning and argumentation characteristic of non-mainstream students and those characteristic of scientific communities. It also emphasizes how the students draw upon their everyday knowledge when engaged in scientific inquiry, reasoning, and argumentation.

The results of these studies highlight ways in which students' ways of knowing and talking are continuous with those of scientific communities. The results also indicate that non-mainstream students deploy sense-making practices—deep questions, vigorous argumentation, situated guesswork, embedded imagining, multiple perspectives, and innovative uses of everyday words to construct new meanings—that can be viewed as intellectual resources in learning science. For example, argumentative discussion is a major feature of social interaction among Haitian adults and can be seen in the way people in Haiti *bay odyans* or "to give talk" (Hudicourt-Barnes, 2003). This adult mode of discourse can be a resource for students as they practice argumentation in science. While Haitian students are typically quiet and respectful in the classroom (Ballenger, 1992), when in a culturally familiar environment, these same students participate in animated arguments about scientific phenomena in a way that is integral to Haitian culture and congruent with scientific practices (Ballenger, 1997; Hudicourt-Barnes, 2003; Warren, Ballenger et al., 2001).

CULTURAL BELIEFS AND PRACTICES

As is made clear by the work of the Chèche Konnen Project among others, by the time students come to school, they already possess knowledge, values, and ways of looking at the world that have developed during their socialization into their families and communities. These intellectual and cultural resources should be acknowledged, understood, and valued in the school context, including the science classroom. The intellectual and cultural resources that non-mainstream students bring to school are often undervalued because they are not easily recognized as relevant or valuable by the mainstream (Lee & Fradd, 1998; Moje, Collazo, Carillo, & Marx, 2001; Warren, Ballenger et al., 2001). Recognition of students' academic strengths and limitations related to their prior knowledge and beliefs enables them to better learn the high-status knowledge that is valued in school science.

Literature on cultural beliefs and practices indicates that students from some cultural communities come to school with experiences and ideas that are sometimes discontinuous with Western science both as it is practiced in the science community and as it is taught in school science. From cross-cultural and multicultural education perspectives, equitable science learning opportunities allow students to successfully participate in Western science, while also validating and building upon the knowledge, beliefs, and problem-solving strategies characteristic of their communities of origin (Aikenhead, 2001a; Aikenhead & Jegede, 1999; Snively & Corsiglia, 2001). When such learning opportunities are provided, students gain access to the high-status knowledge of Western science, without feeling that they must choose between school success and the beliefs and practices of their own cultural group. Science teaching and learning that recognizes and values diverse views of the natural world and diverse ways of knowing can simultaneously promote academic achievement and strengthen students' cultural and linguistic identities.

The literature on non-mainstream students' cultural beliefs and practices and the influences of these beliefs and practices on science learning points to three distinct but related foci: 1) worldviews, 2) communication and interaction patterns, and 3) making the transition between students' cultural beliefs and practices and the culture of Western science.

Worldviews. There is a well-established literature on the worldviews of diverse groups of students both in the U.S. and in other countries (see Cobern, 1991, 1996 for a theoretical discussion of the concept of worldviews as it relates to science and science education). Studies in the U.S. have included worldviews of Kickapoo Native American students in Texas (Allen & Crawley, 1998), Yup'ik students in Alaska (Kawagley, Norris-Tull, & Norris-Tull, 1998), and African American, Hispanic and mainstream White students in the Southeast (Lee, 1999b). There is also a substantial body of literature on science and worldviews of students in countries other than the U.S. Methodologically, the majority of these worldview studies have used questionnaires or interviews to make inferences about students' worldviews. A small number of studies used correlational methods to examine the relationships between students' worldviews and contextual features. Observational studies are rare. The studies on science and worldviews offer several key findings.

First, across cultural groups, there is a broadly held public acceptance of supernatural, spiritual, or animistic views of the working of nature. These views appear strongest among non-mainstream students in the U.S. and in developing countries around the world. For example, Lee (1999b) examined children's worldviews after personally experiencing a hurricane. The study addressed three issues: 1) children's knowledge of the hurricane, 2) children's worldviews with regard to the causality of the hurricane, and 3) children's sources of information about the hurricane. The study involved over 120 fourth- and fifth-grade students in two elementary schools located in areas that were particularly hard-hit by the hurricane.

Students' interpretations of the hurricane differed by ethnicity and SES. African American and Hispanic elementary students were more likely to attribute the cause of the disaster to societal problems (e.g., racism, crime, violence) and spiritual or supernatural forces (e.g., God, the devil, evil spirits). White students were more likely to give explanations in terms of natural phenomena (e.g., weather patterns, ocean conditions). Likewise, low-SES students, regardless of ethnicity, attributed the cause of the hurricane to perceived personal or family wrongdoing (e.g., divorce, fights, drug use), societal problems, or supernatural forces more often than did middle-SES students. This pattern of results was more pronounced when ethnicity and SES were examined together.

White students were more knowledgeable about aspects of the Western scientific explanation of the hurricane than were African American and Hispanic students. Middle-SES students were more knowledgeable than low-SES students. When ethnicity, SES, and gender were examined together, white male students from middle-SES backgrounds were the most knowledgeable about the Western scientific explanation of all groups. Thus, students' worldviews seemed to be related to their canonical science knowledge relevant to the event. Students who expressed alternative worldviews about the causes of the hurricane also tended to have incorrect science knowledge about the hurricane.

Students across demographic subgroups consistently claimed television and parents to be the two most important sources of their knowledge about the hurricane, but there were notable differences in the consistency of information sources. White students generally obtained information from different sources that were relatively consistent with one another as well as with the view of Western science, whereas African American and Hispanic students obtained information from sources that were often incompatible with one another and the view of Western science. Middle-SES students obtained more scientifically consistent information from television as their most important source, whereas low-SES students generally obtained limited or scientifically inconsistent information from parents as their most important source. Again, this pattern of results was more pronounced when ethnicity and SES were examined together.

A second key finding about the studies on worldviews, specifically those conducted in African countries, is that African students often expressed alternative worldviews even after taking science courses. Students with a high level of belief in traditional African worldviews did not perform in science as well as those with a low level of such beliefs, and students who took more science courses expressed more scientific worldviews and had higher science achievement and more positive attitudes than those with fewer science courses.

Okebukola and Jegede (1990) examined the relationships between traditional African cosmology and science learning in Nigeria. They studied secondary school students to test the hypothesis that sociocultural variables influenced students' attainment of science concepts. They considered a number of variables, including the general environment of the community (rural or automated), students' reasoning patterns (empirical or magical/superstitious), students' goal structure preferences (cooperative, competitive, or individualistic), and nature of the home (authoritarian or permissive). The results showed that: 1) students who lived in predominantly automated environments did significantly better in concept attainment than those in predominantly rural environments, 2) students whose reasoning patterns were predominantly empirical did significantly better than those whose reasoning was more magical, 3) students who expressed preference for cooperative learning did significantly better than those who expressed preference for competitive or individual work, and 4) students from permissive homes did significantly better than those from authoritarian homes. Jegede and Okebukola (1991b) also reported that Nigerian high school students with a high level of belief in African traditional cosmology made significantly fewer correct observations of natural phenomena in science classes compared to those with a low level of such belief. However, Jegede and Okebukola (1991a) found that when Nigerian high school students participated in a 6-week instructional intervention that specifically focused on evaluating African traditional beliefs in light of scientific knowledge acquired in inquiry-based biology lessons, the students had higher science achievement and more positive attitudes toward science than students in the control group, who received typical Western science instruction with no connections made to African traditional beliefs. Students did not necessarily replace their traditional beliefs with Western scientific explanations, but rather, they were able to find ways to connect the two.

A third key finding from the study of worldviews is that while conducting scientific inquiry is a challenge for most students, it presents an additional set of challenges for students from cultures that do not encourage young people to question communally held knowledge and beliefs. Many of the studies on worldviews have focused on cultures whose traditional childrearing and formal education practices tend to be authoritarian in nature (e.g., Akatugba & Wallace, 1999; Arellano, Barcenal, Bilbao, Castellano, Nichols, & Tippins, 2001; McKinley, Waiti, & Bell, 1992; Ninnes, 1994, 1995, 2000; Prophet, 1990; Prophet & Rowell, 1993; Shumba, 1999; Waldrip & Taylor, 1999a, 1999b). In these cultures, behavioral norms highlight respect for teachers and other adults as authoritative sources of knowledge. Children are not expected or encouraged to develop their own theories or arguments based on evidence or reasoning Because inquiry and critical questioning are generally not encouraged at home or in school in these cultures, children's discussion about why their answers or ideas were correct or incorrect were rarely observed in science classrooms.

Allen and Crawley (1998) conducted a study of Kickapoo Indians in Texas that is unique in several respects: 1) it is one of a small number of worldview studies conducted in the U.S.; 2) it used ethnographic methods (interviewing, participant observation) over an extensive period of fieldwork; 3) it examined multiple perspectives of participants, including students, teachers who both shared and did not share the students' background, and community members; 4) it was conducted in both science classrooms and community settings, and 5) it highlighted points of congruence between participants' traditional views and modern scientific perspectives, whereas most other studies focused on points of conflict between the two. Key findings included differences between the worldview of Kickapoo members (both middle school students and adults) and the worldview expressed by two science teachers who did not share the students' background. Differences were observed with regard to epistemology, preferred methods of teaching and learning, spatial/temporal orientation, behavioral norms, and perspectives on the place of humans in the natural world. The researchers also noted, however, that some of the views held by the Kickapoo students (e.g., cooperative learning and holistic content) were aligned with modern ecological perspectives that are becoming more broadly accepted in the science community. They concluded that while none of the worldview differences between traditional Kickapoo beliefs and Western modern science would directly prevent students from participating in the science community, many of these differences did seem to hinder the students when it came to being successful in the science classroom. They attributed this lack of success in science largely to the science teachers' failure to recognize and build upon the connections between students' worldviews and scientific beliefs and practices.

Communication and Interaction Patterns. In addition to worldviews, another way to consider cultural knowledge and beliefs is through communication and interaction patterns among students from diverse backgrounds (see the review by Atwater, 1994). Literature reviews have addressed science education among African American (Atwater, 2000; Norman, Ault, Bentz, & Meskimen, 2001), Asian American (Lee, 1996), Hispanic (Rakow & Bermudez, 1993), and Native American students (Kawagley et al., 1998; Nelson-Barber & Estrin, 1995, 1996; Riggs, 2005). Consistent findings from these reviews indicate that cultural norms and expectations for non-mainstream students tend to be inconsistent with the expectations of school and school science. Based on such results, the reviews draw implications for science learning that highlight the importance of building upon students' cultural patterns as a knowledge base for culturally congruent instruction (discussed in Chapter 4).

A small number of studies have examined culturally specific communication and interaction patterns within the context of science instruction. Since the early 1990s, Okhee Lee and colleagues have conducted a programmatic line of research to promote science learning and English language development among elementary students from diverse linguistic and cultural backgrounds (see the details in Lee, 2002). At the start of this research, Lee and Fradd (Lee & Fradd, 1996a, 1996b; Lee, Fradd, & Sutman, 1995) worked with pairs of Hispanic, Haitian, White, and African American elementary students. The students interacted with teachers who were matched in terms of ethnicity, language, and gender (e.g., a pair of Haitian girls with a Haitian female teacher) to work on science tasks outside the classroom setting. The eight participating teachers were selected based on their expertise in working with non-mainstream students, and most had advanced degrees in ESOL/ bilingual education. Interviews were conducted in the language of the students' choice (English, Haitian Creole, and/or Spanish). Results indicated both similarities and differences in communication and interaction patterns among culturally and linguistically diverse groups of elementary students.

Lee, Fradd, and Sutman (1995) examined science vocabulary, science knowledge, and cognitive strategy use among the student groups. Compared to White students, students from non-mainstream backgrounds had more difficulty applying science knowledge and vocabulary to the science tasks. Non-mainstream students were more likely to lack personal experience and prior knowledge relevant to the science tasks under study (e.g., swimming as an example of buoyancy or playing on a seesaw as an example of a lever). In addition, while some non-mainstream students had an understanding of the science concepts, they were more likely to lack the specific vocabulary (in either first or second language) to convey precise meanings. Other participants had only minimal prior schooling, and therefore lacked the background experience engaging in the science tasks. Furthermore, students from different backgrounds used different kinds of cognitive or problem-solving strategies, some of which were more closely aligned with typical Western science practices than others. Despite their challenges, non-mainstream students also demonstrated strengths, such as improved performance when the science tasks related to their prior experiences, a strong desire to engage in and succeed at the science activities, and positive feelings about the teachers.

Lee and Fradd (1996a) also examined mainstream and non-mainstream students' understanding and production of written and pictorial representations of science concepts. Specifically, the study focused on two aspects of literacy related to science performance: 1) students' interpretations of pictorial representations showing a series of science activities and 2) students' written summaries of those science activities. The results indicated that students generally had difficulty interpreting pictorial representations of science activities and communicating their ideas about science in writing. The results also indicated differences across student groups in terms of both the quantity and quality of their written and pictorial communication. A key conclusion of this study is that since written and pictorial representations of scientific ideas are central to successful scientific communication, science instruction needs to simultaneously promote science learning and the development of multiple literacies.

In addition, Lee and Fradd (1996b) examined patterns of verbal and nonverbal communication and engagement in science tasks among student-student-teacher triads. The results indicated consistent patterns within each group but distinct differences across the groups. Consistent patterns of verbal and nonverbal communication were observed within each group with regard to talk (linear or overlapping), turn-taking (sequential or simultaneous), unit of discourse (complete sentences or words/phrases), and nonverbal communication (gestures and facial expressions). Consistent patterns of task engagement were also observed within each group with regard to task performance (step-by-step or overlapping activities), mode of teacher guidance (probing/eliciting or telling/teaching), teacher reinforcement (information feedback or social, motivational statements), and student initiative (task-related or social-personal). The key finding of the study was that teachers and students of the same cultural and linguistic background interacted in ways that were more likely to promote students' participation and engagement. One conclusion that can be drawn is that an effort should be made to give students access to teachers or mentors from similar cultural and linguistic backgrounds. Another conclusion is that teachers of all backgrounds should learn about the cultural and linguistic backgrounds of their students in order to foster more culturally congruent teaching and learning.

Learning experiences in the community may be more or less culturally congruent with practices in the science classroom. According to Lipka (1998), Yup'ik children in Alaska learn science-related skills (e.g., fishing, building fish racks, and using stars to navigate) from observing experienced adults and then actively participating as apprentice-helpers in home and community settings. Children and adults engage in joint activities for long periods of time, during which observation and guided practice, rather than verbal interaction, are central to the learning process. This style of learning may not be optimal within a traditional Western school system that organizes learning around short and frequent class periods and expects students to listen passively to teachers, follow directions, and respond to questions verbally or in writing. The communication and interaction patterns in the Yup'ik and many other indigenous communities are grounded in spiritual, pragmatic, and inductive ways of thinking and problem solving (Kawagley et al., 1998). Natural phenomena are explained in terms of readily observable characteristics or experiences involving a high degree of intuitive thought. Many practices, skills, and values that are instilled in children in indigenous cultures, such as managing natural resources and living in harmony with the environment, have sound scientific rationales that could serve as a bridge for teaching and learning science. In contrast, traditional Western scientific approaches to the natural world, such as an analytical and depersonalized approach to knowledge, can be alienating for Yup'ik and other indigenous youth.

Cultural Transition. The literature on worldviews and communication and interaction patterns in relation to science learning indicate that the culture of Western science is unique in ways that are viewed as foreign to many students, both mainstream and non-mainstream. In addition, the challenges of science learning seem to be greater for students whose worldviews, and cultural and communicative practices are discontinuous with the ways of knowing that are characteristic of both Western science and school science. An additional challenge for non-mainstream students is "to study a Western scientific way of knowing and at the same time respect and access the ideas, beliefs, and values of non-Western cultures" (Snively & Corsiglia, 2001, p. 24).

The ability to shift competently between different cultural contexts, belief systems, and communication styles is critically important to non-mainstream students' academic success. Giroux (1992), among others, has used the notion of *border crossing* to describe this process. To succeed in school, non-mainstream students must learn to negotiate the boundaries that separate their own cultural environments from the culture of Western science and school science (Aikenhead, 2001a; Aikenhead & Jegede, 1999; Costa, 1995; Jegede & Aikenhead, 1999). Even within the cultural mainstream, however, relatively few children's primary socialization is so science oriented as to be perfectly continuous with the demands of school science. At least some degree of border crossing between the culture of Western science and the culture of the everyday world is a challenge for all students (Driver, Asoko, Leach, Mortimer, & Scott, 1994; O'Loughlin, 1992). Still, the metaphorical distance that must be crossed is usually far greater for non-mainstream students, who are likely to find themselves torn between what is expected of them in science classrooms and what they experience at home and in their community. On the one hand, embracing the Western scientific worldview may alienate the child from his or her family or peers. On the other hand, rejecting the Western scientific worldview may marginalize the child from school. A key lesson from this literature is the critical role that teachers, parents, and other community members must play in helping all students to successfully bridge the cultural divide between home and school. While this may be more challenging with some students than others, the alternative is to risk having students become alienated and actively resist learning science.

SOCIOPOLITICAL PROCESS OF SCIENCE LEARNING

As an outgrowth of critical studies of schooling, some research has examined science learning as a sociopolitical process. This literature has several features that distinguish itself from other areas of research, described above.

First, it questions the relevance of science to students who have traditionally been underserved or even oppressed by the education system. This literature argues that science education should begin with the intellectual capital of the learner and his/her lived experiences, not with externally imposed standards. In this way, it attempts to invert the power structure of schooling and its negative effects on students from marginalized groups. Unlike the traditional learning paradigm where science is at the center, as a target to be reached by students at the margins, the sociopolitical approach is one of inclusion where students' experiences and identities remain central to the study of the world.

Second, this literature addresses issues of poverty, as well as cultural and linguistic diversity, from a critical perspective that focuses on the unequal distribution of social and educational resources along lines of class, race, and ethnicity. Researchers in this tradition generally ground their analyses in the political, cultural, and socioeconomic history of the study participants.

Finally, this literature employs critical ethnography as a research methodology that emerges collaboratively from the lives of the researcher and the researched and is centrally about praxis, the notion of action that is informed and driven by theory (Calabrese & Barton, 2001). Explicitly political in nature, critical ethnography allows and necessitates that educators make a political commitment to the struggle for liberation and in defense of human rights. The boundary between research and scholarship, on one hand, and advocacy and activism, on the other hand, is purposely blurred in this literature.

Calabrese Barton (1998a, 1998b, 1998c) and colleagues (Fusco, 2001; Fusco & Calabrese Barton, 2001) have carried out research with children living in poverty, specifically urban homeless children living in shelters who are most at risk for receiving an inequitable education (or no formal education at all). In a series of critical ethnographic studies, they presented narratives of how urban homeless children made sense of science based on their lived experiences.

Calabrese Barton (1998a) points out that science for all students, although egalitarian in theory, proves difficult to actualize among all students, especially those living and learning in poverty, in part because it positions students and science in a relationship where only students must change. Instead, she argues that to make science relevant to these students, both students and science itself must change, and that the relationship between science and students' lives should be central to the science education process. She further argues that educational research, including science education research, should be fundamentally about making a political commitment to the struggle for liberation.

Calabrese Barton (1998b) worked with urban homeless youth in an after-school science program conducted in a homeless shelter. The students took the lead in planning activities, documenting their explorations, and making meaning of their findings. The role of the researcher, as teacher, was to validate the students' experiences by using these experiences as the starting point for their explorations, to help them locate questions in their experiences, and to find ways to critically explore those questions. Through sharing their personal theories of the local community's pollution or the shelter's polices around food, the students in the program used their own personal experiences to define science, in terms of both practice and content. Throughout the teaching and learning process, students' identities remained one central focus, and democratic principles of empowerment remained another. Calabrese Barton argues that urban homeless children arrive at school with a set of struggles that are not reflected in the typical science curriculum or anywhere else in school. To better meet their learning needs, questions of identity and representation should be central to these students' science learning.

In a related study, Calabrese Barton (1998c) described how homeless children's personal constructions of science were demonstrated through acts of invention, such as creating a recipe for soup or making a purse out of beads and other supplies. She interpreted the children's inventive acts in terms of three themes: invention as a social act, invention as a recursive and socially linked process, and invention as embodied agency. From a postmodern perspective, Calabrese Barton argues that the connection between scientific/technological knowledge and power should be carefully examined. She further argues that science/technology education should actively and continually deconstruct the taken-for-granted story or *master narrative* of modern science. A key conclusion of this work is that by encouraging individuals and groups to engage in inventive acts of science, students and teachers together can challenge the imposed definition of science in and out of school as well as challenging broader social, political, and economic conditions.

Pushing the idea of imposed definitions of science further, Fusco (2001) raised the issue of why youth find informal, out-of-school science experiences (i.e., nonschool-, noncurriculum-based interactions with science in environments such as science centers, museums, zoos, parks, and nature centers) more engaging and relevant to their futures than school science. Fusco worked with teenagers from homeless families in an after-school project that involved urban planning and community gardening. In this community-based science project, science became relevant or real to the students because: 1) it was created from their own concerns, interests, and experiences related to science, 2) it was an ongoing process of researching and then enacting ideas, and 3) it was situated within the broader community. A key conclusion was that schools must reconsider how science learning can become more closely connected to students' interests, experiences, and communities if it is to be relevant to the students' lives.

Fusco and Calabrese Barton (2001) further argued that this community-based science project could serve as the context for performance assessment, as students collectively created the community garden and produced a written document about their project. Students' understandings of science content and the nature of science were supported by authentic and meaningful practice. The teens were active producers of science that made sense to them, served a communal purpose, and drew upon their interests and strengths. Conceptions of science and science content emerged from real-world connections. Here, student science learning was supported by a vision of science as socially oriented rather than task oriented. The enactment of science was situated holistically and historically, and the evidence produced was representative of the totality of students' achievements.

Overall, these studies of science learning as a sociopolitical process reject the notion that external standards can make science learning more equitable for students who have been marginalized from science and science education. Instead, this research points to the need for the students to make sense of science based on their lived experiences in social and cultural contexts. The results indicate that a sociopolitical approach to science learning can lead marginalized students to gain knowledge and understanding of science content, to see science as relevant to their lives, and to engage in science in socially relevant and transformative ways.

IDENTITY, DISCOURSE, AND THIRD (OR HYBRID) SPACE

There has been an increasing research interest in the concept of identity as it relates to teaching and learning (J. S. Lee & Anderson, 2009). In science education, research on identity has gained prominence as it relates to discursive identity and third (or hybrid) space.

Identity and Discourse. The work by Brown and colleagues is based on Gee's (2002) definition of identity as "being recognized as a certain 'kind of person' in a given context" (p. 99). Gee specifies four domains of identity. First, *nature identity* indicates a "natural" state of being, given from forces in nature (e.g., being biologically "Asian"). Second, *institutional identity* indicates a position authorized within institutions (e.g., being a student or a teacher). Third, *discourse identity* indicates an individual trait recognized in interactions (e.g., as a result of interaction, either passively or actively taken on). Finally, *affinity identity* indicates a set of shared experiences in practices of "affinity groups" (e.g., being a "tech geek") (J. S. Lee & Anderson, 2009, p. 184).

Of these four domains, the work by Brown and colleagues focuses on discursive identity as an analytical tool for understanding student learning (Brown, 2004, 2006; Brown, Reveles, & Kelly, 2005). This work expands on ideas from the research programs by Chèche Konnen and Lee that explore science learning for marginalized student groups by focusing on the common ways these students act and communicate (described above in this chapter). According to Brown and colleagues, these two research programs use broad cultural frameworks for explaining the behavior of cultural groups of students that have traditionally performed poorly in science education. Instead, Brown and colleagues argue that analyzing classroom interaction from the point of discursive identity allows for the examination of detailed cultural interactions that define individual access to a particular classroom culture. They further argue that this perspective takes into account the cultural co-construction of identities within the classroom context (Brown et al., 2005).

Brown (2004, 2006) conducted his research as a full-time teacher for two class periods of a 9th- and 10th-grade life science course in a large urban high school. He explored how engaging in the cultural practices of science, including the discursive practices of science classrooms, could initiate cultural conflict for marginalized students. Because science has an elitist image, it has the potential to heighten minority students' identity conflicts as they attempt to manage the tension between maintaining their existing discursive and cultural identities and developing new identities as science learners. Specifically, the study examined students' responses to the epistemology of science, practices of science, and discursive norms of science. The results indicated that students experienced relative ease in adopting both the epistemology and the practices of science, whereas they expressed a great deal of difficulty in appropriating the discursive norms of science. Thus, science discourse can be a potential gatekeeper for students who attempt to assimilate into the culture of science. Brown argues that students' attempts to become bicultural through the merging of their own ethnic and discursive identities with that of the culture of science requires them to essentially become bilingual. He further argues that if science educators fail to address the political meaning associated with using science discourse, minority students' identity conflicts with science discourse will continue to be invisible.

Identity and Third (or Hybrid) Space. The work by Calabrese Barton and colleagues addresses issues of identity through the related constructs of voice, agency, discourse, funds of knowledge, and third (or hybrid) space inside and outside the classroom or school. Calabrese Barton bases the notion of identity on the definition by Lave and Wenger (1991)—"a process of coming to be, of forging identities in activity" (p. 3). Students, upon entering a community of practice such as the science classroom, develop identities through engaging in the practices and tasks of the science class.

Tan and Calabrese Barton (2007) explored how and why a sixth-grade Dominican girl transformed herself from a marginalized member of the science class with a failing grade to a highly valued member of the science learning community with a perfect score for the sixth-grade exit project. The results indicated that the different formations of the science classroom, such as whole-class, small-group, and individual work, offered the student different opportunities for identity formation in both productive and unproductive ways. The results also indicated the critical roles that members of her classroom community, in particular teacher and peers, played in supporting and constraining such transformation. Tan and Calabrese Barton conclude that identity formation is an interplay between the student's personal agency and the responses of her community of practice.

Basu (2008a, 2008b; Basu & Calabrese Barton, 2007) used critical ethnography to explore how student voice developed in the context of a ninth-grade conceptual physics class in an experimental school in a major urban city. Almost all the students at the school were of Black Caribbean origin. Basu was a teacher-researcher as a cofounder of the school, science teacher, and assistant principal at the research site. She reported case studies of five immigrant Caribbean youth. The results indicated that in expressing voice, the youth designed science lessons reflective of their identities, leveraged and enhanced their authority, and creatively utilized resources available in the science classroom and at the school. Furthermore, the youth developed *critical subject matter agency* in physics classrooms—they expressed critical agency by envisioning and making change in their lives and world, on one hand, and cultivating subject matter expertise in a specialized field, on the other hand.

In another set of studies that attempted to connect students' lived experiences with science learning, Calabrese Barton and colleagues (Calabrese Barton & Tan, 2009; Calabrese Barton, Tan, & Rivet, 2008) examined the intersection of funds of knowledge, discourse, and third space in identity formation in a low-income urban middle school. The research used a sixth-grade science unit on food and nutrition from the LiFE (Linking Food and the Environment) curriculum that was intended to assist teachers in developing instructional practices that were supportive of students' everyday knowledge and experiences. The results indicated shifts in classroom discourse that were marked by a changing role and understanding of the funds of knowledge students brought to science learning. Furthermore, students strategically used different funds of knowledge and discourse to develop three related third spaces: physical, political, and pedagogical.

This line of research has also examined students' voice and creation of third space related to identity formation in contexts outside the science classroom. Furman and Calabrese Barton (2006) examined the voices of two seventh-grade boys from a low-income urban community as they worked together in an after-school program to create a student-directed video documentary about science. The results indicated that the students used their voices to construct identities that they cared about in school, by reconstructing some aspects of their school identity that did not match who they aspired to be as well as by gaining new resources to enact their desired identities. Furman and Calabrese Barton conclude that integrating student voice can make participation in science a valuable tool in students' identity formation.

Taking a more longitudinal approach to similar questions, Elmesky and Tobin (2005) explored the roles that student researchers created for themselves over 5 years of studies on the teaching and learning of science in urban high schools. The results indicated how students' cultural capital affected their identity formation outside of school, which in turn affected their learning in the science classroom. Elmesky and Tobin conclude that the involvement of students as researchers offers unique insider perspectives on how to improve the teaching and learning of science for urban high school students.

Working to further clarify the relationship between funds of knowledge and the creation of third space, Moje, Ciechanowski, Kramer, Ellis, Carillo, and Collazo (2004) analyzed both the intersections and disjunctions between everyday funds of knowledge and discourse (in the contexts of home, community, and peer group) and school funds of knowledge and discourse. The study involved 30 middle school-aged youth in a predominantly Latino/a urban community across 5 years of an ongoing community ethnography. The results indicated the persistence and strength of various funds of knowledge, both in the community and in the school. Using the funds of knowledge that the youth had available outside of school allowed the construction of third space in science classrooms.

SUMMARY

The literature on science learning and student diversity is varied in its scope, scale, and focus. While some studies have focused on achievement scores as the primary indicator of learning, other studies have focused on sociocultural factors that influence students' inclination to engage in science learning, such as potential conflicts between worldviews, discourse patterns, and identity norms valued at home and in school. When taken together, this body of research indicates that the science learning of non-mainstream students is influenced by a variety of factors associated with their racial, ethnic, cultural, linguistic, and social class backgrounds. These factors include students' cognitive and affective attributes, cognitive processes underlying scientific reasoning and argumentation, cultural beliefs and practices, and sociopolitical features of schools and communities. These factors contribute to the science learning and identity formations of all students, but the relationships between and among the factors are multifaceted and complex. Thus, it is difficult to tease out the influence of each factor, either independently or in interaction with the others. This is especially true given the limited literature within each area to date.

Research grounded in different conceptual and methodological traditions often produces results that are inconsistent or contradictory. This is due, in part, to differences in the focus or emphasis of the studies that reflect differences in the conceptual, ideological, and even political commitments among researchers, individually and collectively.

Even within research that places explicit attention on the intersections between students' linguistic and cultural experiences and scientific practices, some perspectives highlight continuity between students' and scientists' ways of knowing and talking, whereas others focus on discontinuities between the prior cultural and linguistic knowledge of non-mainstream students and Western science. From the *continuity* perspective, non-mainstream students' ways of investigating scientific questions overlap considerably with the way science is practiced in scientific communities. From the *discontinuity* perspective, science learning involves border crossing or making cultural transitions between the home culture and the culture of science. From a sociopolitical perspective, the larger question is not how to bring students' worldviews more in line with the views of Western science, but rather, how science itself should be reconceptualized to better align with the worldviews of people from marginalized groups.

The emerging research on identity formation inside and outside the science classroom illustrates the funds of knowledge and discourse patterns that non-mainstream students bring to science teaching and learning. The contribution of this new body of work is that it can provide directions for how students and teachers can work together to collectively negotiate for third (or hybrid) space where the official school science discourse is challenged and its boundaries are pushed to become more inclusive of students' everyday knowledge and discourse.

This chapter has addressed different traditions of research on science learning with non-mainstream students. How the results from this research lead to instructional approaches and intervention programs is the topic of the next chapter.

ACTIVITIES FOR CHAPTER 3

1. Think about your own childhood experiences with science both in and out of school by answering the following questions:
   A. Where were your favorite places to play as a child? Who did you play with and what did you play?
   B. What trips do you remember taking as a child? Where did you go, who did you go with, and what did you do there?
   C. Did any of these experiences outside of school relate to science? What was your opinion of science based on these out-of-school experiences?
   D. What do you remember about your school science experiences in elementary and middle school? What was your opinion of science based on these school science experiences?
   E. Do you believe that your own race, ethnicity, culture, language, social class, and/or gender influenced your out-of-school experiences with science in any way?
   F. Do you believe that your own race, ethnicity, culture, language, social class, and/or gender influenced your in-school experiences with science in any way?
2. Multiple theoretical perspectives are proposed in this chapter that point to different foci to explain the science learning of non-mainstream students. For each of the perspectives, use the chart below to answer the following questions:
   A. What is unique about this perspective that differentiates it from the others (see the Differences row)?
   B. Think back to your own childhood experiences with science that you discussed above. Describe an example of an experience that relates to each of the foci in the chart (see the Examples row).
   C. Assume you are a classroom teacher who finds one of these perspectives to be the most compelling way to explain and support the science learning of non-mainstream students. What specific actions could you take in your classroom to support this perspective? Do the same for each perspective, assuming you find that one to be the most significant (see the Action Plans row).

	Scientific reasoning and argumentaion	*Cultural beliefs and practices*	*Sociopolitical process of learning*	*Identity formation*
Differences				
Examples				
Action plans				

CHAPTER 4

Science Instruction and Student Diversity

All students come to school with knowledge, experiences, and questions about the natural world. These experiences are bound up with linguistic and cultural practices from home, community, peer group, prior schooling, and other sources. Effective teachers find ways to connect new learning to these prior experiences in ways that are accessible and relevant for students. A limited number of past reviews of literature have addressed the qualities of effective instruction for non-mainstream students, either in general (Garaway, 1994; Lee, 2002, 2003) or for specific groups including African American (Atwater, 2000), Asian American (Lee, 1996), Hispanic (Rakow & Bermudez, 1993), Hmong (Hammond, 2001), and Native American students (Nelson-Barber & Estrin, 1995, 1996; Solano-Flores & Nelson-Barber, 2001; Riggs, 2005).

For mainstream students, the linguistic, cultural, and content knowledge they acquire outside of school is largely continuous with the expectations, assumptions, and privileged knowledge base within school. For non-mainstream students, the linguistic, cultural, and content knowledge they acquire outside of school often appears to be discontinuous with school practices. Nevertheless, as was discussed in Chapter 3, non-mainstream students also bring funds of knowledge (González, Moll, & Amanti, 2005; Moll, 1992) from their home and community environments that can serve as intellectual resources (Lee, 2002; Warren, Ballenger, et al., 2001). Science instruction, if it is to be effective for all students, must identify and build upon intellectual resources in learning science, even when those resources initially seem disconnected from the school knowledge base. Unfortunately, the knowledge and skills of non-mainstream students are frequently overlooked or undervalued by teachers. At the same time, some aspects of students' linguistic and cultural traditions may, in fact, be fundamentally inconsistent with a scientific orientation toward knowledge and problem solving. Such inconsistencies may create difficulties for students learning science and for teachers trying to teach the students (Aikenhead & Jegede, 1999; Atwater, 1994; Lee, 1999a; Moje et al., 2001). Effective science instruction considers students' prior knowledge, experiences, and beliefs and explicitly articulates their relationships with the norms of school science, in order to make science accessible and relevant for all students (Cobern & Aikenhead, 1998; Lee, 2002, 2003; Warren et al., 2001).

A number of research programs have addressed questions related to science instruction with non-mainstream students. Much of this research has been guided by the same or similar conceptual frameworks as those guiding the research on student learning described in Chapter 3. These frameworks include: 1) cognitively-based instruction, 2) culturally congruent instruction, 3) sociopolitical process of instruction, 4) instruction to promote both cultural and science learner identity, and 5) English language and literacy integrated into science instruction. As with the research on student learning, some research projects on effective instruction with non-mainstream students have studied existing practices, while others have created and then studied interventions to improve practices.

COGNITIVELY BASED SCIENCE INSTRUCTION

A cognitive science perspective on effective instruction focuses on multiple relationships between scientific practices and student learning—as similar, different, interactive, and generative (Brown, 1992, 1994; Lehrer & Schauble, 2000). This perspective encourages teachers to begin by examining the everyday experiences and informal language practices that students bring to the learning process. Each student, through his or her lived experience, has developed forms of reasoning and problem solving that can serve as intellectual resources in academic learning, if these skills can be identified and used appropriately.

From the cognitive science perspective, a major problem in teaching non-mainstream students is that teachers fail to recognize the students' intellectual resources in their classrooms. When students' intellectual resources are marginalized during instruction, they may withdraw from classroom interactions and have fewer learning opportunities. On the other hand, if students' out-of-school experiences and informal language practices are recognized as worthwhile resources relevant to science tasks, then a central element of instruction involves identifying the intersections between students' everyday knowledge and scientific practices. Effective teachers learn to build upon intersections between students' everyday knowledge and experiences, on the one hand, and scientific knowledge and practices, on the other hand.

The Chèche Konnen Project has a long history of promoting scientific inquiry among language-minority and low-SES students (Rosebery et al., 1992; Warren & Rosebery, 1995, 1996). The earlier work by this group emphasized how students learned to engage in scientific inquiry and to appropriate scientific argumentation in a collaborative learning community (Rosebery et al., 1992; Warren & Rosebery, 1995, 1996). A central premise of this work has been that school science should be related to science as it is practiced in professional communities. Although scientific practice in school cannot exactly mirror the practice of research scientists, this connection changes the focus of instruction. Instead of teachers disseminating knowledge to their students, they provide students with opportunities to engage in the practice of science. Based on a simplified model of what scientists do in the real world, students learn to use language, think, and act as members of a science learning community.

As is the case in research science, in the Chèche Konnen Project, instruction is not predetermined; rather, inquiry grows directly out of students' own beliefs, observations, and questions. The investigation of one question often leads to additional questions and a new round of inquiry. Because science instruction is organized around students' own questions and inquiries, much of the science curriculum emerges from the questions the students pose, the experiments they design, the arguments they engage in, and the theories they construct. The teachers' role is to facilitate students' investigations of their own questions, while offering guidance and resources as needed. Although this approach to science instruction has sometimes been used for academically advanced students, the Chèche Konnen Project has demonstrated that it is also feasible for non-mainstream students with limited formal science experience.

Over the years, the Chèche Konnen team has studied the informal, everyday knowledge that students of diverse backgrounds bring to the learning process and how teachers can build on that knowledge by connecting it to the practice of science (Ballenger, 1997; Warren, Ballenger, et al., 2001). The results indicate that students use their cultural practices in scientific reasoning and argumentation. For example, when a sixth-grade Haitian student asserted that "The bathrooms in Haiti have mold, the bathrooms here don't get moldy," a classmate challenged this claim and an animated discussion ensued in which students offered arguments and counterarguments and had to defend their positions (Ballenger, 1997).

The work also evolved to consider the role of students' first language in scientific sense-making (Ballenger, 1997; Warren, Ballenger, et al., 2001). The use of a student's mother tongue, such as Haitian Creole or Spanish, when doing science inquiry, serves as a resource for their learning. Students' more nuanced understanding of their home language allows them to express more precise meaning when doing science. In addition, reflecting on the differences in expressing ideas between the home language and English helps students understand the notion of linguistic register to accomplish different purposes in different contexts. For example, Ballenger (1997) described how a fifth-grade Haitian boy, who was learning English as a new language and considered a special education student, used both Haitian Creole and English to understand metamorphosis as a particular kind of change in biology. Speaking in Haitian Creole and using Haitian Creole syntax, the student differentiated the meanings of two terms, *grow* (referring to continuous change) and *develop* (referring to reliably patterned transformation from one discrete stage to the next). Then, the student switched into English and used the terms *grow* and *develop* to further enhance his understanding of these two aspects of change.

Overall, the results from the Chèche Konnen Project indicate that students can and do use diverse languages and cultures in their sense-making practices. They sometimes use vigorous argumentation, situated guesswork, embedded imagining, and innovative uses of everyday words to construct new meanings without realizing that these are all strategies used by research scientists. When teachers identify these intersections between non-mainstream students' everyday knowledge and scientific practices, they can help the students see themselves as potentially successful science learners. When teachers facilitate opportunities for all students to practice doing science, they help their students become members of a science learning community.

CULTURALLY CONGRUENT SCIENCE INSTRUCTION

Children from non-mainstream backgrounds develop cultural norms and practices in their homes, communities, and peer groups that are sometimes incongruent with the cultural norms and practices of school. Teachers begin to bridge this incongruence, both real and perceived, by first being aware of different students' cultural experiences and then building on those experiences. Teachers interact and communicate with students in ways that are familiar to the students in their homes and communities, as well as use cultural artifacts, examples, analogies, and community resources. Strategies of this type, generally known as culturally congruent instruction, serve to make science both more relevant and more intelligible to non-mainstream students. While it is important not to essentialize or stereotype racial, ethnic, or linguistic groups as sharing monolithic or unvarying cultural patterns and experiences (Gutiérrez & Rogoff, 2003), a substantial body of research suggests that when students receive culturally congruent instruction, they respond positively in terms of better communication and higher academic performance (e.g., Au, 1980; Deyhle & Swisher, 1997; Heath, 1983; Ladson-Billings, 1994, 1995; Tharp & Gallimore, 1988).

The initial research on cultural congruence focused on classroom interactions, communication, and literacy development independent of specific content area instruction (Gay, 2002; Ladson-Billings, 1994, 1995; Villegas & Lucas, 2002). Later, studies began to focus on subject-specific instruction, including literature (e.g., C. D. Lee, 2001), mathematics (e.g., Brenner, 1998; Lubienski, 2003), social studies (e.g., McCarty, R. Lynch, Wallace, & Benally, 1991), and science (e.g., Lee & Fradd, 1998). While the following discussion is specific to cultural congruence as it relates to science instruction, many of the same approaches and findings apply to other subject areas as well.

In the science classroom, teachers tend to assume certain prior knowledge on the part of their students. Not only do teachers assume prior knowledge about science content and process, but also prior knowledge about interactions and discourse practices typical of mainstream science learning environments. Students are expected to ask questions, carry out investigations, find answers on their own, and formulate explanations in scientific terms. These practices are typical and essential in scientific inquiry, but are not equally encouraged in all cultures or in the lived experiences of all children (Atwater, 1994; Jegede & Okebukola, 1992; McKinley, 2007; McKinley, Waiti, & Bell, 1992; Solano-Flores & Nelson-Barber, 2001). In addition, the discourse patterns and verbal and written registers associated with scientific inquiry are less familiar to some students (and some teachers) than to others (Lemke, 1990; Moje et al., 2001).

In one set of examples of cultural congruence in science teaching, Parsons (2008) focused on African American students and examined their science achievement in relation to Black Cultural Ethos (BCE). Parsons extended the earlier research on BCE to science education, with a focus on science achievement using the NAEP 2000 assessment in eighth grade. Of the nine dimensions of BCE conceptualized by Boykin and Allen (1988, 1999), this study examined three: social perspective of time, verve, and rhythmic-movement expressiveness. Working with 23 African American students in three classes taught by two teachers, the study involved eight students in the intervention group and 15 students in natural contexts. Parsons provided one of the teachers with the intervention consisting of a short reading and discussions on BCE and three consecutive lessons on force featuring the three dimensions of BCE under investigation. On a science test with a maximum of eight points, the performance of the students in the intervention improved, whereas the performance of the students in natural contexts decreased.

In related studies, Parsons (2000) and Parsons, Foster, Travis, and Simpson (2007) illustrated culturally congruent instruction using science lessons and role-playing with African American students in science classrooms. Parsons and colleagues highlighted how communication patterns within African American communities were incongruent with the communication patterns typically valued and reinforced in school science. Using role-play, they discussed how congruence could be enhanced.

In ongoing research conducted since the early 1990s, Lee and colleagues have extended ideas about cultural congruence and culturally relevant pedagogy through a framework of *instructional congruence*. This framework connects science disciplines with students' languages and cultures (for conceptual discussion, see Lee, 2002, 2003; for methodological discussion, see Luykx & Lee, 2007). It highlights the importance of developing congruence, not only between students' cultural expectations and norms of classroom interaction, but also between students' linguistic and cultural experiences and the specific demands of particular academic disciplines—such as science. Adopting strategies to connect students' linguistic and cultural experiences with the norms of science is especially important when there are potentially discontinuous elements. Thus, instructional congruence emphasizes the work that teachers must do through their instruction to bring students and science together. This framework has served as a conceptual and practical guide for curriculum development, teacher professional development, classroom practices, and student assessment.

Following the instructional congruence framework, effective science instruction should enable students to cross cultural borders between their home cultures and the culture of science (Jegede & Aikenhead, 1999; Jegede & Okebukola, 1991a; Loving, 1998; Shumba, 1999; Snively, 1990). In the multicultural education literature, school knowledge is often represented as the *culture of power* of the dominant society (Au, 1998; Banks, 1993a, 1993b; Delpit, 1988, 1995; Reyes, 1992). The rules of classroom discourse, which are essential for students to access this culture of power, are largely implicit and assumed, making it difficult for students who have not learned the rules at home to figure them out on their own. Teachers need to provide explicit instruction about rules and norms for classroom behavior and academic achievement, rather than assuming the students know and understand these rules. Without this explicit instruction, non-mainstream students lack opportunities to learn the rules and the learning opportunities that knowledge of the rules offers.

In addition to explicit instruction of classroom norms and expectations, explicit instruction of academic content has been advocated with non-mainstream students in literacy instruction (e.g., Au, 1998; Delpit, 1988; Jiménez & Gersten, 1999; Reyes, 1992), literature instruction (e.g., C. Lee, 2001), mathematics instruction (e.g., Brenner, 1998; Lubienski, 2003), and science instruction (e.g., Fradd & Lee, 1999; Lee, 2003). This explicit content area instruction is related to aspects of instructional congruence.

First, explicit instruction of content helps students bridge competing sets of values and practices. For example, teachers point out to students that questioning and argumentation with teachers and peers is encouraged in the science classroom, although it may not be acceptable with adults at home. In the science classroom, teachers encourage students to question and inquire without devaluing the norms and practices of homes and communities, so that students gradually learn to cross cultural borders.

Second, explicit instruction of content provides tools to facilitate the transition from teacher-directed to student-initiated inquiry practices. While explicit instruction implies teacher-directed instruction in which teachers tell students what to do, student-initiated inquiry, in which students ask questions and find answers on their own, is the widely agreed-upon instructional goal. The question, over which there has been ongoing debate, is where to start and what to do to reach this goal with all students, especially with non-mainstream students. Explicit instruction, when done through tasks that students find meaningful, provides needed scaffolding that leads to more open inquiry over time (Buxton, 2006; Moje et al., 2001; Songer, Lee, & McDonald, 2003).

Lee and colleagues proposed the teacher-explicit to student-exploratory continuum for teaching inquiry-based science. This model takes into account students' cultural backgrounds as well as previous science experiences (Fradd & Lee, 1999; Lee, 2002, 2003). Teachers move progressively from explicit to student-centered inquiry experiences. Students are encouraged to take the initiative for different portions of the inquiry process, gradually building toward the full inquiry process, from developing their own questions, to determining how best to communicate their findings. Along the way, teachers maintain a balance between teacher guidance and student initiative, ensuring that all students are successful at each point on the continuum.

Using the models of instructional congruence and the teacher-explicit to student-exploratory continuum, Lee (2004) studied elementary teachers' efforts to bridge school science with the linguistic and cultural experiences of their students. The research involved six bilingual Hispanic elementary teachers who taught predominantly Hispanic students in a large urban school district. The teachers were recommended as exemplary by their principals. During their 3-year collaboration with the research team, the teachers participated in ongoing professional development including the design of instructional units (see Fradd, Lee, Sutman, & Saxton, 2002). Data collection and analysis of classroom observations, interviews, and questionnaires focused on teachers' beliefs and practices with regard to science instruction, incorporation of students' language and culture in science instruction, and English language and literacy development as part of science instruction. The teachers came to view students' linguistic and cultural practices both as intellectual resources for science learning and as challenges that sometimes conflicted with scientific practices. They learned that some of their students came from backgrounds that did not promote children to question or explore. They also acknowledged that they found it difficult to relinquish their own authority and control in favor of increased student autonomy. Thus they found progression along the teacher-explicit to student-exploratory continuum to be a challenge. The teachers described a culturally rooted tension between their students' preference for group collaboration and the school's need for independent performance and assessment. Over the course of the 3-year collaboration, they shifted from emphasizing explicit instruction, whole-group participation, and teacher authority and control to fostering student initiative and autonomy in conducting science inquiry. They also encouraged students to work individually and independently while simultaneously acknowledging the value of the teamwork and collaboration that most of the students preferred.

SOCIOPOLITICAL PROCESS OF SCIENCE INSTRUCTION

The sociopolitical perspective is centered on the claim that typical science instruction reinforces power structures that privilege mainstream students. From this perspective, the substandard performance of non-mainstream students is not due to an inability to perform well, but rather, it is due to an active resistance to science instruction and to schooling more generally.

Hayes and Deyhle (2001) described how science instruction was provided differently at two elementary schools, one serving predominantly middle-class White students and the other serving predominantly non-mainstream students from low-SES backgrounds. At the first school, science instruction was fixed and rigid, and teachers emphasized conceptions of academic success that included raising standardized test scores, ensuring future academic performance, and going to college. At the second school, science instruction was more open, supportive, and personally relevant to students. At the second school, however, teachers did not have specific or well-formed visions of how to prepare their students for standardized tests or for the rigors of future academic settings. Hayes and Deyhle concluded that although the latter type of science instruction might be perceived as better or more effective according to the current conceptions of science instruction, differential curricula and pedagogy between the two schools might actually serve as reconfigurations of social reproduction mechanisms based on existing racial/ethnic, socioeconomic, and political hierarchies. That is, the students from middle-SES backgrounds were getting instruction that focused on and assumed their continuing academic success, while the students from low-SES backgrounds were getting instruction that neither supported nor expected continuing academic success.

Gilbert and Yerrick (2001) described the beliefs and practices of eight students and their teacher in a lower-track Earth science class at a rural high school. The teacher selected eight students (three Black females, three Black males, one White male, and one Cuban-American male) from his class of 28 to participate in weekly focus-group interviews and individual interviews. The results indicated that the quality of science instruction was subverted through a process of negotiation between teacher and students in a context of low expectations and an unsupportive school culture. The teacher expressed concern for his students and a desire to do what he thought was best for them, but he was limited by his lack of practical experience in teaching science to non-mainstream students. Students did not distinguish this teacher from the larger oppressive system he represented, and thus rejected him. They disrupted lessons, provoked disciplinary action, and challenged teacher authority in order to assert their own identities. Student apathy and resistance, coupled with teacher frustration and hostile language, served to reinforce the social distance between the students and teacher. Gilbert and Yerrick argued that whether intentionally or unintentionally, tracking systems that lead to the existence of lower-track science classes serve to reproduce and maintain socioeconomic stratification.

Even when teachers attempt to push non-mainstream students to engage in rigorous inquiry-oriented science, challenges may hinder success. Seiler, Tobin, and Sokolic (2001) explored teaching science through design and technology as a way to support science learning for all students. The study specifically explored the discourse and practices of students and three co-teachers using a curriculum that provided opportunities for students to learn about the physics of motion through designing, building, and testing a model car. The study was conducted in an inner-city Philadelphia high school with primarily African American students. Results indicated that while some students participated in ways that allowed them to develop design and technological competence, other students resisted by participating sporadically and refusing to cooperate with teachers. Analysis of in-class interactions revealed an untapped potential for the emergence of a sciencelike discourse and outcomes. However, a key challenge was students' struggle for respect from peers that permeated their lives on the street and bled into the classroom. Whereas teachers enacted the curriculum as if learning science was the goal for students, students used the class opportunistically to earn and maintain the respect of their peers. The researchers conclude that science teachers must learn to take into account the historical, social, and cultural environments in which their students live and attend school and develop science-related goals that emerge from the knowledge of their students.

In other studies related to the theme of understanding the dynamics of inner-city classroom environments, Sconiers and Rosiek (2000), Tobin (2000), and Tobin, Seiler, and Walls (1999) described personal narratives of teaching science in inner-city secondary schools with predominantly African American students. Sconiers was a middle school science teacher who took up the role of researcher, whereas Tobin was a researcher who took up the role of high school teacher. In two separate studies in two different settings, the researchers described highly similar experiences including: 1) how school systems were structured in ways that failed to connect the curriculum to students' interests or prior knowledge, 2) how students resisted both learning science and conforming to school norms, 3) how teachers with the best intentions and knowledge of subject matter still failed to teach science in ways that were relevant to students and potentially transformative, and 4) how challenging it was to engage students when they lacked motivation and attended school sporadically. Sconiers and Tobin offered suggestions for educating prospective and practicing science teachers of students who were regularly marginalized in science classrooms. Sconiers reflected on why he, as an African American male science teacher, had only marginal success connecting with many of his African American male students. He believed that he failed to make meaningful connections between the school science curriculum and his students. He argued that it was the curriculum, and not the students, that needed to become more responsive. Tobin proposed a number of concrete suggestions for science teachers, such as presenting multiple short activities in each lesson, encouraging alternative ways for students to participate in class, setting up a portfolio system, and involving other individuals who were known to the students (parents, siblings, guardians, and persons from the community) to support science learning in and out of the classroom.

Using ideas from sociology to explain the classroom actions taken by non-mainstream high school students, Seiler and Elmesky (2007) described communalism as a cultural disposition that is common among African American experiences, especially among urban teens. By focusing on a pair of African American male students in an urban high school in Philadelphia, Seiler and Elmesky examined how communal practices allowed for the creation of social and symbolic capital along with positive emotional energy and how the shared goal of learning enhanced participation and understanding in the science classroom. They suggest that communalism and the meanings associated with communal practices originate in peer and community contexts, where urban youth rely on strong bonds in families, in neighborhoods, and among peers. Further, they speculate that communalism and other dimensions of African American culture have emerged from roots in West Africa and have been molded by the experiences of slavery and oppression in the United States. Seiler and Elmesky offer suggestions on how teachers can employ an understanding of the role of communalism, capital, and emotional energy to improve science teaching and learning in their classrooms.

Overall, the sociopolitical perspective on science instruction highlights a deep mistrust of schooling, science instruction, and science teachers among non-mainstream students who have traditionally been at best ignored and at worst oppressed by schooling in general and science education in particular. This mistrust continues to present a serious barrier to science teaching and learning until it is dealt with explicitly in the classroom. Only when new relationships are forged in which students come to see their teachers as allies in a struggle against oppression, rather than part of the oppressive system, can spaces be created in which rigorous learning takes place. Thus, building trusting and caring relationships becomes a prerequisite for all other educational activities.

SCIENCE INSTRUCTION TO PROMOTE CULTURAL AND SCIENCE LEARNER IDENTITY

Many minority students experience identity conflicts in their attempts to learn science. For these students, use of science language can become a symbol of cultural betrayal. As a result, the students avoid the appropriation of science language in order to maintain their cultural identity. Some science education researchers have sought ways to bridge the apparent cultural divide between learning to use the language of science and maintaining cultural identity.

In one example, Reveles and Brown (2008) examined how students whose language, culture, and identity seemed to conflict with the culture of science learned to appropriate identities that supported science learning. They used the metaphor of *contextual shifting* (i.e., changing ways of speaking, acting, and interacting) to underscore the central role of teachers in facilitating student understanding of scientific discourse practices associated with school science. Using a cross-case analysis of two elementary science classrooms with high percentages of non-mainstream students, Reveles and Brown identified ways in which students' academic identities were connected to their affiliation with scientific discourse practices. They conclude that many ethnic and linguistic minority students are not explicitly taught contextual shifting in ways that lead to school success. Furthermore, they argue that as students learn contextual shifting in school science, the students are better able to adopt academic identities as science learners that do not conflict with their own cultural identities.

In two related studies, Brown and colleagues (Brown & Ryoo, 2008; Brown & Spang, 2008) examined how teachers of predominantly African American students used innovative approaches to bridge language, identity, and science content. Brown and Spang identified a particular mode of classroom language used by one teacher to help students manage the dilemma of appropriating science learner identity. The teacher used a hybrid form of vernacular and scientific language, termed *double talk*, while explaining science. The students appropriated this same double-talk strategy when they produced explanations of scientific phenomena. Brown and Spang suggest the value of teaching science explicitly as a second language in urban science classrooms.

Brown and Ryoo (2008) compared two versions of educational technology with two randomly assigned groups of fifth-grade students in an urban elementary school. One version distinguished between conceptual and discursive components, whereas the other version made no effort to separate the conceptual from the discursive. They found that a *content-first* approach to teaching science that used everyday language to introduce the primary content followed by direct language instruction was effective in teaching both science and language to African American students. Brown and Ryoo suggest that when students understand science content first, hearing or reading science language may not produce the same feelings of anxiety and cultural conflict. They propose that when working with ELL students, teachers should focus on scientific concepts in everyday English and then provide instructional scaffolds to help students convert the concepts into scientific language.

In a similar approach to supporting non-mainstream students' science learner identity, Valeras, Becker, Luster, and Wenzel (2002) explored ways to connect science learning with African American students' discourse practices in the forms of plays and hip-hop lyrics. Teachers in this study were able to build bridges for accessing students' identities by encouraging their students to express and work out their scientific understandings in forms that were nontraditional in the science classroom, such as rap songs and plays. This approach assisted students in appropriating science learner identity as well as learning scientific language. As a result, students were able to use their "youth genres to enter the science classroom and disrupted the hegemonic practice of students who do not want to 'act white' (Fordham, 1996) to construct effective science genres" (Valeras et al., 2002, p. 583).

An underlying assumption that serves a guide for the studies by Brown and colleagues and Valeras et al. (2002) is the idea that students' identity and its association with classroom language practices can serve as a gatekeeper for student learning. Teachers in these studies addressed issues of discursive identity with their students by making the norms of classroom language explicit. Students were provided with opportunities to explain and discuss science ideas in everyday language and then make transitions from conceptual instruction to language instruction. Because language instruction was made explicit, students were less apt to perceive the use of scientific language as a symbol of cultural affiliation. In addition, using everyday language to support their learning before using scientific language was established as a normal part of classroom language practices. Thus, teachers provided students with opportunities to learn both the concepts and the language of science, while explicitly establishing the norms of language use.

Several studies address the formation of students' science learner identities by building upon elements of both cognitively based instruction (e.g., the Chèche Konnen Project) and culturally congruent instruction (e.g., Lee), described above. For example, Southerland, Kittleson, Settlage, and Lanier (2005) examined individual and group meaning-making of two small groups of third-grade African American students as they engaged in science inquiry in an urban classroom. They pointed to both continuous and discontinuous features between the cultural practices of these working-class African American students and the practices of science. They argue that to support the formation of both cultural identities and science learner identities of non-mainstream students, instruction needs to be scaffolded in ways that consider both the students' cultural norms and their intellectual resources.

In another attempt to bridge cognitively based and culturally congruent instruction, Moje et al. (2001) described the case of a bilingual middle school science teacher with predominantly Spanish-speaking students in an urban school in a large school district. The teacher taught a project-based science curriculum to promote students' scientific inquiry. Although the school administration expressed a commitment to two-way bilingual education, all instruction was conducted in English. The teacher attempted many of the instructional practices suggested by both the cognitively based literature and the cultural congruence literature. He had extensive science knowledge and his linguistic and cultural background was similar to that of his students. Despite this apparent best-case scenario, the teacher often had difficulties connecting students' everyday knowledge and discourse patterns with scientific knowledge and discourse patterns. The results suggest that it is necessary but difficult for teachers to establish third (or hybrid) spaces in their classroom in which the knowledge bases and discourse patterns from science disciplines, the science classroom, and students' lives can all be brought together in ways that develop the cultural and science learner identities of non-mainstream students.

ENGLISH LANGUAGE AND LITERACY
IN SCIENCE INSTRUCTION

As is the case for other non-mainstream groups, ELL students have generally not been served well by traditional science instruction. Based on observations of 57 randomly selected elementary classrooms serving predominantly Latino students, Barba (1993) found that most ELL students, regardless of their program placement (transitional, bilingual, sheltered English, ESL, and so forth), received instruction predominantly through teacher-directed, expository instruction, rather than student-directed learning or collaborative group work. Teachers in these classrooms usually lacked proficiency in the children's home language, meaning that the bulk of teacher talk was in English. Culturally relevant examples, analogies, and elaborations were used in only 3% of lessons.

In the area of ESOL education, updated standards (TESOL, 2006) specifically target academic language proficiency in core content areas as a central goal. In order not to fall behind their English-speaking peers in both content and academic language development, ELL students need to develop English language and literacy skills in the context of content area instruction (August & Hakuta, 1997; August & Shanahan, 2006; Garcia, 1999). Content area and ESOL/bilingual instruction, however, have traditionally been conceptualized as separate domains. Many teachers, especially at the elementary level, are not sufficiently prepared to meet the learning needs of ELL students in either of these areas (NCES, 1999). In addition, teachers often presume that content area instruction for ELL students must wait until language skills in English have been developed. Thus, it should not be surprising that ELL students frequently fall behind their English-speaking peers in content area learning.

Literature for Science and Literacy Integration with ELL Students. Research and intervention programs have looked at cases where teachers are taking action to support ELL students to learn science content and academic language simultaneously. For example, Kelly and Breton (2001) examined how two bilingual elementary school teachers guided their students to engage in science inquiry through particular ways of framing problems, making observations, and engaging in spoken and written discourse. The teachers constructed science as disciplinary inquiry at the same time that they constructed a community of students as scientists. While one teacher felt constrained in using Spanish because of external pressures, the other teacher regularly code-switched between Spanish and English in her teaching. The results indicated that introducing students to specialized ways of observing, writing, speaking, and understanding in science required a great deal of work with academic language on the part of the teachers. This work included engaging students in conversations through questioning, reframing ideas, varying use of languages, making reference to other classroom experiences, and devising interactional contexts for students to talk science under varying conditions. This linguistic work helped ELL students to engage in science inquiry.

In another study involving code-switching, Luykx, Lee, and Edwards (2008) found that code-switching was used less as a conscious pedagogical strategy for promoting scientific discourse among ELL students, and more as a logical result of constraints imposed by the policy context surrounding the school in the study. The researchers observed science lessons in a class of combined third- and fourth-grade beginning ELL students. The teacher was a monolingual English speaker, assisted by a bilingual co-teacher whose role consisted primarily of providing concurrent Spanish-language translation of the teacher's English-language instruction. The study contrasted classroom discourse between a typical class period when both teachers were present and a nontypical class period when the bilingual co-teacher was absent. The results indicated that the school language policies and practices viewed different languages as essentially equivalent and neutral codes, and viewed science concepts as essentially independent of the language in which they were being constructed or expressed. In contrast, analysis of the bilingual co-teacher's attempts to translate English-based science content into Spanish, and analysis of students' attempts to negotiate language barriers during class discussions of that content, demonstrated that science concepts were tightly tied to the language in which they were constructed.

Luykx, Lee, and Edwards (2008) also examined how the use of concurrent translation in instruction shaped students' opportunities to engage in scientific discourse. During typical class periods, students passively awaited the bilingual co-teacher's translations, and discrepancies between the two languages went unresolved. Surprisingly, when the bilingual co-teacher was absent, the learning environment was more conducive to the development of scientific discourse because students took on a greater role in constructing scientific understandings and actively negotiating meanings with the teacher and with one another. However, pressure to help the teacher understand their discussions, and the teacher's limited ability to understand and make herself understood by students, limited students' learning opportunities. The researchers conclude that concurrent translation is an ineffective teaching strategy, both with regard to teaching science and to helping ELL students develop English proficiency. On the one hand, if the instruction had lived up to its designation of "curriculum content in the home language," students would have had more opportunities to learn science. On the other hand, if the teachers had provided sheltered English immersion, students would have had more opportunities to develop English proficiency. The research suggests that it may not always be possible to effectively combine these two goals of science learning and academic language development in a single lesson or activity.

In other studies focusing on the role of hands-on inquiry, there is evidence that science content and academic language can be developed simultaneously. Hands-on, inquiry-based science provides all students, including ELL students, with opportunities to develop scientific understanding and scientific communication skills simultaneously (Lee & Fradd, 1998; Rosebery et al., 1992). First, hands-on activities depend less on formal mastery of the language of instruction, reducing the linguistic burden on ELL students. Second, hands-on activities promote language acquisition in the context of science knowledge and practice. Third, inquiry-based science requires students to communicate their understanding in a variety of formats, including gestural, oral, pictorial, graphic, and textual. Fourth, the process of science inquiry supports the familiarity with scientific genres of speaking and writing as well as the development of grammar and vocabulary. Finally, language functions, such as describing, hypothesizing, explaining, predicting, and reflecting, can develop simultaneously with science inquiry skills, such as observing, describing, explaining, predicting, estimating, representing, and inferring (Casteel & Isom, 1994).

An emerging body of research on instructional interventions indicates the benefit to ELL students of engaging in inquiry-based science. Some studies examined the impact of instructional interventions on the science achievement of ELL students (Amaral et al., 2002; Cuevas, Lee, Hart, & Deaktor, 2005; Fradd et al., 2002; Hampton & Rodriguez, 2001; Lee, Deaktor, Hart, Cuevas, & Enders, 2005; Lee, Maerten-Rivera, Penfield, LeRoy, & Secada, 2008). Other studies examined the impact of instructional interventions on the literacy (writing) achievement of ELL students in the context of science instruction (Amaral et al., 2002; Lee et al., 2005; Merino & Hammond, 2001). Notably, only a few studies examined the impact on both the science and literacy (writing) achievement of ELL students (Amaral et al., 2002; Lee, Deaktor, Hart, Cuevas, & Enders, 2005). The results have shown promise for improving academic outcomes in both science and literacy, as well as narrowing achievement gaps for ELL students. This emerging literature provides insights for developing interventions for science curriculum materials (see Chapter 5), teacher professional development (see Chapter 7), and classroom practices to simultaneously promote science and literacy achievement of ELL students.

Instructional Strategies for Science and Literacy Integration with ELL Students. Much of the recent literature has focused on an integrated model of instruction to promote science learning and English proficiency simultaneously. In advocating for this integration, researchers usually refer to specific strategies that can be used effectively to promote both science and English proficiency in a reciprocal process. Current research efforts to improve classroom practices are described in five domains below.

First, science instruction should explicitly promote literacy development of all students (Cervetti, Pearson, Bravo, & Barber, 2006; Douglas, Klentschy, Worth, & Binder, 2006; Palincsar & Magnusson, 2001). Instructional strategies include activation of prior knowledge, comprehension of expository science texts, language functions (e.g., explain, compare, contrast, report) in relation to science process skills, scientific genres of writing, graphic organizers (e.g., concept maps, word walls, Venn diagrams, KWL charts), multiple forms of representation, trade books, and writing prompts.

Second, in addition to gaining proficiency in both general and content-specific literacy, ELL students need to develop English proficiency to learn academic content, such as science (Bruna & Gomez, 2008; Buxton, 1998; Carr, Sexton, & Lagunoff, 2006; Fathman & Crowther, 2006; Lee, 2005; Rosebery & Warren, 2008). Science instruction can provide language support strategies for ELL students, typically identified as ESOL strategies. For example, hands-on activities and realia (i.e., demonstration of real objects or events) are especially effective with ELL students. Teachers can guide students to comprehend and use a small number of key science vocabulary words, both content-specific and general academic terms. They can allow students to communicate ideas using multiple modes of representation through gestural, oral, pictorial, graphic, and textual communication. They can also use language in multiple contexts (e.g., introduce, write, repeat, highlight). In addition, they can help ELL students develop English proficiency by focusing on phonological, morphological, and semantic elements in science-specific academic language.

Third, science instruction should provide discourse strategies to enhance ELL students' understanding of academic content (i.e., adjust the level and mode of communication). Unlike the language support or ESOL strategies, described above, which are largely pedagogical in nature, discourse strategies focus specifically on the teacher's role in facilitating ELL students' participation in classroom discourse. The challenge for science teachers is to modify classroom discourse while also maintaining the rigor of science content and processes (Brown & Spang, 2008; Kelly & Breton, 2001). Teachers need to recognize ELL students' varying levels of language proficiency and adjust norms of interaction with students, for example, slower rate of speech, clearer enunciation, or longer periods of wait time. Teachers also provide students with multiple redundancies of the same concepts, for example, using synonyms or paraphrases of difficult language, repeating and rephrasing main ideas, or recasting and elaborating on students' responses. Ideally, teachers should communicate at or slightly above students' level of communicative competence (i.e., comprehensible input according to Krashen, 1981).

Fourth, science instruction should capitalize on students' home language as an instructional support. It is important to draw a distinction between home language instruction (i.e., bilingual education) and home language support (Goldenberg, 2008). Even in the absence of bilingual education programs, ELL students' home language can be used as instructional support for their learning of academic content in English. If teachers share the same home language with their students, they can use the home language to reinforce key science vocabulary and concepts (Hudicourt-Barnes, 2003). Even when the teacher does not speak the students' home language, the home language can still be supported through strategies such as introducing key science vocabulary in both the home language and English; allowing students to code-switch; highlighting cognates as well as false cognates between English and the home language (for example, Spanish and other Romance lexicon is often derived from Latin, the primary language of science); encouraging bilingual students to assist less English-proficient students in their home language as well as in English; allowing ELL students to write about science ideas or experiments in their home language; and inviting family and community members to participate as local experts in classroom literacy events.

Finally, teachers can incorporate the ways in which ELL students' cultural experiences influence science instruction and capitalize on the students' intellectual resources to enhance science learning. By building on students' lived experiences at home and in the community, teachers can ask questions that elicit students' funds of knowledge related to science topics (González, Moll, & Amanti, 2005; Moll, 1992). They can use students' cultural artifacts and community resources in ways that are academically meaningful and culturally relevant (Rodriguez & Berryman, 2002; Solano-Flores & Nelson-Barber, 2001). Examples and analogies drawn from students' lives, and instructional topics that examine issues from the perspectives of multiple cultures, can be of great assistance as students strive to integrate prior experiences with new academic expectations. Teachers need to be aware of culturally based communication and interaction patterns that students have developed in their homes and communities.

SUMMARY

Different theoretical perspectives have led to a range of approaches about how best to meet the instructional needs of non-mainstream students in the science classroom. Research on cognitively based science instruction focuses on the need to understand the relationship between scientific practices and students' everyday knowledge. From this perspective, when teachers identify and incorporate students' cultural and linguistic experiences as intellectual resources for science learning, they provide opportunities for students to learn to use language, think, and act as members of a science learning community.

Research on culturally congruent instruction focuses on the need for teachers to make the rules and norms of school science explicit and visible, so that students learn to cross cultural borders between their home environment and the school environment. When students have limited science experience or come from backgrounds in which questioning and inquiry are not encouraged, teachers and students move progressively along the teacher-explicit to student-exploratory continuum. Over time, students learn to take the initiative and assume responsibility for their own learning.

Research from the sociopolitical perspective focuses on the need for teachers to build trusting relationships with students who have been marginalized in science classrooms. When teachers provide safe environments for students to take part in learning science, they can help their students see science as personally meaningful and relevant to their current and future lives. This reduces the likelihood that students disengage or actively resist learning science.

Research on identity formation focuses on the need to establish both cultural and science learner identities of non-mainstream students. Some researchers highlight a content-first approach to science teaching that explicitly separates conceptual and language components, which can increase students' conceptual understanding and improve students' ability to use scientific language. Other researchers highlight students' everyday knowledge that can serve as intellectual resources, as well as cultural practices that are discontinuous with the practices of science.

Research on science instruction with ELL students focuses on the need for teachers to engage ELL students in hands-on, inquiry-based instruction. In the context of hands-on inquiry, teachers integrate science with English language and literacy for ELL students. Teachers also focus on ELL students' home language as an instructional support and capitalize on the students' cultural experiences as intellectual resources to enhance science learning. Despite the growing number of ELL students in the nation, the spread of English-only policies is hindering science learning for ELL students, especially those in the early stage of acquiring English.

In closing, the research on science instruction and student diversity is varied and multifaceted. It would be difficult, if not impossible, for a classroom teacher to simultaneously act on all of the recommendations for meeting the needs of non-mainstream students that have been outlined in this chapter. Each teacher needs to prioritize, based in part on which of the theoretical orientations that he or she finds most compelling, the instructional approaches that will best meet the learning needs of the students in his or her classroom. The most important point to recognize is that a one-size-fits-all instructional approach fails to meet the unique needs of the variety of students in any classroom. Such an approach is not a viable option given what we know about student learning. Teachers must develop and refine their professional judgments when it comes to making decisions about instructional strategies in their classrooms. In the next chapter, we look more closely at science curriculum designed to meet the needs of diverse student groups.

ACTIVITIES FOR CHAPTER 4

1. This chapter addresses multiple theoretical perspectives on science instruction for non-mainstream students, including: 1) cognitively based instruction, 2) culturally congruent instruction, 3) sociopolitical process of instruction, 4) instruction to support identity formation, and 5) English language and literacy integrated into science instruction. For each perspective, write responses for the following questions:
   A. Explain each perspective in your own words. What is unique about each?
   B. Describe a classroom example or a lesson that a teacher who favors that perspective may use.
2. Conduct a short interview with another teacher who is not familiar with multiple theoretical perspectives on science instruction for non-mainstream students.
   A. Ask her/him the following questions:
      i. What is your opinion about bilingual education? Why?
      ii. What is your opinion about English-only policy? Why?
      iii. Do you think students need to become competent in English before they are taught science? Why or why not?
   B. How are this teacher's responses to these questions similar to and different from your own thinking about each question?
3. Imagine that you have been asked to give a short presentation at a faculty meeting about instructional strategies that can be used to better meet the science learning needs of the non-mainstream students in your school. Pick three specific instructional strategies that have been described in this chapter that you would like to discuss. Consider the following questions:
   A. Describe each of the strategies you have selected.
   B. Why do these three strategies appeal to you? Why did you select them?
   C. What do you think are the biggest challenges of implementing each of these strategies in practice?

CHAPTER 5

Science Curriculum and Student Diversity

Curriculum materials play a critical role in education reform (Ball & Cohen, 1996). Perhaps second only to high-stakes standardized tests, curriculum materials influence the content that is covered and the instructional approaches used in classrooms in both intended and unintended ways. *Educative curriculum materials*, those that specifically aim to guide teacher implementation through extensive scaffolding, can help teachers to more fully realize the intentions of the curriculum in promoting student understanding (Davis & Krajcik, 2005; Remillard, 2005). Although curriculum projects have played a large role in science education reforms since the cold war and the launch of the Soviet Sputnik satellite (Rudolph, 2002), high-quality materials that meet current science education standards are difficult to find. For example, even though the National Science Foundation (NSF) has funded a large number of curriculum reform projects, a comprehensive evaluation of school science curricula by the NSF concluded that most existing materials did not meet the expectations of the National Research Council's (1996) National Science Education Standards (Kesidou & Roseman, 2002; NSF, 1996).

Furthermore, research on the development and use of effective science curriculum is limited. Even studies that involve curriculum materials as an essential component of the research often fail to address the curriculum itself as a research topic. The impending reality of high-stakes testing and accountability in science, however, has highlighted the need to develop more robust science curriculum materials and evaluate their efficacy and effectiveness in improving student achievement across varied educational settings.

In addition to providing high-quality science curricula for all students, science curriculum developers face the additional challenge of meeting the unique learning needs of non-mainstream students, discussed in earlier chapters. For example, NSF (1998) called for "culturally and gender relevant curriculum materials" that recognize "diverse cultural perspectives and contributions so that through example and instruction, the contributions of all groups to science will be understood and valued" (p. 29). The fact that non-mainstream students are less likely to have access to such materials presents a barrier to equitable learning opportunities (Lee & Buxton, 2008). Yet, efforts to develop curriculum materials for culturally and linguistically diverse student groups present a number of challenges.

First, there is an inadequate knowledge base of how the norms and practices of different cultural groups relate to the norms and practices of scientific communities (Chapter 3). There is also limited knowledge of science-related examples, analogies, beliefs, and practices across diverse cultural groups. Where such knowledge has been collected, such as in the case of indigenous Canadians (First Nations groups), instructional materials have been successfully developed and used with students from those specific cultural groups (e.g., Aikenhead, 1997; Matthews & Smith, 1994). However, in educational settings that bring together students from multiple cultural backgrounds it is difficult to incorporate culturally relevant content from each group into curriculum materials without making the materials too cumbersome, expensive, or otherwise impractical.

A second challenge is the risk of fueling stereotypes, biases, and over-generalizations about specific student groups on the basis of limited information. For example, curriculum materials developed to be culturally congruent for Latino students have often highlighted the importance of fostering collaborative group environments, rather than individual or competitive class structures. While such advice may well serve the needs of many Latino students (and many White students as well), it may also reinforce a stereotype that Latino students are not academically independent or competitive, in ways that may disadvantage high-performing Latino students. As another example, ideas for multicultural science curricula often build on historical examples, such as early accomplishments in architecture, agriculture, and navigation. These historical examples may reinforce the false belief that non-mainstream contributions to science are nothing more than interesting historical footnotes.

Third, in addition to content connections between Western and non-Western science, successful multicultural science curricula should consider other cultural influences, such as norms for how resources are accessed, how knowledge is passed on, or how evidence is constructed (Calabrese Barton, 1998a, 1998b; Rahm, 2002).

Finally, the development of curriculum materials that incorporate local linguistic and cultural knowledge runs counter to the current desire for more standardized materials that can be used for large-scale implementation (Lee & Luykx, 2005). There is a movement in some states, however, to ensure that state standards across all the content areas reflect the people and places of the state (Stephens, 2000). Thus, at least some attention is paid to local environments and ecosystems, making it possible for more culturally relevant material to gradually make its way into the curriculum in some states.

Materials developed for wide use, particularly electronic resources, can be implemented across varied settings. Yet, local adaptations are essential for such materials to be used effectively. Thus, there is an inherent tension or trade-off between designing materials that meet the needs of specific local contexts but have limited relevance to other settings, and designing materials that can potentially be implemented across a wide range of settings but require local adaptations. In the end, it falls to teachers to use their experience and knowledge of students as individuals in order to make any curriculum both academically rigorous and culturally meaningful to each and every student.

While curriculum development and research efforts to support diverse student groups have been scarce overall, this work has become less marginalized in the science education community in recent years. These efforts address: 1) culturally relevant science curriculum, 2) science curriculum for students in low-SES settings, and 3) science curriculum for ELL students. For each category, we discuss studies that illustrate key components of the theoretical frameworks underlying curriculum development with non-mainstream students and positive student outcomes based on specific curriculum implementation. Together, the studies highlight formidable challenges as well as promising practices for science educators in their efforts to develop high-quality science curriculum materials for diverse student groups.

One feature that the curriculum materials in these studies have in common is that they are not modifications of existing materials to enhance student diversity components. Instead, developers of these materials each came to the conclusion that existing materials would not suffice and that they would need to conceptualize and design their own materials to meet the needs of their students or their projects. While there is a history of curricular modifications for non-mainstream students that have amounted to little more than watered-down versions of existing curricula, the current generation of curricular studies for student diversity have held curricular rigor as a fundamental goal.

CULTURALLY RELEVANT SCIENCE CURRICULUM

Faced with a shortage of science curriculum materials designed to be culturally relevant to non-mainstream students, a small number of science education research projects have developed materials to incorporate experiences, examples, analogies, and values from specific cultural groups. These projects then field test the curriculum materials in classrooms in hopes of showing positive effects on the science learning of non-mainstream students. The two studies described here took somewhat different approaches to the development and testing of culturally relevant science curriculum materials.

Aikenhead (1997, 2001b) proposed a conceptual framework for designing culturally relevant curriculum materials, using the notion of *cultural border crossing*. In this case, the cultural border was between students' everyday worlds and the culture of science. For non-mainstream students, the cultural border that must be crossed is significantly wider than for mainstream students. Based on this framework, Aikenhead described the development of curriculum units in grades 6 through 11, integrating Western science with Aboriginal sciences of First Nations groups in northern Saskatchewan, Canada. The units focused on two distinct cultural contexts: that of students' Aboriginal communities and that of Western science and technology. Throughout the curriculum, both Western scientific and Aboriginal values were made explicit. Each lesson identified a Western scientific value (e.g., control over nature) and/or an Aboriginal value (e.g., harmony with nature) and pointed out both similarities and contradictions between these two sets of values. The goal of this approach was to give indigenous students access to a Western science and technology and its worldview without requiring them to exclusively or blindly adopt the Western scientific worldview or change their own cultural identity. This type of bicultural curricular model encouraged students to traverse cultural borders between the realm of Western science and their own cultural identity. Informal assessment of classroom practices indicated that students found these units to be engaging and meaningful, but no formal assessment of learning outcomes was reported.

In a study with similar goals but a different structure, Matthews and Smith (1994) considered how currently existing curriculum materials could be modified by teachers in response to the low science achievement test scores of Native American students. They tested the effect of these culturally relevant curriculum materials on the achievement and attitudes of Native American students in grades four through eight at Bureau of Indian Affairs (BIA) schools. They worked with students from nine BIA schools that included students from the Navajo, Sioux, Papago, Hopi, and several other tribal nations. Teachers in these nine schools were randomly assigned to the experimental or control group for the teaching of science. Both groups of teachers used science activities from two NSF-supported curriculum development projects, but the teachers in the experimental group also taught profiles of Native Americans who used science in their daily lives as well as science topics that were specifically related to the Native American community. These culturally relevant materials were developed by teachers of Native American students in an NSF-supported teacher enhancement program. The researchers used a pretest and posttest to examine the effect of the culturally relevant curriculum on students' science achievement and attitudes. They found that the students who were taught the culturally relevant curriculum along with the regular science curriculum showed significantly higher achievement scores and displayed significantly more positive attitudes toward both Native Americans and school science than the students who were taught only the regular science curriculum.

Together, the studies on culturally relevant curriculum with indigenous students point to the value of an additive model where culturally relevant materials are taught in conjunction with more typical science curriculum.

SCIENCE CURRICULUM FOR STUDENTS
IN LOW-SES SETTINGS

The development and use of science curriculum materials for students in low-SES settings overlaps with a focus on meeting the needs of students in urban environments. Some of these materials have been text-based and others have been computer-based, but a common thread is an attempt to explicitly connect school science to students' experiences in urban homes and communities.

Text-Based Curriculum Materials. Some studies using text-based curriculum materials began with commercially available curriculum and then made modifications or additions, while other studies have developed their own curriculum materials as part of the projects. Ruby (2006) examined the impact of a teacher-support model on science achievement of urban middle school students using commercially available NSF-supported materials (Full Option Science System [FOSS] and Science and Technology for Children [STC]). The study included ongoing teacher professional development built around day-to-day lessons, and regular in-class support of teachers by expert peer coaches. One cohort of students at three middle schools using the model was followed from fourth grade through seventh grade. Their gains in science achievement were substantially greater than students at three matched control schools and the 23 district middle schools serving similar student populations. Ruby concludes that long-term support and evaluation of both teachers and students over several years may be a better way of measuring the effects of attempts to improve science instruction and student achievement.

In a study that developed its own curriculum materials, Calabrese Barton, Koch, Contento, and Hagiwara (2005) examined what high-poverty urban children understood and believed about food and food systems and how these children transformed and used that knowledge in their everyday lives. They developed the LiFE (Linking Food and the Environment) curriculum focusing on biology education through inquiry-based investigations of food and the food system for fourth- through sixth-grade students in high-poverty urban settings. The curriculum consisted of five modules: production of food on the farm, food processing and transportation, impacts of food on personal health, food waste and pollution, and the food choices individuals make. Designed for and implemented in high-poverty urban elementary and middle schools, the curriculum explicitly connected scientific and nutritional content with topics that were relevant to students, parents, and community members. The LiFE curriculum was evaluated in 23 classrooms in three schools, and led to student growth on a range of science outcomes including scientific understanding and attitudes toward the natural environment and science. Barton and colleagues conclude that science curriculum that explicitly connects school science to students' experiences outside of school can be effective for simultaneously promoting scientific understanding and positive science attitudes. While valuable for all students, this approach seems particularly relevant in urban communities where both students and parents may feel disconnected from school science.

In a related study, Upadhyay (2006) examined how the LiFE curriculum provided a tool and framework to teach science using lived experiences or funds of knowledge of predominantly Hispanic students in an urban elementary science classroom. The study also examined how an elementary school teacher identified and compared her lived experiences with those of the students in her fourth-grade classroom and integrated these two sets of lived experiences during science teaching. Upadhyay claims that the LiFE curriculum is an example of "connected science" (Bouillion & Gomez, 2001), where scientific knowledge is applied to urban students' real-life situations in a predominantly Hispanic community.

Computer-Based Curriculum Materials. In addition to the text-based curriculum materials described above, other researchers have developed computer-based curriculum materials and examined their impact on students' science outcomes in urban settings. The studies, described below, were conducted by two research teams that have engaged in programmatic lines of research over a number of years. Both research projects have targeted middle school students in urban school districts. In contrast to culturally relevant materials designed for specific groups, these computer-based materials, accompanied by interactive Web-based technology, are intended for large-scale implementation with local adaptations as necessary. The results show positive changes in student achievement on standardized tests.

The Learning Technologies in Urban Schools (LeTUS) project was carried out by a collaboration of researchers and teachers in Detroit and Chicago schools. This project developed and studied the impact of computer-based curriculum materials on science learning in urban settings. The LeTUS team developed project-based curriculum materials that used real-world problems to provide the context for science learning. The curriculum materials also promoted the development of students' science inquiry and computer technology skills. These materials were designed by collaborative teams of researchers and classroom teachers, included teacher professional development, and were revised yearly based on student outcomes and teacher feedback. The units were aligned with national and district curriculum frameworks and met the needs of the two school districts' science improvement plans, which allowed the materials to be scaled up for use in large numbers of classrooms.

While the earlier work by the LeTUS project focused on conceptualizing and implementing inquiry-based curriculum, teaching, and learning in the context of project-based science (Krajcik, Blumenfeld, Marx, & Solloway, 1994; Krajcik, Blumenfeld, Marx, Bass, & Fredricks, 1998), more recent attempts have addressed the characteristics of inquiry teaching practices to promote student learning and achievement in urban schools. While all teachers who carry out project-based science curriculum generally struggle with various issues such as technology use and collaboration, urban school teachers face more severe challenges.

As part of the LeTUS project, Rivet and Krajcik (2004) focused on the sixth-grade unit about machines, which was designed to relate science to the experiences of African American students in their community. This unit was set in the context of developing a new machine to construct large buildings and bridges. After discussing large structures in the city, students took a walking tour of an active construction site near the school and described the different machines they saw and how these machines functioned to help people build large buildings. Students used this anchoring experience to develop a design for a new machine of their own invention. Over the 3-year period of the project, two teachers participated during the 1st year, four teachers during the 2nd year, and 11 teachers during the 3rd year (some of the teachers participated for more than 1 year). Students were then assessed via written science tests. The results showed consistently high achievement gains in students' understanding of science concepts and inquiry process skills.

In addition, Tal, Krajcik, and Blumenfeld (2006) described a detailed case study of LeTUS project teachers whose students achieved high achievement gains on pre- and posttests and who demonstrated a great deal of preparedness and commitment to their students. The study focused on describing students' achievement outcomes and features of classroom practices that seemed particularly effective in urban schools. Tal et al. attributed student achievement outcomes to inquiry-oriented projects and the use of various learning technologies. They argue that for inquiry-based science to succeed in urban schools, teachers must play an important role in considering how best to enact the curriculum while addressing the unique needs of their students.

At the other end of the research spectrum, Marx, Blumenfeld, Krajcik, Fishman, Soloway, Geier, & Tal (2004) conducted a large scale study that examined the impact of the LeTUS project on science achievement with nearly 8,000 middle school students from 14 Detroit schools over a 3-year period. The data consisted of pretest–posttest gain scores based on project-developed achievement tests for four curriculum units (one for sixth grade, two for seventh grade, and one for eighth grade). The team was particularly interested in student outcomes as the project was implemented with larger numbers of teachers and in larger numbers of classrooms over the years (i.e., scaling-up). The results showed statistically significant increases on curriculum-based test scores for each year of teacher participation. In other words, the longer teachers participated in the project, the better their students' test scores became. The study concluded that students from low SES backgrounds in urban schools can succeed in learning challenging science when they are provided with inquiry-based and technology-infused curriculum that makes connections to their real lives and when their teachers are involved in professional development.

While Marx et al. (2004) reported on student outcomes from curriculum-specific achievement tests that were closely aligned to the curriculum, Geier, Blumenfeld, Marx, Krajcik, Fishman, Soloway, & Clay-Chambers (2008) examined the impact of project-based science curriculum on state standardized achievement tests that were not directly tied to the curriculum but were aligned in terms of outcome goals. The study involved approximately 5,000 students of two cohorts of seventh and eighth graders taught by 37 teachers in 18 urban schools. Compared to their peers districtwide, both the initial and scaled-up cohorts showed increases in science content understanding and process skills and significantly higher pass rates on the statewide test. The relative gains continued up to a year and a half after participation and showed little decrease with the second cohort when scaling occurred and the number of teachers increased. The effect of participation in curriculum units at different grade levels was independent and cumulative, with higher levels of participation associated with higher achievement scores. Examination of results by gender revealed that the curriculum effort succeeded in reducing the gender gap in science achievement experienced by urban African American boys. The overall results indicate that standards-based inquiry science curriculum can lead to standardized achievement test gains in historically underserved urban students, when the curriculum is highly specified, developed, and aligned with teacher professional development and administrative support. The researchers argue that scale-up efforts should demonstrate the ability to sustain improvement in student achievement gains on high-stakes assessments for a large number of urban students, while gradually providing less concentrated resources and fading teacher support.

In an unrelated program of research, the Kids as Global Scientists weather program by Songer (H.-S. Lee & Songer, 2003; Songer, H.-S. Lee, & Kam, 2002; Songer, H.-S. Lee, & McDonald, 2003) is also built upon a technology-based curriculum and professional development project. The project used an inquiry-based, technology-rich learning environment focused on weather with middle school students in a large, predominantly African American urban school district and in a mix of other schools across the nation. The work began with a small group of innovative volunteer teachers in mid-SES schools, but later expanded to include a wide range of teacher profiles and school contexts across 40 states.

Songer was interested in studying what happened when the curriculum was scaled up to many classrooms across the nation. Songer et al. (2003) involved one group of 40 "maverick" teachers who had sought out the program on their own and did not receive systematic professional development, and another group of 17 teachers from a high-poverty urban school district who had been involved in a partnership with the research team. From the 57 total classrooms, five successful classrooms were selected for more detailed study on the basis of achievement gains in scientific inquiry and content knowledge. These successful classrooms included three in high-poverty urban environments and two maverick classrooms in middle-class suburban environments.

Although the actual curriculum and patterns of student achievement were similar among the five classrooms, the teachers' classroom practices were somewhat different in each case. The maverick teachers favored having students work in small, self-paced groups, whereas the urban teachers usually had the whole class doing the same activity in unison. The maverick teachers also provided their students with relative autonomy to use open inquiry approaches, whereas the urban teachers tended toward teacher-directed or partial inquiry approaches. The researchers attributed some of these differences between the two groups as being influenced by issues of class size, students' prior experience with science inquiry, and institutional resources and support structures. Songer claims that rather than calling for student-initiated, open science inquiry as a pedagogical ideal (as science standards documents tend to do), different versions of science inquiry should be adapted for different classroom situations and science curriculum can be used to help teachers make those decisions.

SCIENCE CURRICULUM FOR ENGLISH LANGUAGE LEARNERS

Studies of science curriculum for ELL students have generally taken place in urban schools in low-income neighborhoods. Thus, it can sometimes be a challenge to disentangle the role that curriculum plays in addressing the various learning needs of non-mainstream students, including ELL students. For example, Barba (1993) found that when observing 57 randomly selected elementary bilingual/bicultural classrooms in a large metropolitan area of the southwestern United States, students rarely received science instruction using materials that were relevant to their language and culture. No classrooms had Spanish-language textbooks available for student use, and although 61% of the classrooms had science kits available in Spanish, English, or both languages, these materials were used for instructional purposes in only six of the 57 classrooms. In these six classrooms, manipulative materials were used only 12% of the instructional time.

As with the other research on science curriculum, described above, the literature on science curriculum materials for ELL students has generally taken one of two directions. Some studies have involved evaluation of existing curriculum materials and the degree to which these materials meet the needs of ELL students. Other studies have focused on the development of new curriculum materials that focus on hands-on, inquiry-based science as a way to promote science learning and English language development simultaneously for ELL students.

Existing Curriculum Materials. Lynch, Kuipers, Pyke, and Szesze (2005) examined the effect of a highly rated science curriculum unit on diverse student groups. The curriculum unit was not designed to specifically meet the needs of cultural or linguistic relevance to specific groups; instead, it was designed for wide implementation. The researchers used the unit with eighth grade students in five middle schools selected for student diversity. A comparison group of students followed district-approved curriculum materials. Disaggregated achievement data indicated that subgroups of students in the treatment group outscored their comparison group peers in all cases, except for students currently enrolled in ESOL.

Similarly, Hampton and Rodriguez (2001) used the Full Option Science Series (FOSS) with Spanish-speaking elementary children. Using this curriculum, pre-service teachers taught science to students in kindergarten through fifth grade in 62 classrooms at three elementary schools near the U.S.-Mexican border. They taught six 1-hour lessons over the course of 6 weeks, with half of the instruction in Spanish and half in English. Students then took an open-ended written assessment in the language of their choice. Fifty-five percent of the students chose to respond in Spanish and 45% responded in English. There was no significant difference in performance between children who chose to respond in Spanish and those who chose to respond in English. Hampton and Rodriguez concluded that academic language was being developed in both English and Spanish through the use of the FOSS curriculum. Surveys of the preservice teachers, regular classroom teachers, and a sample of the students consistently indicated a strong positive feeling about the value of this inquiry approach for increasing understanding of science concepts in both languages.

The two evaluation studies described above indicate that there is little science curriculum material available to support both the science and language development needs of ELL students. For this reason, a few projects have sought to develop and test their own curriculum materials to support science and language learning of ELL students, as described below.

Curriculum Materials Designed for ELL Students. Merino and Hammond (2001) studied how nine elementary school teachers helped ELL students learn science concepts and skills through writing. The teachers used an interdisciplinary approach in which a series of science inquiry lessons was integrated with other content area curriculum. Merino and Hammond refer to this approach as *sheltered constructivism*. First, students participated in activities under the guidance of teachers who explained tasks in the students' home language. Then, students developed additional activities based on their own questions. Teachers used a variety of classroom activities and strategies to promote students' scientific writing. In addition to producing narrative texts (a common practice in elementary schools), the students were provided with experiences in other genres of writing, such as recording faithfully and in detail what transpired in the science lessons, maintaining careful records to understand what happened, reporting to others so that they could repeat an experiment, keeping a record of an experiment for future use, and providing visual representations of events. Other instructional strategies used by these teachers to promote scientific writing included visual models, student examples, models from the media or literature, video accounts, lab notes, and narrative journals.

Lee and colleagues developed a more structured and comprehensive curriculum designed to meet the needs of ELL students. This project reflects the evolution of the knowledge base in the field of teaching science to ELL students as well as the shifting policy contexts regarding ELL students (e.g., English-only instructional policy) and science education (e.g., the rise of high-stakes testing and accountability policy). As part of their ongoing research program, Lee and colleagues devoted considerable effort to developing curriculum materials to support the simultaneous development of science content and academic language. These curriculum materials then served as the foundation for a series of professional development interventions with elementary teachers. Over the years, the project developed complete science curricula for third, fourth, and fifth grades that were used to fully replace the district science curriculum in schools that participated in the interventions.

During the earlier stage of the work, Fradd et al. (2002) described the development, implementation, and impact of the two curriculum units on matter (culminating in the water cycle) and weather. Teachers used the curriculum over a school year with approximately 500 fourth-grade students from different language backgrounds (Spanish, Haitian Creole, and monolingual English-speaking students) at six elementary schools in a large urban school district. At the beginning and end of each unit, students completed a paper-and-pencil test containing multiple-choice, short-answer, and extended written response items. Students from all language groups showed statistically significant achievement gains in both science knowledge and inquiry skills.

Over the years, the project continued curriculum development for third, fourth, and fifth grades. These included units on measurement and matter for third grade, the water cycle and weather for fourth grade, and the ecosystem and solar system for fifth grade. These topics followed the sequence of instruction from basic skills and concepts (measurement and matter), to variable global systems (the water cycle and weather), to increasingly large-scale systems (the ecosystem and the solar system). The curriculum materials for each science topic included consumable science workbooks for students, teachers' guides (including transparencies), and class sets of consumable and nonconsumable science supplies (including trade books related to the science topics in the units). All the units emphasize three domains relevant to the science learning of ELL students: 1) science inquiry, progressing along a continuum from teacher-explicit instruction to student-initiated inquiry (for details, see Lee, Hart, Cuevas, & Enders, 2004), 2) integration of English language and literacy development in science instruction (for details, see Hart & Lee, 2003), and 3) incorporation of students' home language and cultural experiences in science instruction (for details, see Lee, Luykx, Buxton, & Shaver, 2007). Together, these domains mutually support students' science content and academic language development.

Lee and colleagues examined the impact of the curriculum on student achievement outcomes (Lee, 2005; Lee et al., 2005; Lee, Deaktor, Enders, & Lambert, 2008). The research involved third, fourth, and fifth grade students at six elementary schools. The research addressed three areas of student outcomes: 1) overall science and literacy achievement, 2) achievement gaps among demographic subgroups, and 3) comparison with national (NAEP) and international (TIMSS) samples of students. Significance tests of mean scores between pre- and posttests indicated statistically significant increases each year on all measures of science and literacy at all three grade levels. Achievement gaps among demographic subgroups (defined in terms of ethnicity, home language, ESOL level, SES, special education status, and gender) sometimes narrowed among fourth grade students and remained consistent among third and fifth grade students. At the beginning of the school year, the students performed lower than third/fourth grade national and international samples of students on NAEP and TIMSS items. At the end of the school year, they generally performed higher than third/fourth grade samples, and comparable to or higher than seventh/eighth grade samples. As students advanced from one grade level to the next, the intervention seemed to have cumulative effects on achievement gains and narrowing of achievement gaps.

Using the same curriculum, Cuevas et al. (2005) examined the impact of the intervention on 1) children's ability to conduct science inquiry overall and to use specific skills in inquiry, and 2) narrowing the gaps in children's ability to conduct science inquiry among demographic subgroups of students. The study involved 25 third and fourth grade students taught by seven teachers who were selected for their effectiveness in teaching science and literacy to students of diverse linguistic and cultural backgrounds. The teachers selected these students to represent different achievement levels (high and low) and gender groups. Because the students came from all six schools, they also represented different ethnicities, SES levels, home languages, and levels of English proficiency. At the beginning and end of the school year, the students participated in interviews in which they were asked individually to design an experiment regarding the effect of surface areas on the rate of evaporation. Cuevas and colleagues found that the intervention enhanced the inquiry ability of all students, regardless of demographic background. Particularly, low achieving, low SES, and ESOL students made impressive gains. Detailed analysis indicated that although these students demonstrated enhanced abilities with some aspects of the inquiry task, they continued to have difficulties with other aspects of the task even after instruction (Lee, Buxton, Lewis, & LeRoy, 2006).

In addition to science achievement outcomes, the research also examined literacy (writing) achievement on two related science topics, changes of states of matter for third grade and the water cycle for fourth grade (Lee et al., 2005). The research involved 1,523 third and fourth grade students at six elementary schools. Both third and fourth grade students demonstrated statistically significant gains at the end of the school year. Achievement gaps among demographic subgroups widened with third-grade students at the end of the school year, whereas the gaps narrowed with fourth-grade students. Fourth-grade students showed higher scores on both pre- and posttests than third-grade students. These results suggest cumulative effects of the intervention after a second year of participation.

In the most recent version of this research program, Promoting Science among English Language Learners within a High-Stakes Testing Policy Context (P-SELL), Lee and colleagues have extended their efforts to develop comprehensive curriculum materials for ELL students from grades three, four, and five in urban schools. Their curriculum development efforts respond to the shifting policy context that is increasingly driven by high-stakes testing and accountability across content areas, including science. The curriculum units for third grade include measurement, changes of states of matter, and water cycle and weather; the fourth-grade units include energy, force and motion, and processes of life; and the fifth-grade units include nature of matter, Earth systems, and a comprehensive review and synthesis. The research examines two common assumptions about the teaching of science content to ELL students: 1) Can ELL students learn academic subjects, such as science, while also developing English proficiency? and 2) Can ELL students who learn to think and reason scientifically also perform well on high-stakes assessments? The research involves teachers from grades three through five and their students at 15 elementary schools in a large urban school district. All the schools enroll high proportions of ELL students and students from low socioeconomic status backgrounds, and have traditionally performed poorly according to the state's accountability plan.

Lee, Maerten-Rivera, et al. (2008) examined the impact of the intervention on students' science achievement at the end of the 1st-year implementation. The study involved 1,134 third-grade students at seven treatment schools and 966 third-grade students at eight comparison schools. The results indicated positive achievement outcomes. Students in the treatment group displayed a statistically significant increase in science achievement over the course of the school year. Students who were currently enrolled in ESOL programs performed comparably to students who had existed from ESOL or never been in ESOL. Treatment students showed a higher score on a statewide mathematics test, particularly on the measurement strand emphasized in the intervention, than the comparison group students.

In addition to science achievement outcomes, P-SELL also addresses literacy (writing) achievement outcomes. Lee, Mahotiere, Salinas, Penfield, and Maerten-Rivera (2009) examined third-grade students' writing achievement in the beginning and at the end of each year during the 3-year implementation of the intervention. Writing achievement included form (i.e., conventions, organization, and style/voice) and content (i.e., specific knowledge and understanding of science) in expository writing on the water cycle. From six treatment schools, the study involved 683 third graders during the 1st year, 661 third graders during the 2nd year, and 676 third graders during the 3rd year who completed both the pre- and post-writing test over the course of the school year. Students displayed a statistically significant increase and the gains were larger over the 3-year period. Students who were currently enrolled in ESOL programs made achievement gains comparable to those of students who had exited from ESOL or never been in ESOL.

SUMMARY

High-quality science curriculum has a key role to play in promoting science learning for non-mainstream students. We have described examples of curriculum development efforts that demonstrated positive science outcomes with students from non-mainstream cultures, students in low-SES settings, and ELL students. We have highlighted how alternative, sometimes competing, theoretical views can be brought together, and how curriculum development needs to take into account the current political context such as English-only policy and high-stakes testing and accountability policy.

Efforts to develop curriculum materials that meet the unique learning needs of culturally and linguistically diverse student groups present particular challenges. First, traditional science curriculum materials tend to exclude the cultural and linguistic experiences of non-mainstream students. Despite this shortcoming, curriculum development efforts that target the needs of non-mainstream students have been few and far between. Second, even when culturally relevant materials are developed and proven to be effective, that effectiveness may be limited to the particular cultural or linguistic group for which they are targeted. Conversely, when materials developed for wide use are implemented across a range of educational settings, local adaptations are essential for such materials to be used effectively. This, in turn, requires a level of curricular expertise among teachers that they are unlikely to have received in their teacher preparation or professional development. Teachers, administrators, policy makers, and researchers should be aware of the tension and trade-offs between science curriculum for all students and the curriculum targeted for specific groups.

While efforts have been made to establish design principles to guide the development of standards for high-quality science curriculum materials for all students (Kesidou & Roseman, 2002), other efforts are ongoing to establish guidelines for curriculum development targeted for specific groups. This includes efforts to support culturally relevant curriculum for various groups of Native American students (Aikenhead, 1997, 2001b; Matthews & Smith, 1994; Stephens, 2000), curriculum for students in low-SES settings (Calabrese et al., 2005), and curriculum integrating science and English literacy for ELL students (Lee et al., 2005, 2008). To date, these efforts have emerged independent of one another. Attention should be given to ways in which these multiple sets of guidelines might be compatible and applicable to all students, as well as where divergent approaches might better serve to the needs of specific student groups.

Another important area to consider when developing science curriculum for non-mainstream students is the role of computer-based learning. While educational technology currently plays a large role in science education reform, it has largely been ignored in curriculum development efforts for non-mainstream students. An emerging body of research on science curriculum that employs interactive web-based technology shows promising outcomes for culturally and linguistically diverse students in urban schools (e.g., LeTUS project and Kids as Global Scientists program). Further research may provide detailed descriptions of how non-mainstream students engage with computer technology in science classrooms, and what the impact of large-scale implementation of computer technology is on science outcomes across a range of educational settings.

As science comes to be included in high-stakes testing and accountability policy in increasing numbers of states, a critical question is how to make science curriculum relevant and meaningful for non-mainstream students while also preparing them to perform well on high-stakes science assessments. The research projects described in this chapter have not engaged in curriculum development efforts primarily to prepare students to pass high-stakes assessments. However, given the changes in accountability policy, a commitment to creating equitable learning opportunities requires curricular initiatives that, among other goals, can promote student achievement on high-stakes science assessments. For any curriculum to make an impact on these assessments, it must cover a broad range of science topics in a comprehensive manner and over an extended period of time. This will require new thinking about the role of curriculum materials in relation to teacher professional development, classroom practices, achievement outcomes, and policy contexts affecting non-mainstream students.

ACTIVITIES FOR CHAPTER 5

1. Our images of scientists are shaped by popular media, movies, literature, textbooks, and our own personal experiences. Even young children have images (usually quite stereotypical) of what scientists look like and what scientists do. There is a long history both in research and in teaching of asking students to do "draw a scientist" activities. Try this activity with your class.

   A. Have students close their eyes and imagine a scientist. Ask them to picture what the scientist looks like and what the scientist is doing.
   B. Ask them to open their eyes and draw the scientist and the setting that they pictured.
   C. Ask the students to tape their drawings to the wall and create a scientist "gallery."

D. Ask students to compare and contrast their drawings. What are some common features and what are the differences?

E. Ask students where their ideas about scientists come from. Pay special attention to drawings that are less stereotypical and ask those students what influenced their decisions about what to draw.

F. Ask students why our commonly held stereotypical views of scientists and their work may be problematic both for individuals and for society.

G. As an interesting extension, repeat this activity. Instead of having students draw a scientist, use one or more of the following jobs: *trash collector, nail salon stylist*, and *engineer*.

H. What similarities and differences are there in these drawings? What stereotypes are present? How do they compare with the stereotypes of scientists?

2. The pictures and images in science textbooks have a history of underrepresenting people of color and women. In more recent years, publishers have made an effort to correct this situation. How much of a difference is there?

A. Select one science textbook that is at least 20 years old and another textbook of the same subject and grade level that is less than 5 years old.

B. Pick two chapters at random from each book. Fill out the table below by counting images of people in the two chapters in each book.

C. Then answer the questions below based on the information in the table.

Group	White		Black		Hispanic		Asian		Native American		Unidentified or generic	
Book	Old	New	Old	New	Old	New	Old	New	Old	New	Old	New
Male												
Number												
(%)												
Female												
Number												
(%)												

D. What patterns do you see when you compare the images from the two textbooks?

E. What patterns do you see when you look at the images within each textbook?

F. Do you see any stereotypical roles for any group in either of the textbooks? If yes, describe.

G. What conclusions can you draw about multicultural representation in these science textbooks?

3. Evaluate a science textbook in terms of support provided for ELL students. Select a science textbook that is less than 5 years old. Randomly pick one chapter from the book and answer the following questions.
    A. Calculate the readability of a sample of the text. Type a sample of the text into the website: http://www.standards-schmandards.com/exhibits/rix/ Or use the readability feature in Microsoft Word.
    B. What strategies does the book already utilize to support language and literacy development of the readers?
    C. Other than simplifying the formal readability of the text, what else could the publisher do to increase the readability of the text for ELL students?
    D. What strategies does the book already use that can promote science learning of ELL students?
    E. What additional strategies could the book use to promote science learning of ELL students?

CHAPTER 6

Science Assessment and Student Diversity

The body of literature on educational assessment is extensive, as is the literature on assessment with non-mainstream students. However, research that specifically focuses on science assessment with non-mainstream students is extremely limited (Lee, 1999a; Solano-Flores & Trumbull, 2003). Until recently, science has rarely been part of large-scale or statewide assessments. In addition, because assessment of ELL students tends to concentrate on basic skills in literacy and numeracy, other subjects including science tend to be ignored. Recent changes in science account-ability policy in some states have begun to have significant impact on science education broadly and science assessment specifically with non-mainstream students. It is important to consider how characteristics of non-mainstream students may influence measures of science learning.

A crucial issue in the assessment debate is how to address linguistic and cultural factors to ensure valid and equitable measures for all students. Assessments of science achievement require consideration of fairness to different student groups. Fairness in this context means "the likelihood of any assessment allowing students to show what they understand about the construct being tested" (Lawrenz, Huffman, & Welch, 2001, p. 280).

Assessments of non-mainstream students should be particularly attentive to sociocultural influences that affect students' thinking and meaning-making, as well as the ways that students interpret and respond to assessment items. Students of differing cultural backgrounds may express their ideas in ways that mask their knowledge and abilities in the eyes of teachers who are unfamiliar with the linguistic and cultural norms of students' homes and communities. While mainstream students are also subject to cultural influences, the linguistic and cultural knowledge that they use to express their understanding is more likely to parallel the language and culture of teachers, researchers, and test developers. Thus, the backgrounds of mainstream students are more likely to support their performance on assessments than to interfere with it.

Because instruction and assessment reinforce each other, it is essential to provide high-quality instruction for all students and to assess their learning in ways that can guide subsequent instruction. Likewise, it is important to consider assessment *for* learning (i.e., formative assessment) as well as assessment *of* learning (i.e., summative assessment). While the two serve different purposes, they both provide insights that can improve instruction and learning through a feedback loop. A critical issue involves the fairness of high-stakes assessment and accountability for students who have been underserved in the science classroom. If students have not had access to high-quality science instruction, they cannot be expected to perform as well on assessments as those who have.

Studies of science assessment with non-mainstream students can be divided into two categories: 1) studies that look at science assessment with culturally diverse student groups and 2) studies that focus on science assessment with ELL students. Both advocates and critics of various approaches have based their claims mostly on inferences and insights drawn from related research endeavors, rather than from empirical studies on school science assessments per se (Lee, 1999a; Ruiz-Primo & Shavelson, 1996). Given the limited research on science assessment with non-mainstream students, it is unclear whether new assessment technologies and innovations present greater opportunities or greater obstacles to students being able to demonstrate their knowledge and abilities.

SCIENCE ASSESSMENT WITH CULTURALLY DIVERSE STUDENT GROUPS

Valid and equitable assessments should consider the knowledge and abilities that students bring from their home and community cultures, while measuring the science standards expected of all students (i.e., the content of assessment). In addition, assessments should allow students to demonstrate their knowledge and abilities in ways that are compatible with their backgrounds and experiences, while they acquire the ways of demonstrating knowledge and abilities that are expected by school science and the science community (i.e., the format of assessment). All students must learn to adopt these practices, but for non-mainstream students, the practices may be less culturally and linguistically congruent, making it a greater challenge to adapt to both the content and format of assessment.

Content of Assessment. One approach to promoting valid and equitable assessment is to make assessments more relevant to the knowledge and experiences of diverse student groups in their homes and communities. This approach focuses on the content of science assessments. Proponents of this approach criticize traditional science assessments for making few, if any, connections to non-mainstream students' lives. This may be due to the fact that few teachers or test developers have an in-depth knowledge of non-mainstream students' cultural beliefs and practices. In addition, because science is often thought to be universal and culture-free, the idea that cultural backgrounds should influence science instruction or assessment is an alien concept to many teachers and test developers. Proponents argue that authentic tasks drawn from students' real-life situations, rather than decontextualized textbook knowledge, may motivate students and enhance their performance (García & Pearson, 1994; Lacelle-Peterson & Rivera, 1994). Skeptics, however, claim that measuring performance on open-ended tasks favor privileged students who typically have more opportunities to participate in science-rich environments (Hamilton, 1998; Shavelson, Baxter, & Pine, 1992). This group has argued that assessment tasks based entirely on classroom content and experiences are fairer than those requiring students to draw upon knowledge acquired outside the classroom because the classroom tasks have been experienced by all students. This argument, however, holds only if all students have had equal access to high-quality science instruction within the school environment. Unfortunately, this is rarely the case because non-mainstream students tend to be concentrated in urban schools with limited access to highly qualified teachers and resources needed to support high-quality science instruction (Hewson, Kahle, Scantlebury, & Davies, 2001; Kahle, Meece, & Scantlebury, 2000; Spillane et al., 2001).

Many forms of validity are considered when constructing assessments. Solano-Flores and Nelson-Barber (2001) propose the idea of *cultural validity* to address sociocultural influences that may shape the ways in which students interpret and respond to science test items. These sociocultural influences include the values, beliefs, experiences, communication patterns, teaching and learning styles, community ways of knowing, and socioeconomic conditions in which students live. Furthermore, students of differing cultural backgrounds may have alternative ways of expressing what they know. Grounded in cross-cultural studies of science learning and assessment, Solano-Flores and Nelson-Barber identify five areas in which cultural validity can contribute to improving science assessment: 1) student epistemology, 2) student language proficiency, 3) cultural worldviews, 4) cultural communication and socialization styles, and 5) student life context and values. They suggest that "ideally, if cultural validity issues were addressed properly at the inception of an assessment and throughout its entire process of development, there would be no cultural bias and providing accommodations for cultural minorities would not be necessary" (p. 557). Still, the question of what it means to properly address such issues is far from simple. Even teachers who know their students well as individuals would likely struggle to balance and include all five areas of cultural validity when constructing classroom assessments. The idea that standardized tests, constructed at a distance from individual students, could meet such a measure of cultural validity seems even more challenging.

The areas identified by Solano-Flores and Nelson-Barber are addressed (though sliced rather differently) in a study by Luykx, Lee, Mahotiere, Lester, Hart, & Deaktor (2007), which examined cultural and home language influences on students' written responses on paper-and-pencil science tests. The assessment instruments measured third- and fourth-grade students' science knowledge and inquiry skills after participating in culturally congruent curriculum units on measurement, matter, the water cycle, and weather. The results revealed a wide range of linguistic and cultural influences in students' responses to science test items. These influences reflected the knowledge, beliefs, and implicit assumptions derived from students' homes and communities. Linguistic and cultural features of student responses skewed assessments of individual students' science knowledge and inquiry skills. Linguistic features included 1) nonstandard spellings of English words that reflected the phonology of the students' home language but were often unintelligible to adult readers unfamiliar with the home language, and 2) semantic confusion about science terms with more than one possible meaning (e.g., *state*, *gas*, and *record*). Cultural features included: 1) genre confusion regarding the interpretation of scenario-based science test items and 2) responses reflecting the practices of students' home environments, rather than those assumed by the test developers. The results also indicated that the assessment instruments were shaped by the researchers' own cultural assumptions and linguistic practices, to a greater degree than they had realized. If researchers who are engaged in the study of language and culture struggle with some aspects of cultural validity in designing assessments, it seems unlikely that mainstream test developers, who are less attuned to these issues, would do better in this regard.

Based on the student test results, Luykx et al. (2007) drew several conclusions. First, assessment instruments are inevitably cultural products, whose content and organization are built on cultural knowledge that different groups of students may not share. While attempts to avoid obvious and blatant cultural bias are now common practice in test design, they can never achieve complete cultural neutrality. Second, many of the cultural and linguistic influences present in students' responses are unintelligible to test developers and scorers who are unfamiliar with students' home language and culture. Students' limited English proficiency or lack of familiarity with mainstream culture may masquerade as a lack of science knowledge or inquiry skills. Finally, attempts to ground assessment items in students' real-world experience or cultural norms may be misguided, given that cultural norms and experiences can differ greatly, even among students who are perceived to be from the same cultural and linguistic backgrounds. In the end, attempts to ensure that all students have access to high-quality science instruction in school may be the best way to support equitable science assessment.

Format of Assessment. Another approach proposed to promote valid and equitable assessments is to reconsider the formats used for assessing student achievement. Traditional multiple-choice tests have been criticized for failing to adequately measure the types of knowledge and abilities that science students are expected to learn (AAAS, 1989, 1993; NRC, 1996). Instead, alternative or performance assessments have been proposed that include open-ended or constructed response items, laboratory-based practical tests, construction of portfolios or exhibitions, and opportunities to design and conduct experiments (Ruiz-Primo & Shavelson, 1996). Advocates of performance assessments claim that they provide students with flexible and multiple opportunities consistent with cultural preferences, and permit students to communicate ideas in multiple ways (Darling-Hammond, 1994; García & Pearson, 1994; Lacelle-Peterson & Rivera, 1994). However, performance assessments tend to rely heavily on students' ability to read and write in particular genres, confounding academic literacy skills with content knowledge. This is particularly problematic for ELL students, as well as for speakers of nonstandard varieties of English (Ruiz-Primo & Shavelson, 1996; Shaw, 1997). Furthermore, regardless of their pedagogical value, performance assessments may be too costly and time-consuming to implement on a large scale (Stecher & Klein, 1997). Thus, large-scale assessments continue to rely primarily on multiple-choice items.

Given the limited research on performance assessments in science with non-mainstream students, both advocates and critics have relied on inferences drawn from related research (see the discussion in Ruiz-Primo & Shavelson, 1996). Furthermore, the few relevant studies on science assessments show inconsistent results with regard to the effect of assessment formats on science outcomes of students from different ethnic groups (Klein, Jovanovic, Stecher, McCaffrey, Shavelson, Haertel, Solano-Flores, & Comfort, 1997; Lawrenz et al., 2001).

Klein et al. (1997) examined whether the differences in mean scores across demographic subgroups on science performance assessments were comparable to the differences that are typically found across these subgroups on multiple-choice tests. The research, which involved over 2,400 students in grades five, six, and nine from 90 classrooms across 30 schools, was part of a field test of California's statewide testing program, the California Learning Assessment System (CLAS). Students completed several hands-on science performance assessments as well as state-created multiple-choice items. Additionally, fifth- and sixth-grade students took the multiple-choice science subtest of the Iowa Tests of Basic Skills (ITBS). The results indicated that differences in mean scores across demographic subgroups were not related to the test formats (i.e., performance assessment vs. multiple-choice items). Regardless of test format, Whites and Asians had significantly higher mean scores than Blacks or Hispanics. These results remained consistent when other factors were taken into account, such as variations among schools or teachers. Klein and colleagues conclude that simply changing test format is unlikely to have much effect on the differences in mean scores among demographic subgroups. These results should be interpreted with caution, however, because the researchers did not control for other characteristics of students, such as SES or parents' educational level, which are likely to influence students' academic performance. In addition, the research on the content of assessment discussed earlier would support the argument that simply changing the format of assessment from multiple choice to performance, without considering cultural or linguistic factors in assessment or inequities in instruction, should not be expected to lead to improved performance of non-mainstream students.

Lawrenz, Huffman, and Welch (2001) also examined science achievement outcomes for demographic subgroups of students using different assessment formats. A nationally representative sample of approximately 3,500 ninth-grade science students from 13 high schools throughout the U.S. completed a series of science assessments designed to measure their level of achievement on the national science education standards. All participating schools used a curriculum designed to meet the *National Science Education Standards* (NRC, 1996). Teachers from each school were involved in the curriculum development, and the resulting materials were provided to all participating classrooms. All assessment items were selected from existing sources, such as the NAEP, the International Assessment of Educational Progress (IAEP), and the Second International Science Study (SISS). The assessments covered a range of formats, including a multiple-choice test, an open-ended written test, a hands-on lab skills test, and a full hands-on investigation test. The results showed that the different assessment formats measured different student competencies. In particular, the hands-on formats seemed to measure different competencies than the multiple-choice and open-ended formats.

In contrast to the study by Klein et al. (1997), the results of Lawrenz et al. (2001) indicated that the achievement of students from different demographic subgroups did vary somewhat by assessment formats. The typical trend of higher achievement for White and Asian American students and lower achievement for African American and Hispanic students was still found in all assessment formats. However, on the hands-on lab skills and full hands-on investigation assessments, there were switches in relative order within the two higher-performing groups and within the two lower-performing groups. These results suggest that using different assessment formats may affect the science outcomes of students from different demographic subgroups. As was the case with the study by Klein et al. (1997), these results should be interpreted with caution for multiple reasons. First, the study did not control for other characteristics of students, such as SES or parents' educational level. Second, the study considered variations in the format of assessment without considering variations in the content of assessment, issues of cultural validity, or variations in the preparation of teachers serving the different demographic subgroups of students.

SCIENCE ASSESSMENT WITH ENGLISH LANGUAGE LEARNERS

In addition to the questions of content and form of assessment that are relevant to the valid and equitable assessment of all non-mainstream students, discussed above, assessment of ELL students requires additional consideration of language-related issues. First, should assessments be given in English and/or in the ELL students' home language? Second, what kinds of accommodations are needed to enable ELL students to demonstrate their knowledge and abilities in science? In other words, when assessment is done in English, how can assessment distinguish between science knowledge and English proficiency?

Language of Assessment. To address the complexities of linguistic and cultural factors in assessment more effectively, Solano-Flores and Trumbull (2003) propose a new paradigm to promote valid and equitable assessment of ELL students and other non-mainstream students. Most current efforts toward valid and equitable assessment focus on assuring test validity by attempting to eliminate the confounding effects of non-mainstream students' language and culture. Under the proposed new paradigm in assessment of ELL students, efforts should be oriented in the opposite direction. As discussed earlier, it is virtually impossible to construct tests that are free from cultural and linguistic influences. Therefore, understanding how best to account for the inevitable influences of mainstream and non-mainstream languages and cultures, rather than futilely trying to exclude those influences, should guide all elements of the assessment process, including test development, test review, test use, and test interpretation.

One possible approach is to translate assessment instruments from English into a student's home language and then administer the assessment in both languages. Assessing students' knowledge in both the home language and the language of instruction allows students a more balanced opportunity to demonstrate their content knowledge while reducing the confounding effect of language. One challenge with this approach is that ensuring the comparability of assessment instruments between two languages is complicated, raising issues of validity. Also, this approach may still fail to give an accurate picture of students' content knowledge if students have not developed grade-appropriate literacy skills in the home language. This is often the case because ELL students rarely have the opportunity to receive academic language instruction in their home language. In addition, translating assessment instruments would not eliminate all sources of possible linguistic and cultural confusion, and may well introduce new ones. Despite these concerns, the approach of dual-language assessment should be weighed against the threats to validity inherent in English-only assessment. Dual-language assessment has the potential to produce clearer understandings of the interactions among first and second language proficiency, students' content knowledge, and the linguistic and content demands of test items. Research in this vein has illustrated the proposed paradigm using science topics assessed in English, Chinese, Haitian Creole, and Spanish (Solano-Flores, Lara, Sexton, & Navarrete, 2001). This perspective, however, has so far gained little ground in policy and assessment circles in the U.S. education system.

Assessment Accommodations. When assessment of ELL students is done in English, attempts should be made to distinguish between students' science knowledge and English language proficiency. It is challenging to avoid confounding English language proficiency with science knowledge, however, and the attempt has rarely been made in research on assessment programs. In practice, the issue of distinguishing between content and language with ELL students is generally addressed through testing accommodations.

When developing testing accommodations for ELL students, the goal should be to decrease the language load while keeping the content the same. This is a difficult goal because language and content are closely linked (Siegel, 2007). Much of the research on academic assessment of ELL students has focused on the effectiveness of various testing accommodations. Building on studies of testing accommodations for students with special needs, accommodations for ELL students involve questions such as which students should be included in accountability systems and which accommodation strategies assist students in demonstrating their knowledge and abilities (Abedi, 2004; Abedi et al., 2004).

A range of accommodation strategies can be used to support ELL students. For example, accommodations given to ELL students during the 2005 NAEP science test included the use of bilingual dictionaries, bilingual texts, subject-specific glossaries, English-language dictionaries, extra time to complete assessments, having test items read aloud, allowing students to ask clarifying questions, allowing students to work in small groups, and allowing students to dictate oral responses to a scribe (NCES, 2008). Although assessments could be made more comprehensible to ELL students by allowing for translation of test items or by simplifying the language of the test through avoiding unnecessarily complex grammatical constructions, polysemic terms (i.e., terms with more than one meaning), and idiomatic expressions, such accommodations are not regularly employed.

In one recent study of testing accommodations, Kieffer, Lesaux, Rivera, and Francis (2009) examined the effectiveness and the validity of specific testing accommodations in improving the performance of ELL students on large-scale assessments. Effectiveness was defined in terms of whether ELL students who received an accommodation outperformed ELL students who did not receive the accommodation. Validity was defined in terms of whether an accommodation altered the construct validity of a test—whether non-ELL students who received an accommodation outperformed non-ELL students who did not receive the accommodation. The researchers analyzed data from other studies of the effects of accommodations for ELL students on NAEP, TIMSS, and state accountability test items in mathematics and science at fourth and eighth grades. Kieffer and colleagues examined 11 other studies of accommodations, including extra time, a dual language booklet, dual language questions, a Spanish version of the test, use of a bilingual dictionary, use of an English dictionary, and simplified English language versions of test questions. Results indicated that of all the accommodations studied, only providing students with English dictionaries led to improved performance for ELL students. Results also indicated little evidence of threat to validity.

In contrast to testing accommodations on large-scale assessments by Kieffer et al. (2009), Siegel (2007) studied accommodations for ELL students on classroom assessments. Unlike large-scale assessments that attempt to contain and reduce the language factor, the goal of these classroom assessments was to improve written assessment items in as many ways as possible to make the items more accessible and equitable for ELL students. The study was conducted in two middle school life science classes that used NSF-supported science curriculum materials for a full academic year between the pretest and posttest. The advanced ELL students participating in the study had some proficiency in reading and writing in English. Since changes to written, open-ended items were designed especially for ELL students, the study compared how the ELL and non-ELL students performed on those items.

Siegel developed and used an equity framework for written classroom assessments that was composed of five principles: 1) match the learning goals of the original items and match the language of instruction, 2) be comprehensible for ELL students both linguistically and culturally; 3) challenge students to think about difficult ideas without watering down content, 4) elicit student understanding, and 5) scaffold the use of language and support student learning. Ways to improve two written assessments for advanced ELL students were developed through teacher research and tested with a pretest/posttest design. Based on these five principles, 11 kinds of modifications to the items were made to support linguistic (e.g., reducing the number of words), cognitive (e.g., adding a graphic organizer), and visual (e.g., including a picture) improvements.

Results indicated that both English-only and advanced ELL students scored significantly higher on the modified classroom assessments. Because modifications to test items were targeted for ELL students, the performance of ELL students should have improved, whereas the performance of English-only students should have remained the same, thus reducing the performance gap. One possible interpretation of the finding is that because language and content are so closely linked, it is difficult to tease them apart. Another possible interpretation is that the wording and formatting of science test items can be confusing to English-only as well as ELL students. Thus, strategies to improve the comprehension of test items may benefit all students.

Shaw (1997) examined the degree to which classroom science assessment functioned as a measure of science knowledge or as a measure of English language proficiency. The study used science performance assessments with two classes of ELL students in a high school in a large metropolitan area of northern California. The school was unusual in that it implemented bilingual education programs with extensive human and material resources for effective instruction of ELL students. The two teachers who participated in the research had training and experience in the teaching of hands-on inquiry science to ELL students, and both were fluent in English and Spanish. The study focused specifically on a 4-day performance assessment task in the sheltered science classes taught by the two teachers. The assessment task on heat energy involved an open-ended inquiry and hands-on investigation by students working in small groups. Using a scoring rubric, Shaw and the two teachers scored student responses on assessment items. The results indicated that students' ability to develop an inquiry procedure, which was the most text-dependent item scored, was significantly affected by students' level of English proficiency. In contrast, each of the other measures scored, including the use of graphs, calculations, equations, data tables, and final summary questions, was not significantly affected by students' level of English proficiency, but was significantly affected by students' level of science knowledge. Thus, there was no simple answer to the question of whether performance assessments accurately measure ELL students' science knowledge. The answer seems to depend on the assessment task in question.

The studies by Kieffer et al. (2009) and Siegel (2007) indicate tensions between the purpose of enhancing the validity of measures by using accommodations for ELL students in standardized assessments and the purpose of improving the performance of all students, both ELL and non-ELL students, in classroom assessments. The studies by Siegel (2007) and Shaw (1997) highlight the difficulty of separating the language and content of assessments with ELL students. Collectively, the results of these studies suggest the need to take into account multiple factors when offering testing accommodations for ELL students on science assessments, such as developing and refining test items in both English and students' home language at the same time so that both versions are validated throughout the assessment process (Solano-Flores, 2006, 2008; Solano-Flores & Trumbull, 2003). In making these decisions, issues of validity, equity, and practicality should be considered for both standardized and classroom assessments.

SUMMARY

Given the limited research on science assessments with non-mainstream students, it is difficult to draw conclusions about how to provide more valid and equitable science assessments for these students. The few studies that have directly addressed this issue have shown inconsistent results (e.g., Klein et al., 1997; Lawrenz et al., 2001).

There has been considerable debate about the question of cultural bias in science assessments. While some see cultural bias as a serious inequity in assessment, others attribute differences in academic performance across student demographic subgroups to deficiencies in students' cognitive abilities or limitations in students' experiences or home environments. Among those who believe that cultural bias is a serious problem in assessment, there seem to be two opposing perspectives on how best to address the concern. Advocates of one position aim to increase test validity by removing cultural bias from assessment instruments and practices. In contrast, advocates of the other position claim that because cultural bias cannot be removed, non-mainstream students' cultural beliefs and practices should be incorporated throughout the assessment process (Solano-Flores & Nelson-Barber, 2001; Solano-Flores & Trumbull, 2003).

Although the second approach has the potential to solve some problems regarding cultural bias, it presents its own challenges. First, test developers and even teachers generally do not know enough about non-mainstream students' communities, histories, and backgrounds to design assessments that are relevant to students' lives outside of school. Second, attempts to define typical cultural practices of any group always run the risk of stereotyping. Third, because most schools and nearly all school districts educate students from a wide range of cultural backgrounds, attempts to create assessment instruments that are culturally relevant for some students may make them culturally inappropriate for others. Fourth, the use of different versions of assessment instruments with different student groups raises obvious problems with regard to validity across groups. Finally, even assuming that these other issues can be resolved, the large-scale standardization of academic assessments means that there is unlikely to be political or institutional support for widespread tailoring of assessments to meet the needs of specific cultural groups.

For students who are acquiring English as a new language, cultural bias in assessments is likely to be compounded by language-related issues. For ELL students who are assessed in a language they are not yet proficient, there is no easy solution to the problem of valid and equitable assessment. The language, science concepts, and assessment practices commonly used in U.S. schools are closely tied to the usage of American English. Thus, until ELL students have mastered that language (a process that takes quite a bit longer than the 1 or 2 years of ESOL instruction students typically receive), assessing them in English should not be assumed to provide an accurate picture of their science knowledge. On the other hand, assessing them in their home language raises problems of validity, resources, and compatibility with the language of instruction (Solano-Flores, 2006, 2008). Even if assessments are administered to ELL students in both English and the home language, ensuring the comparability of assessment instruments in the two languages is complicated.

In the current policy context of standardization, high-stakes assessment, and accountability, designing and implementing assessments for specific cultural and linguistic groups would not only be expensive and politically unpopular but also open to psychometric and other technical problems (Abedi, 2004; Abedi et al., 2004; Penfield & Lee, in press; Solano-Flores & Trumbull, 2003). For ELL students, possible solutions to this dilemma are further reduced by the spread of English-only legislation that prioritizes students' acquisition of English over content knowledge in subject areas (Gutiérrez et al., 2002). In light of all of these challenges, designing valid and equitable approaches to assess the academic learning of non-mainstream students remains one of the more difficult issues in educational policy and practice.

As well as being an equity issue for non-mainstream students, the challenge of valid and equitable assessment is a problem for educators as well. Much of the existing knowledge base concerning achievement gaps among demographic subgroups (racial, ethnic, cultural, linguistic, socioeconomic, or gender) is derived from large-scale studies that depend on standardized assessment of students' content knowledge in subject areas. Because these large-scale studies involve heterogeneous populations, the question of how to achieve more valid and equitable assessment results represents a fundamental dilemma. When researchers attempt to combine large-scale assessment with a concern for cultural and linguistic diversity, they are forced to make choices and draw conclusions based on assessment measures that may not paint an accurate picture of what non-mainstream students know and can do.

ACTIVITIES FOR CHAPTER 6

1. The following questions are taken from two intelligence tests from Australia. The first 5 questions come from a standard Western European test and the second 5 questions come from a test developed by members of the Edward River Aboriginal community in North Queensland.

   A. *Standard Western European Test*
       i. How many weeks are in a year? _____
       ii. Filthy is to disease as clean is to _____
       iii. Which items may be classified with clock? (circle as many as apply)
           a. Ruler
           b. Thermometer
           c. Rain gauge
           d. Tachometer
       iv. If Mary's aunt is my mother, what relation is Mary's father to my sister? _____
       v. Why should you keep away from bad company?
   B. *Test Developed by Edward River Aboriginal Community*
       i. How many lunar months are in a year? _____
       ii. As wallaby is to animal so cigarette is to _____
       iii. Which items may be classified with salt-water crocodile? (circle as many as apply)
           a. Marine turtle
           b. Brolga

    c. Frilled lizard

    d. Black snake

   iv. You are out in the bush with your wife and young children and you are all hungry. You have a rifle and bullets. You see three animals all within range—a young emu, a large kangaroo and a small female wallaby. Which should you shoot for food?

   v. Why should you be careful of your cousins?

Now, consider the following discussion questions:

  A. How did you feel when you were answering each set of questions?

  B. Are these tests a fair measure of intelligence? Why or why not?

  C. How does this relate to how non-mainstream students might feel when taking standardized tests in school?

  D. As a teacher, how would you work with a student who scored very low on a test such as the first one but very high on a test such as the second one?

2. ELL students are generally eligible for testing accommodations on standardized tests such as the current high-stakes assessments given in most states.

  A. Find out what testing accommodations can be used with ELL students in your state. Make a list of the possible accommodations.

  B. Talk to teachers at two or more different schools and ask them which of the possible state-approved testing accommodations are actually used with ELL students in their schools. Try to get information from schools in more than one school district, ideally from one district that serves a large population of ELL students and another district that serves a small population of ELL students.

  C. What differences, if any, do you see between schools?

PART III

School and Home Environments

To create more equitable learning environments for non-mainstream students, teachers' knowledge, beliefs, and practices need to continually evolve throughout their professional careers. As our understanding of student diversity and its effects on student learning grows through further research, highly effective teachers look for ways to apply this new knowledge to classroom practice. Administrators and policy makers at the state, district, and school level also need to take the new knowledge into account if they are to act in ways that are supportive of the learning needs of non-mainstream students. When policies and practices at any level of the education system fail to provide this support, teachers face added difficulties in promoting students' science learning. For example, there is a growing understanding that school science should be connected more closely to the knowledge and experiences that non-mainstream students develop in their homes and communities. Current policies and practices, however, rarely provide explicit support or resources for developing those connections as an avenue for improving students' science learning. In this part, we discuss results of research and development projects in the following areas: 1) science teacher education, 2) school organization and educational policy, and 3) home and community connections to school science.

CHAPTER 7

Science Teacher Education and Student Diversity

As our nation's schools educate increasing numbers of non-mainstream students, there is a growing awareness that today's teachers need a new set of knowledge, skills, and dispositions to provide equitable learning opportunities for all students. In contrast to the shifting demographics in the student population, the teaching profession continues to be dominated by White female teachers. Jorgenson (2000) states that "school districts across the United States confront an urgent shortage of minority educators, while the number of minority students in the public schools steadily increases. This imbalance is expected to worsen" (pp. 1–2). Haberman (1988) further states that "[h]aving too few minority teachers is merely one manifestation of under-educating minority children and youth in inadequate elementary and secondary schools" (p. 39).

Teachers need not come from the same racial, ethnic, cultural, linguistic, or socioeconomic background as their students in order to teach effectively (Ladson-Billings, 1994, 1995). Given the student diversity within individual classrooms, matching teachers with students of similar backgrounds is often not feasible. However, teachers of all backgrounds need to increase their awareness of the cultural and linguistic knowledge that non-mainstream students bring to the classroom (Gay, 2002; Villegas & Lucas, 2002). To do this, they need opportunities to reflect upon how students' minority or immigrant status may affect educational experience (Cochran-Smith, 1995a, 1995b; Valli, 1995). In short, there is a critical need for teacher education that specifically addresses both pre-service and in-service teachers' beliefs and practices with regard to student diversity as it relates to subject areas.

Despite the call to address issues of student diversity in teacher education for two decades or more, limited progress has been made in preparing teachers to succeed in today's culturally and linguistically diverse classrooms. One reason is that teacher education tends to be *strategy-focused* and rarely attempts to address the multiple challenges of promoting classroom practices that are both academically rigorous and equitable for all students. Another reason is that even when teacher education does address multiple challenges simultaneously, this does not easily translate into a workable model of classroom practices. Such a model should consider a range of factors, including 1) the need to address both academic content and student diversity (Bryan & Atwater, 2002; Rodriguez & Kitchen, 2005),

2) the context of urban schools with limited resources and high rates of student and teacher mobility (Hewson et al., 2001; Spillane et al., 2001), and 3) the role of high-stakes testing and accountability with its attendant conJstraints on how teachers are asked to spend instructional time (Marx & Harris, 2006; McNeil, 2000).

Teacher education should equip teachers with knowledge of academic content, ways in which academic content may align with students' cultural and linguistic experiences, teaching strategies appropriate to multicultural and multilingual settings, awareness of how traditional educational practices have marginalized certain groups of students and limited their learning opportunities, and allocation of resources within the constraints of urban schooling and accountability policies. Below, three areas of research on teacher education are addressed: 1) pre-service teacher preparation, 2) in-service teacher professional development, and 3) teacher education with regard to ELL students.

TEACHER PREPARATION

In their review of the literature on pre-service teachers' beliefs about multicultural issues, Bryan and Atwater (2002) conclude that science teacher preparation programs that aim to support the education of an increasingly diverse student population tend to focus on three categories of beliefs: 1) student characteristics, 2) external influences on student learning, and 3) appropriate teacher responses to student diversity. Many pre-service teachers believe that students from non-mainstream backgrounds are less capable of academic success than mainstream students. Pre-service teachers also tend to ascribe problems associated with students' learning to students' lives outside of school, rather than to events that take place in the classroom. In addition, many pre-service teachers are largely unaware of cultural and linguistic influences on student learning, do not consider teaching for diversity as part of their job as a teacher, overlook racial/ethnic and cultural differences in the classroom, accept inequities as a given condition, or actively resist multicultural views of learning.

The literature review by Bryan and Atwater (2002) is largely based on the context of elementary reading and language arts education, due to limited literature specifically addressing science or mathematics education. Bryan and Atwater conclude that most pre-service science teachers enter their teacher preparation programs with little or no intercultural experience and with beliefs and assumptions that undermine the goal of providing an equitable education for all students. More troubling, many pre-service teachers graduate from their teacher preparation programs without fundamentally changing their beliefs and assumptions about students who are linguistically and culturally different from themselves. The research concludes that teacher preparation programs should provide pre-service teachers with more intercultural experiences to challenge their beliefs and assumptions about student diversity, if program completers are to learn to teach all students effectively.

Rethinking teacher preparation to support the science learning needs of non-mainstream students requires new models and new features in science teacher education. Based on the emerging literature on critical theory and multicultural science education, Ferguson (2008) proposes six categories for *multicultural science teacher education standards* to be used as an organizing structure for science methods course instructors. These categories include dialogic conversations; authentic activities; transformative skills; reflexivity; and knowing self, others, and epistemology. Development and application of standards in these categories would result in science methods courses with a very different emphasis than most current methods courses.

The literature based on studies of science teacher preparation supports the conclusions by Bryan and Atwater (2002) and Ferguson (2008) regarding the need for more explicit preparation in multicultural science teacher education. Overall, the results of these studies indicate that pre-service science teachers mostly come from mainstream backgrounds and encounter the challenge of relating to students with backgrounds different than their own for the first time in a university course or in a classroom setting. These pre-service teachers often exhibit resistance to change and experience difficulties making transformative changes in their beliefs and practices with regard to student diversity throughout their teacher preparation programs. Even when significant changes in teacher beliefs and practices occur, such changes are demanding and slow.

Science Methods Courses. One set of studies deals with science methods courses designed to help pre-service science teachers foster positive beliefs and effective practices with regard to non-mainstream students. Southerland and Gess-Newsome (1999) taught a science methods course with 22 pre-service elementary teachers who were almost all from mainstream backgrounds. They used a variety of teaching methods to focus on issues related to inclusive science teaching practices. The results indicated that pre-service science teachers held a traditional view of knowledge, teaching, and learning. They believed that the goal of inclusive science teaching was to make a fixed and clearly defined body of scientific knowledge accessible to all students, presumably within the confines of the students' fixed abilities. These pre-service teachers also believed that a goal of inclusive science teaching was to help non-mainstream students think like mainstream students and to eliminate as much of the diversity as possible.

In a similar study focusing on pre-service secondary science teachers, Yerrick and Hoving (2003) taught a field-based science methods course with teachers who were almost all from mainstream backgrounds. The field experience involved working with predominantly rural Black high school students in a lower-track earth science class. Initially, the teachers designed, taught, and reflected upon their lessons from an egocentric perspective, using their own experiences as learners as a guide to good teaching. They demonstrated similar practices, made similar inferences about teaching and learning, and relied on similar domains of knowledge to gauge their teaching. Then, Yerrick and Hoving worked explicitly with the pre-service teachers to consider alternative practices based on gaining a better knowledge of their students' learning needs and prior experiences with science. By the end of the course, two discrete categories of pre-service teachers emerged: 1) those who demonstrated an ability to reflect on and revise their practices in response to their non-mainstream students' experiences, and 2) those who resisted efforts to shift their thinking and instead reproduced their own educational experience with a new student population.

Similar to the work of Yerrick and Hoving, but addressing the role of teacher educators rather than the teachers themselves, Rodriguez (2001a) urged science teacher educators and researchers to (re)examine the roles they play in the reproduction of social and educational inequities in our schools. He addressed how to improve the preparation of science teachers in order to reduce gaps in science achievement and science careers for non-mainstream students. To do so, he deconstructed the notion of educators as cultural workers and, instead, proposed the role of cultural warriors. Specifically, he called for teacher educators to show the courage to challenge pre-service teachers' resistance to both pedagogical and ideological change. Rodriguez insists that learning to teach for student diversity and social justice must be central to the ongoing work of science teacher education, regardless of pre-service teachers' background or the context in which they believe they will be teaching.

In a practical example of this approach, Rodriguez (1998b) reported on his work with pre-service secondary science teachers from mainstream backgrounds in a year-long science methods course. Unlike typical methods courses, this course was organized around a political theory of social justice as well as a pedagogical theory of social constructivism. Rodriguez hoped that this model would help prepare pre-service teachers to teach for both student diversity (through culturally inclusive and socially relevant pedagogy) and scientific understanding (through critically engaging and intellectually meaningful pedagogy). The results showed that this approach did cause pre-service teachers to critically examine their prior beliefs about what it meant to be a successful science teacher. Most of the participants came to value the importance of creating science classrooms where all students would be provided with opportunities for successful learning. However, several of the pre-service teachers demonstrated strong resistance to ideological change and became defensive when asked to confront ideas of racism and their own racial privilege as Anglo-Europeans. Some of these pre-service teachers also demonstrated resistance to pedagogical change, citing the conflicting messages they felt they were receiving about what was expected of them from their cooperating teachers (i.e., cover the curriculum and maintain class control) and from their university supervisors (i.e., implement student-centered, constructivist class activities).

In contrast to studies that have described challenges and difficulties that pre-service science teachers experienced in their science methods courses, Howes (2002) focused on the strengths that could assist pre-service teachers in developing an effective, inclusive science pedagogy. She worked with four pre-service elementary teachers (two White and two African American) in an elementary science methods course. The positive characteristics that these pre-service teachers demonstrated included a propensity for inquiry, a concern for children, and an awareness of school/society relationships. In particular, the two African American teachers expressed a belief that schooling tends to work against social justice, a desire to use schooling to work for social justice, and a willingness to bring historical and cultural examples into the science classroom.

Moore (2007a, 2008a, 2008b, in press) reported a set of results from her research with 23 preservice elementary teachers regarding issues of multiculturalism and social justice in teaching science in urban elementary classrooms. The pre-service teachers were enrolled in a 16-week elementary science methods course in a master's degree program at a large urban university. Participants came from a wide range of ethnic backgrounds. The majority had very little to no prior experiences in teaching elementary science. They were placed in urban elementary classrooms to do field observations and to teach one science lesson. As part of the methods course, they participated in a book club while reading *Ways with Words: Language, Life, and Work in Communities and Classrooms* written by Heath (1983). The book club met approximately once per month for three times over the semester.

Moore (in press) defined the book club as an informal, peer-directed group discussion that met regularly to discuss an ethnographic, multicultural text regarding issues pertinent to science teaching and learning in urban elementary classrooms. The book club incorporated five theoretical constructs for promoting multicultural understandings in science teacher education: the principle of ideology, critical pedagogy, critical reflective inquiry, multicultural education, and issues of diversity. The results highlighted how the book club structure and theoretical foundation fostered critical inquiry and served as a method for effecting ideological change, as pre-service teachers embraced issues of diversity in urban science education. Moore advocates the use of book clubs as a strategy for preparing pre-service elementary teachers for diverse urban classrooms.

In another report of the workings of the book club, Moore (2007a) described how the pre-service elementary teachers revealed their cultural biases, connected and applied their knowledge of diversity, and realized the importance of getting to know their students for teaching science in urban elementary classrooms. Through their participation in the book club, they came to understand how their cultural biases could impede student learning and gained new knowledge of diversity as they challenged their own cultural biases. Moore argues that pre-service teachers need opportunities to reveal, confront, challenge, and change their cultural models and to develop new models for teaching science in urban elementary classrooms.

Using critical and feminist poststructuralist perspectives on language, Moore (2008a) analyzed the pre-service elementary teachers' understanding of linguistic diversity for teaching science in urban elementary classrooms. The study was based on the premise that pre-service teachers should know the culture of power of language, the culture of power of science, how the language of science affects student learning, and how teachers can empower students by explicitly teaching the language of science. The results indicate that the pre-service elementary teachers in the study learned the importance of language to their role as science teachers in urban elementary classrooms. The results also indicate that pre-service teachers need explicit conversations and tasks to connect science and linguistic diversity to science teaching. Moore argues that pre-service teachers need to discuss scientific language and linguistic diversity in terms of power and its implications for science teaching and learning in urban classrooms.

Moore (2008b) further explored intersections of identity, agency, and social justice as perceived by pre-service elementary teachers. The study examined pre-service teachers' conceptions as agents of change and how their perceptions as change agents framed their identities as soon-to-be elementary science teachers and their understanding of teaching science for social justice in urban elementary classrooms. The results indicated that the pre-service teachers had varying goals and perspectives as agents of change. For the majority of them, being an agent of change predominantly took place at the classroom level. Here they felt that they had more agency or control over teaching practices through modifying curriculum and meeting the needs of students. They did not, however, perceive their agency as extending beyond the classroom because they did not see themselves as being in positions of power or authority to effect change as pre-service teachers. Moore argues that science teacher education programs should play an immediate, fundamental, and emancipatory role in developing science teacher identities and a stance toward social justice.

Student Teaching. Several studies have explored the student teaching component of science teacher preparation programs. The results of these studies are consistent with the results of the studies conducted in science methods courses, described above. Student teachers in these studies demonstrate either resistance to change or an unrealistically high self-efficacy of their teaching compared to their actual abilities to teach. Furthermore, even those pre-service science teachers who are committed to educational equity still face a number of challenges related to implementing classroom practices that support student diversity during their student teaching.

Luft, Bragg, and Peters (1999) presented a case study of a pre-service secondary science teacher who was concerned with equitable instruction in her classroom. The study specifically examined her student teaching semester and the challenges she faced as a White teacher working with predominantly Hispanic, Native American, and African American students. The teacher experienced: 1) unfamiliarity with her students and their life experiences, 2) marginalization by her students and colleagues as she tried to create new science lessons for her students, and 3) struggles to make her science instruction more relevant to her students. Over the course of her student teaching experience, some of the difficulties within each of these three areas were resolved, while others persisted. The results reveal the complexity of learning to teach in a school where most students come from cultural backgrounds different from one's own, even when a pre-service teacher is committed to addressing issues of cultural diversity in the classroom.

Luft (1999) interpreted these same results using the idea of cultural border crossing, in which cultural borders existed between: 1) the teacher and her Hispanic students, 2) the teacher's instructional philosophy and that of the other teachers at the school, and 3) the teacher and the school culture. While some of the teacher's efforts at border crossing were successful, others were not. This study suggests that even when pre-service teachers receive training in cultural differences and culturally congruent teaching, they are unlikely to be fully prepared for the range of cultural contexts they will encounter in schools. Luft concludes that teacher educators need to recognize the multiple cultural borders that pre-service teachers will encounter when working with non-mainstream students, and encourage them to examine their beliefs about teaching and learning as a means to acknowledge and understand these borders.

Similarly, Bullock (1997) designed a program to provide pre-service science teachers with opportunities to examine their beliefs and practices regarding gender, ethnicity, and science education during student teaching. She worked with six secondary science student teachers on four topics: 1) equitable representation in curriculum materials, 2) equitable treatment within the classroom, 3) equitable opportunities in the laboratory setting, and 4) equitable evaluation of student performance. While the student teachers initially approved the program, they grew increasingly dismissive of some issues, such as gender and ethnic equity, once they began struggling with the inadequate academic preparation of their students and the scant material resources available in their classrooms. By the end of their student teaching experience, the six participants all recognized that the program provided them with specific tools for developing more equitable classrooms. They realized the value of active learning opportunities for applying educational theories in meaningful ways and expressed the view that activities focusing on equity should begin earlier in the teacher preparation program.

In another study of student teachers' beliefs about diversity, Brand and Glasson (2004) explored the development of belief systems in relation to racial and ethnic identity formation in the early life experiences of pre-service teachers. They questioned how these belief systems influenced pre-service teachers' views about diversity in science classrooms and science teaching pedagogy. The study involved three pre-service science teachers enrolled in a graduate certification program. The three participants were an Asian male from a suburban setting, an African American male from an urban setting, and a White male from rural Appalachia. The three were selected because their racial, ethnic, and cultural backgrounds were distinct and none of them fit the profile of the typical science teacher. As part of two secondary science teaching methods courses, the participants completed two internship placements in rural, suburban, and urban areas. The results of this study indicated that the three participants were reluctant to embrace issues of diversity in their teaching because of negative personal experiences related to race and ethnicity in their own lives. In addition, the notion of cultural border crossing was threatening to them because they felt that accepting a new set of norms or beliefs might imply that something was wrong with their original beliefs. Brand and Glasson conclude that science teacher preparation programs need to challenge and expand teachers' beliefs about racial and ethnic identities throughout the program in order to promote an awareness of the impact of such beliefs on science teaching. Still, in keeping with the findings of many of the studies described in this chapter, they caution that attempts to change teacher beliefs is difficult, time-consuming, and often met with resistance.

In a recent study with implications for how we think about the importance of field experience and measurement of pre-service teachers' beliefs, Settlage, Southerland, Smith, and Ceglie (2009) examined the impact of field placements on pre-service elementary teachers' beliefs about teaching science to non-mainstream students. Data were gathered at three points during the participants' final year in their teacher preparation program in order to chart changes over time. Teaching self-efficacy scores revealed only marginal changes over time, and individual interviews revealed no discernible influence on the teachers' perceptions of science teaching that could be attributed to the student demographics of their field placements. Prior to and throughout their student teaching, pre-service science teachers held extraordinarily high self-efficacy beliefs about their science teaching, which were incongruous with their actual teaching abilities. The results cast doubt on two commonly held views in teacher preparation programs: first, the ability of multicultural field experiences, in and of themselves, to transform pre-service teachers' views about student diversity; and second, the utility of reports of teacher self-efficacy as an indicator of individual or programmatic success. Instead, Settlage and colleagues suggest the value of self-doubt as a factor in motivating pre-service science teachers to seek opportunities for further professional growth.

Similar to the questions raised by Settlage et al., Buck and Cordes (2005) critically examined the value of providing pre-service teachers with experiences in teaching science to at risk youth in a nonformal educational setting. Participants engaged in an out-of-school field placement, explored these experiences in a seminar setting, and engaged in on-line discussions in an attempt to increase the pre-service teachers' confidence and knowledge in regard to teaching science to non-mainstream children. The 20 pre-service teachers, working toward teacher certification in elementary or middle grades, participated in a collaborative project between a school of education and community-based organizations during their final year of the teacher preparation program. The community-based experience allowed pre-service teachers to teach in a situation in which at risk youth were the majority, thus spotlighting their needs in a manner not typically experienced by pre-service teachers. Buck et al. concluded that the effect of the community-based field experience did lead participants to gain confidence about teaching non-mainstream students. They noted, however, a lack of critical and constructive reflection by the pre-service teachers about experiences in the program, and questioned the applicability of such results to actual classroom practice.

In conclusion, while teacher preparation programs often look to student teaching and other field experiences to play a major role in the development of pre-service teachers' beliefs and practices in teaching science to non-mainstream students, the studies outlined here highlight a number of challenges that may call into question just how effective student teaching experience can be in learning to teach science to diverse student groups. There may simply be too many pressing issues that student teachers face for issues of diversity to receive the necessary attention. It is because of challenges such as these that teacher induction programs have gained more popularity in recent years, as described next.

Beginning Years of Teaching. Several studies of beginning teachers in master's degree teacher education programs indicate that the challenges pre-service teachers experience in providing equitable learning opportunities for non-mainstream students continue into their beginning years as classroom teachers.

Bianchini and colleagues (Bianchini & Cavazos, 2007; Bianchini, Cavazos, & Rivas, 2003; Bianchini, Johnston, Oram, & Cavazos, 2003; Bianchini & Solomon, 2003) conducted a series of studies with cohorts of teachers as they advanced from an intensive 5th-year teacher education program into their 1st year of teaching, and then after 2 years of teaching science in secondary schools. The program placed issues of diversity and equity at the core of the teacher education process.

Bianchini, Cavazos, and Rivas (2003) worked with a cohort of 12 science student teachers who took part in a science methods course on the nature of science and equitable educational practices. The study examined student teachers' understandings of topics, such as who scientists are; how science is practiced; how science is situated in social, cultural, and political contexts; and how best to teach science to all students. The results indicated that the student teachers varied widely in their engagement with issues of equity—some made great strides toward aligning their views of science and science teaching with equity goals, whereas others did not. Bianchini and colleagues speculate that they needed to provide additional opportunities for student teachers to engage in explicit discussions about equity concerns and how student teachers were addressing those concerns in their classrooms.

Bianchini and colleagues then expanded their study to include the nature of the science course, a science methods course, and a course on professional issues. Bianchini and Solomon (2003) worked with a cohort of eight beginning secondary science teachers (five European-American, two Asian American, and one Latino). The study examined the teachers' views of science and science teaching as they related to issues of equity and diversity along three dimensions: personal, social, and political. The personal dimension focused on how to use personal experiences to support students' science learning and also how to represent science in ways that are meaningful to all students. The social dimension centered on the question of how to broaden notions of who does science. The political dimension involved science as cultural production. The researchers propose that all three of these dimensions need to be considered in any science teacher education program that aims to be inclusive of all students. The beginning teachers frequently drew from their own personal experiences to support their views of the nature of science and to find ways to represent science to all students, but that they rarely moved beyond the personal dimension to include the social or political dimension. Again, this raises the point that beginning teachers are hard pressed to consider the complex nature of teaching for diversity in the face of all the other challenges of learning to manage a science classroom.

Continuing this line of work, Bianchini, Johnston, Oram, and Cavazos (2003) followed three secondary science teachers (all European-Americans) into their first year of teaching. They explored these beginning teachers' attempts to teach the nature of science and to implement equitable instructional strategies in their classrooms. The results indicated a set of common themes across the beginning teachers' successes and struggles in learning to teach science in equitable ways. The teachers had closely examined the nature of science and issues of equitable and inclusive science instruction in their science teacher preparation program, and were able to translate some of what they had learned into their teaching practices during their first year. There were other aspects, however, that had been examined in the program but were rarely addressed in their teaching, such as the ways in which social values and cultural biases shape scientists' research or the kinds of knowledge and practices that indigenous cultures contribute to science. The beginning teachers heard repeatedly from more experienced colleagues in their schools that they needed to focus on the science content and skills outlined in the state science standards. Furthermore, many of the topics introduced in the teacher preparation program were not clearly addressed in the standards, creating another obstacle even if the beginning teachers were committed to implementing these topics.

Finally, Bianchini and Cavazos (2007) reported on the work with two beginning secondary science teachers in their efforts to teach science in ways that built upon and empowered the ethnic, gender, and academic diversity of their students. The study examined successes and challenges they encountered in learning to teach science for all from the perspectives of: 1) their students, 2) inquiring into their own practice, and 3) participating in professional communities. The study followed these two teachers for 4 years, starting from the 5th-year teacher education program, into the beginning year of teaching, and during 2 additional years. The results indicated that the two teachers adopted a critical stance toward teaching starting from their pre-service year. With the exception of one radical and abrupt change (a shift from seeing science education as value-neutral and acultural to recognition that values and culture play a role in teaching and learning science), other changes in their views were slow and incremental. The teachers perceived themselves as being on a long trajectory toward teaching science to all students. These results suggest that learning to teach science in equitable and diverse ways, even for teachers committed to doing so, takes persistence, practice, and time.

The overall research program by Bianchini and colleagues provides an example of how a teacher education program can be conceptualized, designed, and implemented to address issues of diversity and equity. Bianchini, Cavazos, and Rivas (2003) described how the program continued to be revised and refined on the basis of their ongoing research and development efforts with beginning teachers.

In another approach to working with beginning teachers to support science teaching with non-mainstream students, Tobin and colleagues (Edmin, 2008; Roth, Tobin, Carambo, & Dalland, 2004; Tobin, Roth, & Zimmermann, 2001; Tobin et al., 1999) have proposed co-teaching and co-generative dialogue as a model for teacher preparation and professional development of urban science teachers. They conducted a series of case studies involving student teachers during year-long field experience in a master's degree program in science education. The studies were conducted at an inner-city high school with African American students in a low academic track program of study in Philadelphia.

Co-teaching, or working at the elbow of someone else, allows student teachers to experience appropriate and timely action. The student teacher not only learns by doing but also has opportunities to experience teaching of others as it is done in a co-participatory way. Co-teaching enables the student teacher to experience success and failure while teaching in the same space as another. Co-teachers can be another student teacher, a cooperating teacher, a methods instructor, a college supervisor, or even a student. The important feature is that the knowledge of teaching is shared and adapted by co-teachers. In addition, co-teaching sessions are followed by co-generative dialogue sessions, in which all co-teachers discuss their experiences with the intent to design changes. The shared experiences associated with co-teaching are starting points for conversations about practice, discussions about events and issues associated with practice, and the reflective possibilities for future teaching episodes.

Tobin, Seiler, and Smith (1999) described the co-teaching efforts of a university professor (Tobin), a doctoral student (Seiler), and a student teacher (Smith) during their initial attempts at conceptualizing a model of co-teaching. The researchers described their failures in teaching science in the face of student resistance. For example, they concluded that their efforts to implement inquiry-oriented science were far too open and unstructured for the students. Instead, the students expected to be told what to learn and to reproduce facts on tests. The students did not deal well with the uncertainty and ambiguity of inquiry and the necessity of creating their own structure for undertaking longitudinal investigations. These initial co-teaching experiences provided a rich resource for conversations that led to a professional discourse for teaching science in the inner-city high school.

In a subsequent study, Tobin et al. (2001) described the experiences of a student teacher as she enacted a curriculum that was designed to be culturally relevant to her students, responsive to their interests, acknowledge their minority status with regard to science, and help them meet school district standards in science. In addition, Roth et al. (2004) described how a student teacher and a cooperating teacher co-taught chemistry in ways that addressed student interests and cultural resources. They also explored the underlying value of co-teaching and co-generative dialogue. The presence of a co-teacher increased access to social and material resources, and thereby increased opportunities for actions that otherwise would not have occurred. Co-teaching also permitted co-generative dialogue, which created the context for considering and planning further action.

In conclusion, studies that have examined the beliefs and practices of beginning teachers and supported them through induction programs continue to bump up against the challenge that new teachers are struggling to put many aspects of their practice together at the same time. Despite some positive results in which beginning teachers took actions to create environments conducive to the academic success of non-mainstream students, most efforts in the first few years of teaching are slow and gradual. Other studies have focused on professional development with more experienced teachers who have already established classroom rhythms and practices, as described next.

TEACHER PROFESSIONAL DEVELOPMENT

Professional development with in-service teachers aims to expand and improve the learning opportunities that they provide to their students by enhancing their knowledge of subject matter and enabling them to provide reform-oriented or standards-based teaching practices (Richardson & Placier, 2001; Wilson & Berne, 1999). Some professional development has focused on teachers participating in university graduate degree programs, while others have recruited participants from the broader teaching force. Research on professional development has often focused on the form and structure of professional development activities, such as the total number of contact hours, whether contact hours are concentrated or distributed, and whether consultation or coaching occurs during classroom visits or entirely outside of the classroom (Desimone, Porter, Garet, Yoon, & Birman, 2002; Garet, Porter, Desimone, Birman, & Yoon, 2001). However, more recent research has placed greater emphasis on the substance of professional development activities. Cohen and Hill (2000) have argued that what teachers actually learn in professional development experiences has the greatest impact on their beliefs and practices and, eventually, on student learning outcomes. According to recent literature, the most effective professional development enhances teachers' knowledge of specific subject matter content, their understanding of how children learn that content, and reform-based instructional practices.

Research on professional development indicates that teachers need to engage in reform-oriented practices themselves in order to feel comfortable and confident using those practices with their students. For example, teachers need opportunities to develop their own deep and complex understandings of science concepts, recognize how students' misconceptions cause learning difficulties (Kennedy, 1998; Loucks-Horsley, Hewson, Love, & Stiles, 1998), engage in their own science inquiry (NRC, 2000), and practice sharing and negotiating ideas and constructing collective meanings about science (Lemke, 1990).

Effecting changes in one's knowledge, beliefs, and practices with regard to science instruction is a demanding and arduous process. Teachers who engage in professional development often end up blending a repertoire of reform-oriented practices and traditional practices (Cohen & Hill, 2000; Knapp, 1997). Thus, teachers may implement specific features of reform-oriented practices in isolation, such as encouraging students to pose their own questions or using hands-on activities, but they are less likely to implement systematic changes to multiple practices simultaneously. Because many teachers of science, especially in the elementary and middle grades, have been insufficiently prepared in terms of their own knowledge of science content and content-specific teaching strategies (Kennedy, 1998; Garet et al., 2001; Loucks-Horsley et al., 1998), implementing reform-oriented practices presents challenges for many teachers in science classrooms.

Even within professional development efforts that emphasize academic achievement for all students, attempts to link subject matter content to the specific linguistic and cultural experiences of non-mainstream students have been limited. Professional development programs focusing on subject matter content rarely address the ways in which students from diverse backgrounds engage that content, whereas programs that focus on student diversity seldom consider the subject-specific demands of content learning. This is especially true in science and mathematics, which have traditionally been treated as culture-free subject areas in terms of both epistemology and pedagogy.

Despite the critical need to better understand the qualities of effective professional development for science teachers working with non-mainstream students, the literature in this area remains limited. A small number of studies have examined the professional development of science teachers working with non-mainstream students, often in urban schools or districts. The professional development results with in-service teachers working with non-mainstream students are inconsistent across projects. This inconsistency is partly due to the fact that some projects engage volunteer teachers in intensive and long-term professional development, whereas others engage a wider cross-section of teachers in limited professional development opportunities. Even those teachers who are committed to diversity and equity more generally have difficulty connecting the multiple domains of science, language, culture, and urban education simultaneously.

In an example of working intensely with groups of volunteer teachers, Buxton (2005, 2006) developed a pair of professional development projects aimed at helping in-service teachers reconsider their beliefs and practices about how to make inquiry-based science both accessible and meaningful for their non-mainstream students in low-SES urban school contexts. Although the majority of teachers in both projects were experienced veterans, many of them expressed frustration at their inability to engage students in learning science. One project took place in an elementary school and the other in a high school.

The first project was developed around a model of authentic science inquiry at an academically low-performing inner-city elementary school. Using a framework of contextually authentic science inquiry, Buxton (2006) guided teachers in linking the strengths of a canonical model of science inquiry (grounded in the Western scientific canon) with the strengths of a youth-centered model of authenticity grounded in student-generated inquiry. The goal of the project was to bring together the science content standards to which teachers and students were held accountable with topics that had critical social relevance and might be motivational to low-performing students. Buxton used this framework to examine how 14 elementary teachers from this school, participating as a cohort in a site-based master's degree program, worked with their upper elementary grade students to interpret and enact ideas about authenticity and collaboration. Over a 2½-year period he investigated what structures in the professional development activities were necessary to support contextually authentic science learning. He identified several general principles in the areas of curriculum, instruction, and assessment that frequently led teachers to engage their students in authentic science learning. Curricular principles included a focus on highly localized neighborhood environments and connections to students' families. Instructional principles included learning to ask testable questions and a focus on how doing science together could help foster communal relationships. Assessment principles included increasing students' choice over how to document their learning and supporting the use of multimedia technologies as assessment tools. Despite pointing to positive examples of how authentic science learning resulted from this professional development project, Buxton also painted a rather bleak picture of how the professional development efforts were undermined by high-stakes testing, accountability policies, and administrative mandates. The study highlights challenges to implementing professional development that is responsive to the needs of inner-city teachers and their students within the policy context currently faced in many urban schools.

In the second project, Buxton (2005) worked over a 3-year period with the teachers at an urban science, mathematics, and technology magnet high school to consider how student identities were constructed and how teachers could aid non-mainstream students in developing good student identities that would foster their academic success. One key finding of the study was that teachers and their non-mainstream students defined ideas such as learning, achievement, success, and resistance in very different ways. Buxton worked with the teachers to better understand the discrepancy between teacher and student ideas about being a good student, and the implications of these differences for students' academic success. Professional development efforts then focused on collaboratively inventing ways for teachers and students to come to shared understandings of ideas such as *good student work* and *good student identity*.

In analyzing the professional development project, Buxton, Carlone, and Carlone (2005) borrowed from research in organizational studies to propose the concept of boundary spanners, or "individuals, objects, media, and other experiences that link an organization to its environment" (p. 304), as a theoretical model to guide further professional development activities. They argue that boundary spanners can have both practical and theoretical utility in organizing professional development that better meets the needs of non-mainstream students. Practically, boundary spanners can act as tools for enhancing meaning-making among students, teachers, and parents. Theoretically, boundary spanners can act as guidelines for understanding both the reproductive and the transformative aspects of urban science teaching.

Moore (2007b, 2007c) reported a set of results from her research with three experienced African American (two female and one male) science teachers from two high schools in a small rural county in the Southeast. The school district had predominantly African American students from poverty. The two high schools were described as critically low-performing, according to the state accountability system. Moore provided professional development opportunities with and for the teachers in the form of co-teaching, planning inquiry-based science lessons, and discussing multicultural approaches to teaching for two academic years.

Moore (2007b) examined how the three teachers used their personal knowledge and experiences of the school district and their students to cope with teaching science under stressful conditions associated with economic, social, and institutional challenges. The teachers brought different pedagogical strengths and ways of relating to students, as they focused on helping students overcome negative perceptions, value the importance of an education, build strong relationships with teachers, and connect science to students' lives and communities. To complement and enhance the strengths of the teachers, Moore proposed a model of multicultural science teacher professional development that incorporates multicultural science education, feminist pedagogy, and culturally responsive and culturally relevant pedagogies.

Moore (2008c) also examined how positional identity or positionality (defined in terms of race, ethnicity, economic status, gender, religion, and age) created and shaped the lives and professional development of the three teachers. The context of the study, described above, added to the significance of how positionality influenced where the teachers worked and how they approached professional development. Thus, the focus of the study was to examine how multiple personal and social variables affected teaching, learning, and professional development in science education. The results indicated that although the three teachers came from similar social backgrounds and were members of the same racial/ethnic group, their positionality was manifested in different ways: different meanings of their life experiences, different orientations to professional development, and different career goals in science education (e.g., attending conferences, participating in workshops, and aspiring for advanced degrees and national science teacher certification). The results highlight the value of incorporating positionality as a way of understanding and meeting personal and professional goals when conceptualizing professional development for teachers of non-mainstream students.

Moore (2007c) further examined how language functioned as a gatekeeper, keeping the teachers out of "mainstream" discourses of science that also kept them from teaching and learning science in their classrooms and in their professional development. The study indicated four findings. First, the teachers experienced the gatekeeping function of language in their students' learning of science, in achieving professional honors in teaching science (e.g., national science teacher certification), and in teaching science to ELL students. Second, the various uses of language revealed complex dynamics related to the culture of power of language and the culture of power of science along race/ethnicity, gender, and class dimensions of teachers. Third, the teachers did not see fully that language had distinct purposes and uses in science teaching, learning, and professional development. This further maintained the gatekeeping function of language and perhaps led to misunderstandings of language-power-knowledge relationships. Finally, there are strong implications for looking closely at language(s) for student learning and teacher professional development in science classrooms. Together, Moore's studies highlight the importance of considering individual teacher differences that lie beneath shared personal and school demographic features when designing and implementing professional development projects.

Lee and colleagues implemented a large-scale instructional intervention aimed at promoting achievement and equity in science, particularly focusing on science inquiry and English language and literacy development for culturally and linguistically diverse elementary students. Grounded in the framework of instructional congruence and the teacher-explicit to student-exploratory continuum, the ongoing professional development intervention emphasized the integration of three domains: 1) inquiry-based science instruction, 2) English language and literacy, and 3) students' home language and culture. Together, these aspects were designed to support teacher and student growth across varied classroom contexts. The intervention involved all third-, fourth-, and fifth-grade teachers (over 75) and their students from six elementary schools serving students from a wide range of linguistic and cultural backgrounds. A series of studies examined both the professional development process and the impact of the intervention on participating teachers.

Lee, Hart, Cuevas, and Enders (2004) focused specifically on professional development efforts in the domain of science instruction. They examined 1) teachers' initial beliefs and practices related to inquiry-based science and 2) the impact of the professional development intervention on teachers' beliefs and practices over the course of the school year. As a school-wide initiative, the study involved all third- and fourth-grade teachers (53 total) at six elementary schools in a large urban school district. The intervention consisted of two instructional units, including all needed supplies and materials, for each grade level and four full-day teacher workshops over the course of the school year. In the science instruction domain, the professional development emphasized ways to promote scientific understanding, inquiry, and discourse with elementary students from non-mainstream backgrounds. Teachers' beliefs were examined using a questionnaire and focus group interviews at the beginning and end of the school year, while participating teachers' instructional practices were examined during one classroom observation in the fall and one in the spring. At the end of the school year, teachers reported significantly enhanced knowledge of science content and stronger beliefs about the importance of science instruction. Their classroom practices, however, did not show statistically significant changes from the fall to the spring.

Lee, Luyxk, Buxton, and Shaver (2007) also examined the impact of their professional development intervention on teachers' beliefs and practices related to incorporating students' home language and culture into science instruction. The study involved 43 third- and fourth-grade teachers as they participated in the professional development for 2 consecutive years. The results indicate that as teachers began their participation in the intervention, they rarely incorporated students' home language or culture into science instruction. During the 2-year period of the intervention, teachers did not show significant change related to using students' home language and culture. The researchers discuss a range of possible explanations for the limited effectiveness of the professional development and make suggestions for improving future professional development efforts related to students' home language and culture.

The results of the ongoing professional development efforts by Lee and colleagues indicate an overall receptiveness of teachers to the intervention, as well as both strengths and weaknesses with regard to the professional development goals. For example, like many of the other studies outlined in this chapter, state science standards served both as a guide for which science was taught and as an obstacle to reform-oriented teaching practices. Given that the research included all third-, fourth-, and fifth-grade teachers within the six participating schools, rather than a self-selected group of volunteer teachers, participants' beliefs and practices regarding teaching science for diversity were varied and might be more representative of teachers in general. Thus, the results have implications for the scaling-up of this or related interventions focused on teaching science to non-mainstream students in urban schools.

Also investigating teacher professional development, Kahle and colleagues conducted a series of studies to examine the impact of standards-based teaching practices (i.e., extended inquiry, problem solving, open-ended questioning, and cooperative learning) on the science achievement and attitudes/perceptions of urban African American middle school students (Boone & Kahle, 1998; Damnjonovic, 1998; Kahle, Meece, & Scantlebury, 2000). These studies were part of the NSF-supported Ohio statewide systemic initiative (SSI) known as Discovery. A centerpiece of this reform initiative was sustained professional development for middle school science and mathematics teachers. The Ohio SSI's professional development programs were very intensive, consisting of 6-week summer institutes in physics, life science, and mathematics, and six full-day seminars during the academic year.

To examine the impact of the professional development programs, Kahle, Meece, and Scantlebury (2000) involved a random sample of 126 schools drawn from all schools in Ohio. These selected schools enrolled students from grades five through nine and had at least one teacher who participated in the Ohio SSI's professional development programs. Then, a subsample of eight middle schools was identified on the basis of at least 30% minority student enrollment. At each of these eight schools, one teacher was randomly selected from among those who had completed the SSI's professional development program. Each SSI teacher was then matched with a non-SSI teacher in the same school who taught similar classes. The non-SSI teachers volunteered to administer student achievement (based on NAEP public release items) and attitude measures to their seventh- and eighth-grade students and to complete the same teacher questionnaire that the SSI teachers completed. A total of 18 teachers (8 SSI and 10 non-SSI) reported data for their students. Fifteen were White (6 SSI teachers and 9 non-SSI teachers), and three were African American (2 SSI teachers and 1 non-SSI teacher).

The student sample used in the study consisted of all of the African American seventh- and eighth-grade students enrolled in the SSI and non-SSI teachers' classes. Students' science achievement was measured using a total of 29 NAEP public release items, of which 20 involved solving problems or conducting science inquiry. In addition, students responded to questionnaires focusing on: 1) their attitudes toward science, 2) their teachers' use of standards-based science teaching practices, 3) their parents' involvement in science homework and projects, and 4) their peers' participation in science activities. Results indicate that students of SSI teachers rated their teachers as using standards-based teaching practices more frequently than did students in non-SSI teachers' classes. In addition, students of SSI teachers scored higher on the science achievement test and had more positive attitudes toward science. Notably, these improvements were most pronounced with African American boys. The results suggest that professional development designed to enhance teachers' content knowledge and use of standards-based teaching practices can not only improve science achievement overall, but can also reduce inequities in achievement patterns for urban African American students.

In another study of the Ohio SSI, Damnjanovic (1998) analyzed the impact of the professional development programs on science achievement by race and gender. A total of 610 seventh- and eighth-grade students enrolled in the SSI teachers' classes participated in the study, including 190 African American females, 131 White females, 168 African American males, and 121 White males. Three sets of results were reported. First, on the NAEP public release items, females scored significantly higher on the science achievement test than males, and White students of both sexes scored higher than African American students, but there was no interaction of race and gender. Second, for the student sample as a whole, reform-oriented classroom teaching, students' positive attitudes toward science, and students' participation in hands-on activities were significant predictors of high science achievement. In contrast, low peer interest and involvement in science was a significant predictor of low science achievement. Finally, predictors for science achievement varied for each race and gender group.

In another related study, Boone and Kahle (1998) analyzed the impact of the Ohio SSI's professional development programs on students' perceptions of science, disaggregating the data by race and gender. In total, over 900 middle school science students completed the questionnaires in 1995 and 1996. Responses of African American and White students of both genders indicate that students actively participated in those science classes taught by SSI teachers. With the exception of White boys, students were more involved in active learning in SSI classes compared to non-SSI classes, implying the SSI-trained teachers were reducing the science participation gap between mainstream and non-mainstream students.

Based on these results, Kahle and colleagues (Boone & Kahle, 1998; Damnjonovic, 1998; Kahle et al., 2000) offered policy recommendations to support the use of inquiry-based science instruction with urban African American students.

They advocated for consistent policies at the state and district levels with regard to length of science classes, availability of appropriate materials and supplies, and use of performance-based and other types of authentic assessments. They also offered policy suggestions to facilitate teachers' participation in sustained professional development efforts. Sustained professional development is seen as a critical feature of success in the Ohio SSI project, but one that requires clear policies to address support and incentives for teacher participants, appropriate mechanisms for evaluating teachers who use standards-based instruction, and possible negative effects of traditional norm-referenced tests on inquiry teaching.

TEACHER PREPARATION AND PROFESSIONAL DEVELOPMENT WITH ENGLISH LANGUAGE LEARNERS

Thus far, the discussion in this chapter has focused on working with teachers across the continuum of the teaching profession to support the science learning of non-mainstream students. This final section focuses specifically on the need to help teachers prepare to teach science to ELL students. Teachers of ELL students need to promote students' English language and literacy development as well as their academic achievement in content areas. This requires teachers to use subject-specific instructional strategies that go beyond the general language strategies that many teachers learn through English to Speakers of Other Languages (ESOL) or bilingual education training. Unfortunately, a majority of teachers working with ELL students believe they are not adequately prepared to meet their students' learning needs, particularly in academically demanding subjects such as science, mathematics, and reading (NCES, 1999). Most teachers also assume that ELL students must acquire English before learning subject matter, even though this approach almost always leads the students to fall further behind their English-speaking peers (August & Hakuta, 1997; August & Shanahan, 2006; Garcia, 1999). Because all students are now being asked to make adequate yearly progress in content area learning under the NCLB guidelines, it is no longer possible to require ELL students to miss content area instruction while they develop English language proficiency.

Professional development to promote science as well as English language and literacy development with ELL students is desperately needed. Such professional development should involve teacher knowledge and practices in multiple areas. First, in addition to ensuring that ELL students acquire the language skills necessary for social communication, teachers need to promote ELL students' development of general and content-specific academic language functions, such as describing, explaining, comparing, and concluding (Wong-Fillmore & Snow, 2002). Second, teachers must be able to formulate developmentally appropriate expectations about language comprehension and production over the course of students' learning of English. A high school ELL student who is newly arrived and has limited English proficiency needs a different approach to both English and content area learning when compared to a first-grade ELL student. Finally, teachers need to be able to apply this knowledge to the teaching of general and content-specific academic language. The combination of these three knowledge sources should result in teaching practices that 1) engage students of all levels of English proficiency in academic language learning, 2) engage students in learning activities that have multiple points of entry for students of differing levels of English proficiency, 3) provide multiple modes for students to display learning, and 4) ensure that students participate in a manner that allows for maximum language development at their own level.

As a practical example of this philosophy, Buck, Mast, Ehlers, and Franklin (2005) explored the process a beginning teacher went through to establish a classroom conducive to the academic, linguistic, and social needs of middle-grade ELL students in the science classroom. An action research team consisting of a science educator, an ELL educator, a 1st-year science teacher, and a graduate assistant planned and sometimes taught together. The analysis of 5 months of classroom data revealed that: 1) strategies that a beginning teacher must use for teaching middle-grade ELL students in a mainstream classroom involved complex considerations that were not part of typical teacher preparation programs; 2) learning naturally increased for all students over time, but there were differences in learning between ELL and non-ELL students; and 3) student and peer feedback proved to be effective means of enhancing the growth of a beginning teacher seeking to increase her skills in teaching ELL students.

A limited number of studies have addressed professional development efforts to help in-service teachers expand their beliefs and practices in integrating science with English language development for ELL students. These studies range from large-scale professional development at the school or district level to intensive teacher research with small numbers of participants. A common feature, however, is that these studies all acknowledge that science and literacy skills must be developed in tandem. Without gaining literacy skills, it is impossible for students to gain grade-appropriate science content knowledge. At the same time, rigorous content learning in science and other subjects provides authentic context for gaining academic language.

While the literature in bilingual education supports content area instruction in ELL students' home language, Stoddart, Pinal, Latzke, and Canaday (2002) argue that it is often not possible to teach academic subjects to ELL students in their native language while they are acquiring proficiency in English. A chronic shortage of bilingual teachers, particularly teachers qualified to teach academic content such as science, means that few ELL students receive content area instruction in their home language. In addition, English-only legislation in an increasing number of states severely limits the teaching of academic subjects in languages other than English. Also, students may not have the academic language in their native language to engage in grade-appropriate academic discourse. As an alternative, Stoddart and colleagues attempted to integrate the teaching of academic subjects, such as science, with second language (i.e., English) development. The idea was that inquiry-based science would provide a particularly powerful instructional context for the integration of science content and second language development with ELL students.

As part of an NSF-supported local systemic initiative, Stoddart et al. (2002) studied 24 elementary school teachers of predominantly Latino ELL students. The analysis of teachers' work during a 5-week summer professional development program indicated changes in teachers' understanding of science and language integration. Prior to their participation, the majority of participating teachers viewed themselves as well prepared to teach either science or language, but not both. After their participation in the professional development program, the majority of teachers believed they had improved in the domain in which they had initially felt less prepared. This change typically involved a shift from a restricted view of the connections between science instruction and second language instruction to a more complex reasoning about the different ways that the two areas could be integrated.

In a similar study, Amaral et al. (2002) enacted professional development that promoted science and literacy with predominantly Spanish-speaking elementary students as part of a districtwide local systemic reform initiative. The inquiry-based science program started with 14 volunteer teachers from two school sites. As the program progressed, more teachers and sites were added to the program until it gradually became available to all teachers at all elementary schools in the school district. Over 4 years, teachers were provided with at least 100 hours of professional development designed to deepen their understanding of science, address pedagogical issues, and prepare them to teach science at their grade level. Teachers also received on-site professional support from resource teachers, and complete materials and supplies to carry out hands-on inquiry-based science teaching.

The researchers examined the impact of the professional development over a 4-year period. The five areas of emphasis in the project included high-quality curriculum, sustained professional development and support for teachers and school administrators, materials support, community and district administrative support, and program assessment and evaluation. Although teachers and students had the freedom to use Spanish for facilitation of instruction, most instruction was done in English, even in the "bilingual" classes. All students were assessed in science using the Stanford Achievement Test (SAT), the statewide science assessment. Assessments in writing were conducted using the district writing proficiency test. All assessment instruments were in English.

This study involved only those students who had been enrolled in the school district for the previous 4 years, during which time the reform initiative gradually expanded to cover the entire district. Student achievement in science and writing for 615 students in fourth grade and 635 students in sixth grade was compared 1) across the five levels of students' duration in the program (0–4 years), and 2) among five levels of English proficiency. The results indicated that both science and writing achievement increased significantly for fourth- and sixth-grade students, in proportion to the number of years they participated in the program. English proficient students, however, performed significantly better than limited English proficient students in both science and writing. The study suggests that districtwide implementation of reforms involving science curriculum, professional development, and classroom instruction can have positive effects for ELL students on both science learning and writing skills simultaneously. This study of professional development by Amaral et al. (2002) is particularly noteworthy because it is one of only a few studies that examined the impact of a districtwide reform initiative on student achievement. However, the study also suggests that districtwide implementation of comprehensive reform initiatives presents challenges in terms of research design and interpretation of the results.

As part of the ongoing research by Lee and her colleagues, Lee (2004) examined patterns of change in elementary teachers' beliefs and practices as they learned to teach English language and literacy as part of science instruction throughout their 3-year professional development experience. Working with six bilingual Hispanic teachers of fourth-grade Hispanic students at two elementary schools, Lee described changes in teachers' beliefs and practices regarding the use of literacy as part of science instruction. Although teachers initially spoke in very broad and general terms about integration of science and literacy, they gradually came to focus on specific aspects of English language and literacy in the context of science instruction. Teachers began to adapt their literacy instruction and provide linguistic scaffolding to meet students' learning needs. They also helped students to gain the conventions of standard oral and written English, including syntax, spelling, and punctuation, in both social and academic contexts. In addition, teachers learned to use multiple representational formats in oral and written communication to promote both literacy and science learning. Overall, the professional development experience helped teachers see science instruction as a meaningful context for English language and literacy development, and language processes as the medium for understanding science.

As an expansion of the Lee (2004) study, Hart and Lee (2003) provided similar, but less intensive, professional development opportunities to all third- and fourth-grade teachers (53 total) from six elementary schools serving students from a range of ethnic, linguistic, and SES backgrounds and varying levels of English proficiency. This study was focused specifically on assisting teachers in integrating English language and literacy development as part of science instruction with ELL students. Hart and Lee examined teachers' initial beliefs and practices, and the extent of change in teachers' beliefs and practices, following the first year of the professional development. They focused on how teachers learned to incorporate reading and writing into science instruction, to integrate appropriate (English) grammar into science instruction, and to provide linguistic scaffolding to enhance science meaning. Results indicated positive change in teachers' beliefs and practices, as teachers came to place greater emphasis on the importance of reading and writing in science instruction, to express a more integrated conceptualization of literacy in science, and to provide more effective linguistic scaffolding to enhance scientific understanding.

In their current Promoting Science among English Language Learners (P-SELL) project, Lee and colleagues involve teachers from grades 3 through 5 and their students at 15 elementary schools in a large urban school district. All of the schools enrolled high proportions of ELL students and students from low-SES backgrounds, and traditionally performed poorly according to the state's accountability plan. Based on the challenges from the previous project, the researchers conceptualized the professional development for the subsequent P-SELL project as responses to a series of competing tensions in three categories: 1) balancing science content and inquiry; 2) supporting content areas of English language and literacy and mathematics; and 3) recognizing contextual features common to urban settings, and high-stakes testing and accountability (Buxton, Lee, & Santau, 2008).

Lee, Lewis, Adamson, Maerten-Rivera, and Secada (2008) examined urban elementary teachers' knowledge and practices in teaching science while supporting English language development of ELL students. The study involved 38 third-grade teachers who participated in the 1st-year implementation of the professional development. The study examined four areas—teacher knowledge of science content, teaching science for understanding, teaching science for inquiry, and teacher support for English language development—using a questionnaire, classroom observations, and postobservation interviews. Results indicate that teachers' knowledge and practices were generally aligned with the goals supported by the intervention. However, only a small fraction of the teachers were able to move beyond the explicit instruction that served as the starting point of the professional development model to exhibit stronger reform-oriented practices in science instruction (NRC, 1996, 2000) or English language and literacy development in content area instruction (TESOL, 1997, 2006). The results, consistent with much of the other literature in this chapter, suggest that when teachers attempt new practices to address complex sets of issues, their practices may initially fall short of the goal of reform-oriented practices.

At the end of the 1st year of the 5-year intervention, however, the same third-grade teachers believed that the intervention had effectively promoted students' science learning along with English language development (Lee, LeRoy, Thornton, Adamson, Maerten-Rivera, & Lewis, 2008). Teachers highlighted many strengths as well as areas needing improvement in the intervention, and teachers' perspectives were subsequently incorporated into ongoing professional development efforts.

Because the P-SELL research is still in progress, the results reported here are preliminary. At the completion of the project, the impact of the professional development intervention on teacher change and student achievement will be examined using a longitudinal research design.

SUMMARY

The last decade has seen the development of a small but growing body of research on science teacher education for non-mainstream students. The literature to date points to several notable patterns. First, the studies on pre-service science teacher preparation were nearly all small-scale studies conducted by researchers who were either instructors for science methods courses or supervisors for student teaching. In other words, the researchers conducted research on their own practices and students. In most cases, the pre-service science teachers were nearly all from mainstream backgrounds and were considering the topic of student diversity for the first time. These studies examined pre-service teachers' beliefs and practices as they interacted with course instructors and peers in a university setting or with students in a classroom setting.

Second, research on in-service teacher professional development included both small-scale and large-scale studies involving teachers across multiple schools and districts. These studies examined a wider range of features of teachers' knowledge and practices and were more likely to include longitudinal components of professional development. Unlike the results with pre-service teachers, the results with in-service teachers are inconsistent and variable. This is partly due to the range of scale of projects (e.g., a few graduate students to statewide initiatives), variability of participants (e.g., volunteers or nonvolunteers), and relative areas of emphasis in professional development activities (e.g., focus on science, culture, English literacy, urban education).

Finally, the small number of studies dealing specifically with teacher education for ELL students focused primarily on in-service teacher professional development interventions. These studies included both small-scale research with individual participants and large-scale research on school- or districtwide initiatives. The studies were generally conducted in the context of ESOL instruction to promote ELL students' acquisition of English as part of science instruction, but not to build students' home language for science learning.

Across the three areas of the research on pre-service teacher preparation and in-service professional development with diverse student groups, the results indicate several consistent patterns in teachers' beliefs and practices after their participation in teacher education programs or activities: 1) teachers who were already committed to embracing student diversity in science education became more committed and better prepared as a result of professional development op-portunities, 2) teachers who had not considered student diversity as being related to science education came to recognize and accept issues of diversity as important in science education; 3) teachers who were skeptical of the role that language and culture played in science education remained unconvinced of the importance of considering student diversity, and 4) teachers who actively resisted the need to consider student diversity in general failed to embrace the need to consider diver-sity issues in science education in particular. Even those teachers who came from racial or ethnic minority backgrounds (e.g., Brand & Glasson, 2004) and those who were committed to educational equity (e.g., Buxton, 2006; Luft, 1999; Luft, Bragg, & Peters, 1999) still faced significant challenges related to student diversity in their science teaching. Even when changes in teachers' beliefs and practices oc-curred, such changes were demanding and slow.

A few studies involved all teachers in a given grade or from entire schools, rather than volunteer teachers (Amaral et al., 2002; the studies by Lee and col-leagues). Research on schoolwide professional development initiatives reveals both advantages and limitations of such programs (Gamoran, Anderson, Quiroz, Secada, Williams, & Ashmann, 2003; Garet et al., 2001). On the one hand, col-lective participation of all teachers from the same school or grade level in pro-fessional development activities allows teachers to develop common goals, share instructional materials and assessment tools, and exchange ideas and experiences arising from a common context. Also, findings from these studies may be more representative of how a professional development intervention would be received by a random selection of typical teachers. On the other hand, unlike programs comprised of volunteer teachers seeking opportunities for professional growth, programs that are implemented schoolwide inevitably include teachers who are not interested in participation. In addition, the intensity of professional develop-ment activities may have to be reduced due to limits on the number of days teach-ers may be out of their classrooms, the difficulty of finding sufficient numbers of substitute teachers, the pressure to prepare students for high-stakes assessment, and other related constraints. Despite these hurdles, schoolwide professional de-velopment can provide valuable insights for large-scale implementation.

ACTIVITIES FOR CHAPTER 7

1. Think about your own teacher preparation experience. Write some notes in response to the following questions. Then get in a group of 3 or 4 and compare your experiences.

   A. Describe your teacher preparation program. Was it a traditional undergrad-uate program? A graduate certification program? A fast-track program?

    B. What do you feel were the overall strengths and weaknesses of your teacher preparation program? Explain.

    C. What did your program do to prepare you to teach science? What do you think was effective and what was not?

    D. What did your program do to prepare you to teach non-mainstream students? What do you think was effective and what was not?

    E. What did your program do to prepare you to teach ELL students? What do you think was effective and what was not?

2. Think about your experience as a 1st-year teacher. Write some notes in response to the following questions. Then get in a group of 3 or 4 and compare your experiences.

    A. Describe your school, classroom, and students during your 1st year. How do you think these were assigned to you?

    B. In what ways did you feel well prepared during your 1st year? In what ways did you feel underprepared?

    C. Who had the greatest influence over what you did when you faced challenges during your 1st year?

    D. What were some of the challenges that you remember from your 1st year?

    E. What resources from your teacher preparation program did you make use of during your 1st year teaching?

    F. What professional development from your school, district, and so forth do you remember from your 1st year teaching? What do you remember about it?

3. Suppose you were a district professional development consultant who was being hired to help teachers in your district improve their science instruction for non-mainstream students. Work with a partner to outline a professional development program that you would want to implement. Think about the following guiding questions.

    A. How would you balance the need to focus on science and the need to focus on culture, language, or other diversity issues?

    B. What specific science-related issues do you think would be most important for teachers to work on? Why?

    C. What specific culture- and/or language-related issues do you think would be most important for teachers to work on? Why?

    D. What would you do to work with teachers who seem uncertain about or resistant to the idea that they should pay special attention to the needs of non-mainstream students in their teaching?

    E. Describe one activity you would have teachers do in a workshop setting to help them think about teaching science to non-mainstream students.

    F. Describe one activity you would have teachers do to help them think about teaching science to non-mainstream students in their classrooms.

CHAPTER 8

Educational Policies and Student Diversity

Classroom practices and teacher decision making occur in the context of school policies and institutional structures, which are shaped by policies mandated by the school district, the state, and the nation. Policies are interpreted and modified by individuals at every level of their implementation, to the extent that they are sometimes implemented in ways that are directly contrary to their presumed goals or opposite to their original intent. While the literature on the impacts of educational policies on classroom practices has expanded greatly following the NCLB legislation, the literature focusing on science teaching for non-mainstream students remains scarce. Of this limited literature, some studies focus on school organization, while others describe how district, state, and federal policies influence classroom practices and student learning.

SCHOOL ORGANIZATION

Studies of school organization that relate to science education for diverse student populations have addressed such issues as school restructuring, school leadership, and resources to promote change in classroom practices and student learning. In general, these factors are likely to have a greater impact on the learning opportunities of non-mainstream students than mainstream students. This is because mainstream students are more likely to have the benefits of other supports for their science learning, such as better-equipped schools, more resources at home, and highly educated parents. In contrast, the academic success of non-mainstream students depends more heavily on the quality of their school environment, and yet it is non-mainstream students who are less likely to have access to high-quality learning environments. Studies of school organization focusing on diverse student populations have largely been carried out in urban contexts where inequitable resources are a central concern.

School Restructuring. School restructuring efforts have the potential to narrow SES- and ethnicity-based achievement gaps. Valerie Lee and colleagues (Lee & Smith, 1993, 1995; Lee, Smith, Croninger, & Robert, 1997) conducted a series of studies to examine how the structure of high schools affects both overall student learning and equitable distribution of learning by SES in mathematics and science education.

V. Lee and Smith (1995) examined how practices that were advocated by the school restructuring movement influenced the learning and academic engagement of high school students. Using a national sample of schools, the researchers asked principals to report on the use of 30 specific practices in their schools. Twelve of these practices were classified as being consistent with the school restructuring movement, and the other 18 practices were classified as being representative of traditional practices not aligned with the school restructuring movement. The results indicated that student achievement was higher in schools that reported regularly using at least three of the 12 reform-oriented practices than those schools that reported using two or less. In those schools that used more of the reform-oriented practices, achievement and engagement were significantly higher (i.e., schools were more effective) and differences in achievement and engagement among students from different SES backgrounds were reduced (i.e., schools were more equitable). These results suggest that schools that enacted reform-oriented practices produced higher achievement and created more equitable learning environments.

In a related study, V. Lee, Smith, and Croninger (1997) examined the link between broader school organizational practices and student learning in mathematics and science. The study examined differences in the social and academic organization of high schools and whether those differences might help to explain the higher student achievement and engagement found in the earlier study (Lee & Smith, 1995). The results indicated that academic achievement was influenced by practices consistent with the restructuring movement (replicating the results in Lee & Smith, 1995). However, academic achievement was even more strongly influenced by broader organizational attributes, such as the creation of smaller organizational units within larger schools. This *schools within schools* model created learning environments that resembled communities more than bureaucracies, and promoted teacher professional communities that focused on the quality of instruction. Schools within schools tended to have a strong academic focus, and all students were more likely to take a highly academic curriculum with limited tracking options.

Together, these studies by V. Lee and colleagues indicated that when schools both maintained high expectations for student achievement and provided students with strong and supportive learning environments, student achievement in mathematics and science increased and social class-based achievement gaps narrowed. In addition, these schools formed strong professional communities that focused on the quality of their curriculum and instruction.

School Leadership and Resource Use. School reform and restructuring can take root and persist through difficult periods when there is strong and committed leadership. School leaders must sometimes make decisions that will initially be unpopular with teachers, parents, or higher administrators. Many challenging decisions have to do with the allocation and use of limited resources. In the urban schools inhabited by the majority of non-mainstream students, resources are usually more limited than in suburban schools, making these decisions even more challenging.

Knapp and Plecki (2001) provide a conceptual framework for understanding what is involved in renewing urban science teaching. Not surprising, a central feature of this framework involves resource allocation. At the classroom level, student learning in any given subject is supported by teachers and students who make choices to invest the available resources, including instructional time, intellectual resources, and social resources. To improve science education, there must be a proper balance in the allocation of materials, human capital, and social capital. At the school level, a school's capacity for improving science education (or any content area) includes allocation of material resources (such as time for teacher professional development), intellectual resources (such as availability of subject area specialists), and social resources (such as the building of trust and collaboration between administrators and teachers). Knapp and Plecki basically interpret school reform using an economic model. Attempts to improve teaching involve strategically investing resources while establishing conditions that favor a return on this investment.

Several studies of schools and districts have applied similar models to examine how schools make decisions about the allocation of materials, human capital, and social capital to promote change in science education. Spillane, Diamond, Walker, Halverson, and Jita (2001) examined how leaders (including administrators and lead teachers) at one urban elementary school successfully brought together resources to enhance science instruction. Similar to Knapp and Plecki (2001), they found that promoting change in science education involved the combination of 1) the allocation of material resources (i.e., money and other material assets, 2) the development and use of human capital of teachers and school leaders (i.e., the individual knowledge, skills, and expertise that comprise the resources available in an organization), and 3) the development and use of social capital (i.e., the relations among individuals in a group or organization, and such norms as trust, collaboration, and a sense of obligation). Each of these factors had to be managed simultaneously and with an eye toward accountability measures that caused other subjects (i.e., reading, writing, and mathematics) to command the bulk of the school resources.

To enact this model, Spillane and colleagues emphasized the importance of distributed leadership, in which different formal and informal leaders brought different knowledge and skills needed to support instructional change. This distributed leadership looked very different from individual leadership typified by the school principal making all key school-level decisions unilaterally. Furthermore, they argued that individuals who trust one another are more likely to pool their knowledge and skills to promote change. Thus, materials, human capital, and so-cial capital all play critical roles in school reform efforts.

In a study focused on collaborative leadership, Gamoran and associates (2003) examined how teachers from elementary through high schools in six school districts across the nation taught mathematics and science with non-mainstream students. The research involved six case studies of schools that had participated in design collaboratives, in which teams of researchers collaborated with teachers and administrators to design classroom environments in order to support student learning with understanding. The six schools varied in terms of community de-mographics, reform context, school organization, number of participating teach-ers, and the nature of the relationships formed with the research teams. Three of the schools were in urban settings and had large numbers of non-mainstream students. The other three were suburban schools with predominantly mainstream students. In addition, the research topics among the six schools varied in terms of subject (mathematics or science) and grade level. The researchers used obser-vations, interviews, and questionnaires with teachers and administrators over a 5-year period.

Teachers at the three urban schools had varying conceptions of student diver-sity and equity. They differed widely in their thinking about topics such as ability grouping (tracking) of students; differences in learning styles; relevance of factors such as race, ethnicity, culture, language, and SES; differentiated curriculum; and structural inequalities influencing student learning. Teachers' conceptions of di-versity and equity were also connected to the availability of human, social, and ma-terial resources. School-level efforts to increase the availability and access to such resources seemed to positively support change among teachers, and particularly made a difference with teachers who initially expressed a resistance to change. The challenges related to the strategic use of resources were, however, greater in urban schools. Because resources and funding were scarcer in the three urban schools, there was more competition for human, social, and material resources that were also needed to support other subjects in addition to mathematics and science. Like Spillane et al. (2001), Gamoran and his colleagues (2003) concluded that distrib-uted leadership among school administrators, teachers, and staff was essential to supporting and sustaining a professional school community and bringing about change in school policies and practices.

In another study of school leadership and resource use, Lee et al. (2009) ex-amined urban elementary school teachers' perceptions of their science content knowledge, science teaching practices, and support for language development of ELL students. At the same time, they explored teachers' perceptions of organiza-tional supports and barriers associated with teaching science to non-mainstream students. The study involved 221 third- through fifth-grade teachers from 15 urban elementary schools in a large school district. The teachers reported that they gen-erally felt knowledgeable about science topics at their grade level. They reported that they taught science with the goal of promoting students' use of inquiry in most science lessons, while also using traditional/conventional approaches in some lessons. Furthermore, the teachers generally agreed that their principals supported science instruction and that teachers at their schools collaborated in their teaching of science. In contrast to the high ratings they generally gave themselves on their science teaching practices, the teachers reported infrequently using ESOL strategies or home language resources with their ELL students to promote English language development. In addition, the teachers claimed that they rarely discussed issues of student diversity, such as inclusion of girls, ESE students, ELL students, or culturally diverse students, in their conversations about teaching science with other teachers at their schools. Lee and colleagues (2009) noted that the teachers' lack of attention to student diversity was a particular concern, considering that the majority of both the teachers themselves and their students were from non-mainstream backgrounds.

In terms of school leadership and resources, the teachers in this study generally felt supported by their school administrators and other teachers regarding teaching science. However, they reported what they felt to be a number of moderate barriers to their teaching of science. These barriers included school-level constraints (e.g., shortage of science supplies, large class size, lack of time to teach science, pull-out programs during science); the emphasis on statewide assessments in reading, writing, and mathematics, accompanied by students' poor academic skills in these subjects; and a perceived lack of support from parents, family, and community. The last of these perceived barriers was especially surprising, considering that many of the teachers in this study came from backgrounds and communities similar to those of many of their students. These results are consistent, however, with the rest of the literature on elementary science instruction in urban schools, in that they indicate a lack of science instructional materials and supplies (Knapp & Plecki, 2001; Spillane et al., 2001), limited science instructional time due to the urgency of developing basic literacy and numeracy in the context of high-stakes assessment and accountability policies (Settlage & Meadows, 2002; Shaver, Cuevas, Lee, & Avalos, 2007), and teachers' tendency to ascribe problems associated with non-mainstream students' learning to the students' lives outside of school involving parents, family, and community (Bryan & Atwater, 2002).

EDUCATIONAL POLICIES

Due largely to the demographics of urban, suburban, and rural schools in the United States, the limited literature on policies addressing student diversity in science education has focused exclusively on urban contexts. Ensuring equitable science learning experiences for students in urban schools is particularly urgent, considering that urban school districts educate 43% of all K–12 students, 68% of all students living in poverty, 71% of all ELL students, and 65% of all ethnic minority students (National Clearinghouse for English Language Acquisition, 2007). Thus, policy studies addressing student diversity have examined three main issues in urban contexts: 1) systemic reform, 2) scaling-up of educational innovations, and 3) accountability. Although these educational policies influence all districts and all schools, their consequences are especially critical in urban schools because of the sheer number of students attending urban schools, the array and scope of the obstacles facing urban schools, and the institutional precariousness under which urban schools operate.

Systemic Reform. A set of studies has examined systemic reform to improve science education in urban schools. Systemic reform generally means the simultaneous restructuring of various components of an education system in interactive and coherent ways to improve the quality of the curriculum and instruction delivered to students (Smith & O'Day, 1991). One concern of many systemic reforms has been the impact on educational equity, for example, how a system of reforms deals with linguistic, cultural, and socioeconomic diversity and how nonmainstream students fare under such a system (McLaughlin, Shepard, & O'Day, 1995; Porter, 1995).

Grounded in the belief that educational reforms should be both systemic and equitable, Kahle (1998) developed an equity metric to monitor the progress of reform toward or away from educational equity over time. She proposed indicators of equity that are applicable for states, districts, schools, and classrooms. Key indicators are grouped into three categories that Kahle views as critical for equitable education: *access*, *retention*, and *achievement* of all students in high-quality science and mathematics programs. Each state, district, school, or class that aims to equitably meet the needs of all students would select and use the indicators that are most appropriate for its situation. As is the case in many educational reforms, when progress is made with some groups, other groups of students may suffer setbacks, so that a balance of different indicators and criteria must be continually monitored and adjusted.

Kahle's equity metric has been applied to assess the progress toward equitable systemic reform in several school districts and individual schools (Hewson, Kahle, Scantlebury, Davies, 2001; Kahle & Kelly, 2001; Rodriguez, 2001b). Using the equity metric, Hewson et al. (2001) assessed the progress toward equity of two urban middle schools engaged in the systemic reform of science education. They reported case studies of these two schools, which were part of the Ohio Statewide Systemic Initiative. The equity metric provided a framework for mapping each school's readiness for and progress toward reform, as well as barriers and opportunities that impeded and facilitated reform. The results indicated that the culture and climate of the two schools affected their progress toward equitable science education reform in different ways. At one school, a combination of factors consumed the attention of science teachers, leaving them with little time or energy to teach science. At the other school, in contrast, science teachers worked in a cooperative, stable environment that provided the time and space to focus their energies on teaching science. Hewson et al. (2001) concluded that equitable systemic reform of science education in urban schools was greatly facilitated by several key features, including collaboration between the school and community around clearly understood and accepted goals; responsible and accessible leadership; teachers who feel empowered and respected; and a community that is supportive and involved. A hallmark of a school that has successfully instituted equitable systemic reform is the school's visible progress toward goals that are clearly understood and accepted by all major stakeholders and that are consistent with state and district criteria.

Rodriguez (2001b) extended Kahle's notion of an equity metric by identifying strategies that have the potential to affect issues of access, retention, and achievement of non-mainstream urban students in science and mathematics education. He proposed a conceptual framework that incorporates ideological, pedagogical, and operational approaches to systemic reform. Rodriguez (2001b) argued that systemic reform should address the following key components: 1) policy, curriculum, and assessment, 2) growth in student achievement and participation, 3) professional development to change the culture of teaching and encourage community support and participation, and 4) strategies for scaling-up and for making systemic change self-sustaining.

Rodriguez (2001b) then applied this framework to explore how these components of systemic reform were implemented and how progress toward equity could be measured in a school district. The case study was conducted in a large urban school district with support from the NSF Urban Systemic Initiative (NSF-USI), which was aimed at improving the science and mathematics achievement of all students in the district. The results of the study illustrated how the multiple components in the conceptual framework were interdependent and how each was necessary to move reform efforts forward. Rodriguez concluded that the goal of systemic reform should not be to follow a one-model-fits-all approach. Because the complex variables in large school systems are always changing, the goal cannot be to control all the variables. Instead, insights generated from positive reform initiatives can stimulate other school districts to design equitable and inclusive systemic reform efforts tailored to their own unique contexts and needs.

Scaling-Up of Educational Innovations. While systemic reform efforts in mathematics and science have been supported by the National Science Foundation since the early 1990s, strategies for scaling-up of educational innovations have emerged more recently. Driven by the current policy context of NCLB, scaling up involves designing and implementing specific educational innovations or interventions on a large scale. For example, taking an intervention that has been effective in a few schools and implementing it across an entire school district or in numerous schools scattered across districts are examples of scale-up. Standards-based systemic reforms often require the scaling-up of educational innovations or interventions to bring about system-wide improvements (Elmore, 1996; Schneider & McDonald, 2007a, 2007b).

Despite the urgent need for systemwide improvements, scale-up research in educational settings is an emergent field that requires conceptual and methodological grounding. First, the conceptualization of scale-up research is currently under development. For example, Coburn (2003) challenges traditional definitions that equate scaling-up with simply increasing the numbers of teachers, schools, or districts involved in a project. Instead, she proposes that scaling up needs to address "the complex challenges of reaching out broadly while simultaneously cultivating the depth of change necessary to support and sustain consequential change" (p. 3). In other words, depth of change that has made a smaller-scale innovation successful is often built on specific features, such as the strength of personal relationships, which may be sacrificed when more and more teachers, classrooms, or schools are added to a larger-scale innovation.

Second, stages of going to scale are also under development (Raudenbush, 2007). In the model that is used by the U.S. Department of Education Institute of Education Sciences, the first stage involves designing an innovation, whether a whole-school reform program, a professional development initiative, curriculum materials, instructional strategies, computer technology, or some combination of these. Once an innovation is designed, the next stage involves testing its efficacy, which means how well the innovation works under extremely favorable conditions. This type of *efficacy study* demonstrates that the innovation can have a significant impact on desired outcomes (i.e., to test the theory underlying the innovation). Efficacy studies also involve the designers of the innovation in the implementation, such as in the facilitation of professional development activities. Once efficacy studies show that an innovation works under favorable conditions, the next stage involves testing its effectiveness, which means how well the innovation works under resource constraints in typical settings (i.e., to test implementation of the innovation). This type of *effectiveness study* demonstrates that the innovation has the ability to go to scale. Effectiveness studies usually do not involve the original designers of the innovation in the implementation. If an effectiveness study demonstrates a positive impact, then the innovation has proven itself to be robust enough to be scaled up across districts and even states. This multistep approach is important to ensure that the large amount of resources needed to scale up an innovation are used only when there is good evidence that the innovation will be successful on a large scale.

Third, scale-up research is methodologically complex. McDonald, Keesler, Kauffman, and Schneider (2006) argue that a key component of scale-up research is developing research designs that can realistically be executed in field settings. They point out three main methodological concerns facing scale-up research:

1) internal and external validity, 2) statistical power and sample size, and 3) methodological tools that researchers can use to produce robust, generalizable findings.

Finally, there are policy issues that should be considered. Scaling-up efforts occur within the demands and constraints of educational policies, local institutional conditions, limited resources, individual teacher practices, expectations of local stakeholders, and other factors. Scaling up compromises some of the conceptual rigor and fidelity of implementation by subjecting the innovation to the realities of varied educational contexts. Furthermore, scaling up the innovation in multilingual, multicultural, urban contexts involves an additional layer of complexity, due to conflicts and inconsistencies in defining what constitutes effective educational policy and practice as well as inequitable distribution of educational resources and funding.

As one concrete example, Blumenfeld, Fishman, Krajcik, and Marx (2000) and Fishman, Marx, Blumenfeld, Krajcik, and Soloway (2004) describe numerous challenges involved in their ongoing attempts at scaling up computer technology innovations for science education in a large urban school district. The research team created an innovation to promote an inquiry-focused, technology-rich middle school science curriculum and teacher professional development, utilizing a number of design experiments. They developed a conceptual framework, and identified issues and concerns in scaling up this innovation in a systemic urban school reform setting.

Blumenfeld et al. (2000) described a diagnostic framework that the project developed for identifying challenges to adopting and sustaining educational innovations in a systemic reform setting. The framework contains three dimensions. The *policy and management* dimension describes the extent to which established district policies and management systems are favorable to the demands of the innovation. The *capability* dimension describes the extent to which users have the conceptual and practical knowledge necessary to carry out the innovation. The *culture* dimension describes the extent to which the innovation adheres to or diverges from the existing norms, beliefs, values, and expectations for practice within the system or organization. Blumenfeld et al. illustrated how this framework was relevant to their own experiences in scaling up. They emphasized the importance of collaborating with teachers and administrators to adapt the innovation to make it feasible within the constraints of the context, while also keeping it true to its underlying philosophy. Simultaneous coordination of the different elements of the innovation, such as technology, professional development, and instruction, was also imperative. Finally, coordination of administrative and organizational functions was crucial.

Based on their experiences with scaling-up efforts, Fishman et al. (2004) examined why computer technology innovations that have been shown to successfully promote understanding have not become widespread in K–12 schools. One key reason is that the research conducted on these technologies has focused on cognitively oriented innovations, but has not adequately addressed practical issues of scalability, sustainability, and usability. There is not a strong bridge between research and development of learning technologies, on one hand, and the implementation of these innovations in schools, on the other hand. While there is value in exploring cutting-edge technologies that may not be ready for widespread use in schools, it is also important to engage in systemic research on scaling up well-established technology innovations in schools.

In another framing of challenges inherent in scaling up educational interventions, Lee and Luykx (2005) map out major difficulties that arise in scaling-up efforts, specifically with regard to elementary school science and students' linguistic, cultural, and socioeconomic diversity. As their intervention gradually scaled up over the years, policies and practices to promote high-stakes assessment and accountability in reading, writing, and mathematics became increasingly prevalent. Despite the overall effectiveness of their intervention with regard to students' science achievement and changes in teachers' beliefs and practices in teaching science, the project continued to experience challenges hindering its fuller implementation. First, scaling up in contexts of student diversity requires considerable conceptual work. The knowledge base needed to translate an educational innovation that integrates science inquiry, English language development, and student diversity into self-sustaining educational policy and practice remains limited. Second, standards-based instruction and accountability policies in a growing number of states reinforce the mainstream view that non-mainstream students should simply be assimilated into the dominant culture. Third, continued shifts toward English-only policies fail to consider students' resources in their home languages, limiting the viability of scaling-up projects that place a value on home language as a tool for enhanced content learning. Finally, because non-mainstream students disproportionately attend inner-city schools, scaling-up efforts need to confront the practical, day-to-day challenges that characterize teaching and learning in these schools, including high rates of administrator and teacher mobility, disproportionate numbers of beginning or inexperienced teachers, high rates of student mobility, inadequate infrastructure, and insufficient funding. It will be difficult to ensure the sustainability of any innovation beyond the research period, if these features are not carefully considered. Lee and Luykx (2005) conclude that the existing tensions and conflicts around educational policies and practices for non-mainstream students in elementary school science will continue to be major challenges to the scaling-up of innovations of this kind. The factors influencing both the feasibility and fidelity of implementation of scaling-up efforts must become a subject of open debate and analysis in the educational community if innovations in science education are to have a chance of reaching non-mainstream students.

The question of fidelity of implementation, raised by Lee and Luykx (2005), among others, is a critical feature to consider in all scale-up efforts. Fidelity of implementation is defined as the determination of how well an innovation is implemented according to its original program design (Dane & Schneider, 1998; Dusenbury, Brannigan, Falco, & Hansen, 2003; Mowbray, Holter, Teague, & Bybee, 2003). A good deal of research on fidelity of implementation has been conducted in the field of public and mental health interventions, but the concept is a relatively recent addition to conceptualizing K–12 educational interventions (see the literature review in O'Donnell, 2008). Fidelity of implementation is essential to understanding the effects of an intervention on the outcomes. When an innovation fails to produce the expected results, the researchers should determine whether the nonsignificant results were due to poor conceptualization (i.e., a failure of theory or a failure of program) or due to inadequate or incomplete delivery (i.e., a failure of implementation) (Raudenbush, 2007). A poorly conceptualized program would not be successful even under the best of conditions and with a high fidelity of implementation. If there is a failure to implement the program as planned, however, then the nonsignificant results may not be due to poor conceptualization, but due to inadequate or incomplete implementation. Researchers should determine whether an innovation was implemented completely, whether some components were implemented accurately while others were not, or whether modifications (intended or unintended) were made to the innovation that effected the outcomes. In addition, fidelity of implementation provides important information about the feasibility of an innovation. If it is difficult to achieve fidelity of implementation in an efficacy or effectiveness study, then the chances of successfully scaling up the innovation are small. On the other hand, if an innovation is implemented with high levels of fidelity but fails to produce desired effects, it needs to be redesigned.

With growing interest in the scaling-up of educational innovations, researchers should consider the fidelity of implementation in efficacy and effectiveness studies (O'Donnell, 2008; Schneider & McDonald, 2007a & b). The need to consider fidelity of implementation has been increasingly noted in the current standards-based accountability systems. In order to attribute changes in outcome to an educational innovation, researchers need to verify whether the intervention was implemented as planned. If fidelity data are not collected during implementation, it is difficult to determine the impact of the intervention on the outcomes. The importance of examining fidelity of implementation in an educational intervention is greater with increasing student diversity because the impact of the intervention may vary among diverse student groups and the overall outcomes may mask differential achievement outcomes among the groups.

In one example of the study that explicitly investigated fidelity of implementation, Lee, Penfield and Maerten-Rivera (2009) examined the effect of fidelity of implementation on the science achievement gains of third-grade students broadly and students with limited literacy in English specifically. An earlier study with these same third-grade students demonstrated the effectiveness of the intervention on students' science achievement (see Lee, Maerten-Rivera, Penfield, LeRoy, & Secada, 2008). Based the positive effects of the intervention on multiple measures of students' science achievement, this study tested the hypothesis that teachers' fidelity of implementation would predict students' science achievement gains. The study was conducted in the context of a professional development intervention with elementary school teachers to promote science achievement of ELL students in urban schools. As the criterion for measuring fidelity, the study focused on the quality of instruction in teaching science to ELL students. Fidelity was measured using teachers' self-reports and third-party classroom observations. Science achievement was measured by a pretest and posttest over the school year. Contrary to the hypothesis, the results of the study indicated that none of the measures of fidelity using teachers' self-reports of teaching practices or third-party classroom observations had significant effects on students' science achievement gains. The results also indicated that the effect of fidelity on achievement gains was not dependent on the classroom composition of ELL students. The results raise questions about the conceptualization and measurement of fidelity in the study. Given the soundness of conceptual grounding for the study, however, methodological limitations, including the small number of classroom observations and the low reliability of the science test scores, might account for nonsignificant effects of fidelity of implementation on students' science achievement gains. Lee, Penfield, and Maerten-Rivera (2009) conclude that scale-up research should consider *measurement failure*, in addition to theory or program failure and/or implementation failure.

With increasing accountability based on achievement outcomes of all students, educational interventions are being created to address various needs of diverse student groups. As a result, the call for measuring fidelity is receiving increased attention (O'Donnell, 2008). The link between fidelity of implementation and student achievement outcomes has often been ignored in research designs and is difficult to measure. Fidelity of implementation, however, may be a key to evaluating the impact of any intervention. Furthermore, student diversity makes the establishment of this link both problematic and critically important. While the literature on fidelity focuses on guarding against theory or program failure and implementation failure (Raudenbush, 2007), more attention should be paid to measurement failure (Lee, Penfield, & Maerten-Rivera, 2009).

Accountability Policy. Under current education reforms that place a heavy emphasis on standards-based instruction, state content standards and curriculum frameworks offer guidelines for school curricula and classroom instruction (Cohen & Hill, 2000; Knapp, 1997; Smith & O'Day, 1991). After almost a decade of high-stakes assessment in reading, writing, and mathematics, state and national policies are now shifting to include science and social studies as well.

Policy makers continue to promote high-stakes assessment as a way of addressing what has historically been a dual challenge for schools: simultaneously promoting high achievement in academic subject areas and educational equity for an increasingly diverse student population (Darling-Hammond, 1996; McLaughlin et al., 1995). The inclusion of all students in high-stakes tests, and then reporting results disaggregated by demographic subgroups, is an attempt to ensure that all students have at least basic opportunities to encounter the same content. However, critics charge that high-stakes assessments, in effect, stratify students by race, ethnicity, SES, and linguistic background, given that these factors largely determine students' access to learning opportunities (Amrein & Berliner, 2002; McNeil, 2000).

As states increasingly turn to standardized tests for accountability, high-stakes assessments play a bigger role in influencing instructional practices both in subject areas being tested and in those that are not tested. When science is not included in accountability measures, it is taught minimally in the elementary grades (Knapp & Plecki, 2001; Spillane et al., 2001). Even when science is included in accountability measures, it is often tested at specific grade levels (e.g., 5th, 8th, and 10th grades), meaning that science is not given equal weight as reading and mathematics, which are tested at every grade level. In particular, schools serving ELL students and low-SES students are pressed to ensure basic proficiency in standard English literacy and numeracy, often at the expense of other subjects such as science and social studies (Lee & Luykx, 2005).

Current accountability policy, according to NCLB, holds all students to the same academic standards in core subjects. This policy involves annually assessing all students in core subjects and holding schools accountable for adequate progress of all students by implementing sanctions when adequate progress is not met. The theory behind NCLB is that by mandating reporting of assessment scores for all students, the education system at the school, district, and state levels will be motivated to allocate resources in a way that gives all groups of students the chance of meeting the established standards.

NCLB is unprecedented in terms of its broad jurisdiction of test-based accountability. It is also unprecedented in terms of its expectation of high academic standards for all students and reporting of annual yearly progress (AYP) for non-mainstream students who have traditionally been underserved in the education system. While reading and mathematics have been the core subjects in education reforms during the past several decades, science has recently been added as part of high-stakes assessment and accountability systems in some states. It is still uncertain whether science will be considered part of the AYP calculation in the upcoming reauthorization of NCLB, but states were mandated to begin administration of science assessments in 2007.

The current mandated science assessments in NCLB, and the prospects of future inclusion of science in AYP calculation, indicate that science assessment is likely to play a major role in current and future accountability systems. There are several potential benefits stemming from the current inclusion of science assessment in NCLB mandates and the potential future inclusion in AYP calculation.

Major benefits include: 1) science counting in determination of whether adequate achievement levels have been attained, 2) a concerted focus on reducing science achievement gaps between mainstream and non-mainstream student subgroups in science, and 3) all students counting in evaluations of school and district science achievement levels. In theory, this policy should mean that at the elementary school level, science will be given a more prominent role in the school curriculum and that at all levels, all students will be given more rigorous science learning experiences. This policy should also mean that states, districts, and schools will strategically allocate resources to science education for non-mainstream students who have traditionally performed poorly in science.

Despite the intended benefits of NCLB, numerous issues arise with respect to its effective implementation. NCLB is based on assumptions that science accountability policy will result in improved science curriculum and instruction (Desimone, Smith, & Phillips, 2007; Lee & Luykx, 2005), and that improved curriculum and instruction will positively influence gains in science learning as well as producing higher test scores (Brickhouse, 2006; Champagne, 2006; Geier et al., 2008). It remains to be seen whether these assumptions will hold true over time.

In addition, there are a number of issues concerning the validity, reliability, and fairness of measurement in science learning for non-mainstream students in the context of NCLB. These measurement issues may impede the intended benefits of NCLB for non-mainstream students (Penfield & Lee, in press). There is a clear risk that the potential benefits of including science in NCLB for non-mainstream students will be limited by an inadequacy of the science assessments for these students. In particular, the less than ideal measurement properties of the assessments for non-mainstream students (discussed in Chapter 6) jeopardize the accuracy and appropriateness of the inferences of science knowledge and abilities made about these students. In other words, a test that is a fair measure of knowledge and skills for mainstream students may not be a fair measure of knowledge and skills for non-mainstream students.

Despite the potential benefits of using assessments and accountability as the basis for educational policy, basing that policy on assessments that are developed for a target population of White, middle-class, and native English speaking students raises serious questions of equity when those assessments are applied to non-mainstream students. There exists a paradox; while non-mainstream students are intended to be beneficiaries of the test-based accountability policy through the allocation of increased resources, the same students are at the greatest risk of experiencing a systematic bias in the accountability system. In addition, the approaches used to prepare students to succeed on the assessments may differ between mainstream and non-mainstream students.

The literature on high-stakes assessment and accountability in science education is limited (Deboer, 2002; Wideen, O'Shea, Pye, & Ivany, 1997), especially with regard to non-mainstream students. Marx and Harris (2006) expressed the concern clearly:

> We worry that standards-based science instruction, with its emphasis on scientific thinking and reasoning skills in the context of meaningful real-world investigations, will become a kind of "upper-class science" available primarily to students in high-performing schools and districts and less common in schools that serve poor and minority students. (p. 471)

Similarly, Southerland et al. (2007) argue that the area of science education research that has been most affected by NCLB policies is research on student diversity. Given negative consequences for schools with demographic diversity, an unintended outcome may involve reinforcing a deficit view of multiculturalism and the abilities of non-mainstream students. This view does not support teachers in building on the cultural and linguistic resources of non-mainstream students in curricular or teaching strategies. In addition, although NCLB focuses attention on achievement gaps of specific demographic groups, limited funding often fails to provide schools with the resources necessary to meet the accountability standards. Identifying gaps is of limited use if the political will and resources necessary to take action in reducing those gaps are lacking. Thus, NCLB mandates can produce more negative consequences for non-mainstream students than their mainstream counterparts.

In a concrete example of increased negative consequences, Settlage and Meadows (2002) examined the influences of standards-based reforms and standardized testing as experienced by four science teachers in urban schools in Cleveland, Ohio, and Birmingham, Alabama. Three of the four teachers were African American; two taught in elementary schools and two in high schools. All four were exemplary teachers, respected by their peers, dedicated to their students, and determined to improve themselves and the systems in which they worked. Through classroom observations and teacher interviews, the researchers identified several unintended and harmful consequences of standards-based reform and standardized testing. These included: 1) the erosion of teacher professionalism, 2) the disruption of interpersonal relationships between teachers and their students, 3) the trivialization of science instruction, and 4) the adoption of an educational triage mentality, in which schools focused attention on students whose test scores were on the edge of moving to the next achievement level and gave less attention to students who were less likely to move levels. The researchers propose strategies that university-based science educators might employ, such as assisting teachers in resisting these reform-induced perils and treating the conditions faced by urban schools as a substantive aspect of science teacher education.

In an example focusing on teachers' perceptions of accountability policy, Shaver et al. (2007) asked elementary school teachers how educational policies affected their science instruction with ELL and low-SES students. Through repeated

administration of a questionnaire and focus group interviews over a 2-year period, the study tracked changes in the perceptions of 43 urban third- and fourth-
grade teachers in regard to high-stakes assessment and accountability policy. As
the state enforced stronger measures of accountability over time, a key finding
of the study was a shift in teachers' perceptions regarding the effects on science
instruction of policies related to standards, state assessment, and accountability in
reading, writing, and mathematics. Teachers consistently expressed positive perceptions of science standards, seeing them as supportive guidelines for science
instruction. However, their perceptions of the state assessments and accountability policies that were connected to those standards grew progressively more negative. Although the teachers approved of the standards, they disapproved of how
those standards were used to drive state assessments and accountability policies.
Such negative perceptions became stronger over the course of the study. Particularly, teachers expressed exasperation with their own loss of authority concerning
whether students were promoted or retained in grade.

SUMMARY

The literature on school organization in science education has been developed
primarily in urban contexts. Despite the limited scope of this research to date,
there are several consistent findings with regard to effective and equitable school
organization for non-mainstream students. Schools that promote high academic
achievement for all students (effective) while also narrowing achievement gaps
(equitable) display reform-oriented practices that are consistent with the school
restructuring movement. Such schools are likely to have a strong academic focus,
offer a highly academic curriculum with limited use of tracking, create smaller
organizational units (schools within schools), and support strong professional
communities of teachers with a focus on the quality of instruction. These schools
also emphasize strategic use of human, social, and material resources and distributed leadership among administrators and teachers. Although these effective
practices seem to be clearly defined, there are many challenges that make these
practices difficult to enact in urban schools.

In response to recent educational policies that promote standards-based instruction, systemic reform, and accountability, there is also an emerging literature
on educational policies in science education. Like the research focusing on school
organization, these studies have largely occurred in urban contexts. This research
has been strongly influenced by federal policy initiatives in recent years. Substantial funding for systemic reform of mathematics and science education, including
the NSF-funded Statewide Systemic Initiative and the Urban Systemic Initiative,
has provided multiple examples of how policy changes can result in changes in science teaching and learning. Under the current policy initiatives for research-based

practice, there is a new focus on scaling up effective practices and testing the impact of large-scale initiatives across varied educational settings. In addition, as science has been included in NCLB (although not included in AYP) since 2007, research on the influences of high-stakes assessment and accountability on science instruction has been on the rise.

Current educational policies are unique in terms of federal and state mandates for accountability in state education systems, which have historically been driven by local decisions. Research in science education must make both conceptual and methodological advances to better address evolving policy issues. To answer the question of what constitutes best policies and practices in science education for diverse student populations, greater attention must be paid to a range of challenges facing schools and teachers, such as the challenge of bringing together an understanding of science disciplines with an awareness of the linguistic and cultural experiences of non-mainstream students (Lee & Luykx, 2005). While there are potential benefits of increased accountability for academic achievement of non-mainstream students, there are also ways in which new assessment and accountability policies may place non-mainstream students at even greater risk of academic failure.

Teachers, administrators, and policy makers need to understand the range of challenges facing non-mainstream students and the schools serving them. They must recognize how statewide science assessments, primarily designed for mainstream students and native speakers of English, may present obstacles and pitfalls to ELL students and other non-mainstream students in science (Penfield & Lee, in press). They must also learn to distinguish between students' science knowledge and linguistic and cultural experiences, and develop ways to assist students in demonstrating what the students do know about science rather than focusing so much attention on identifying what students do not know. This may require the development of new tools and new assessments that are critical to creating more effective and equitable assessment and accountability policy for non-mainstream students.

ACTIVITIES FOR CHAPTER 8

1. Using your school Web site, school improvement plan, and other available resources, review the science education programs at your school. Consider the following issues related to policy and practice:
    A. What messages does the school administration/leadership team provide about the role of science teaching and learning in your school?
    B. What material resources are provided to support science teaching and learning in your school?
    C. How is human capital (i.e., resources to support the individual knowledge, skills, and expertise available in the organization) developed to support science teaching and learning in your school?

D. How is social capital (i.e., support for relationships among individuals in the organization) developed to support science teaching and learning in your school?

E. What role does science play in your school improvement plan?

F. What special programs/intervention programs/research programs, etc. to support science teaching and learning are currently or have recently been implemented in your school?

Write a paragraph that summarizes the formal policies and informal messages regarding the importance of science teaching and learning in your school.

2. Explore your State Department of Education Web site and obtain the following information regarding the role of science testing as part of the state accountability plan:

A. At what grade levels are state science tests administered?

B. How are state science tests scored and reported?

C. How are state science test scores factored into school grades or other school level accountability (if at all)?

D. What information is available to the public about state science test results at the school, district, and state levels?

E. What information is available to the public about the nature of state science tests, such as publicly released tests or test items, or item specifications used to develop test items, and so forth?

F. Do state science tests include constructed response items, or do they include only multiple-choice items?

Write a paragraph that summarizes the formal policies and informal messages regarding the importance of science testing as part of the accountability plan in your state.

3. With a partner, develop a 5-to-10-question interview that could be conducted with parents or community members to get their opinions about the pros and cons of the high-stakes testing and accountability policies in your state. Potential topics include the following:

A. perceptions of the purposes of the accountability policies

B. perceptions of the strengths and potential benefits of the accountability policies

C. perceptions of the weaknesses and potential costs of the accountability policies

D. the actual effects they have seen as a result of the accountability policies

E. changes they would like to see in the high-stakes testing and accountability policies

F. any other related topics of interest to you

Conduct your interview with at least three different parents or community members. If possible, include parents with different demographic backgrounds. Write a short summary that compares and contrasts the responses you obtained and how you interpret them.

CHAPTER 9

Home Connections
and Student Diversity

The relationship between students' academic success and parental involvement in schooling has long been understood (Baker & Stevenson, 1986; Epstein, 1987). Subsequent research has tried to better understand how home connections can be supported and whether certain types of family or community involvement might be particularly helpful to support student achievement. For example, Bloome, Katz, Solsken, Willett, and Wilson-Keenan (2000) explored how the dominant relationship between schools and families is a school-centered model where school-based intellectual practices are presented to parents as best practices that should be reinforced in the home. Bloome and colleagues advocated a community-centered model where the cultural and intellectual practices of family, community, school, business, and so forth are all valued and accepted. These two models are not easily resolved, however, and raise tensions, such as the desire of families to maintain in their children the cultural and linguistic practices of their heritage while also wanting their children to participate fully in the dominant school culture. Thus, while it has long been recognized that building home-school connections is important for the academic success of non-mainstream students, in practice, this is rarely done in an effective manner.

In the context of science education, several studies have examined the influences of families and home environments on students' science achievement. As noted in the earlier chapters on curriculum and instructional practices, a major challenge facing many schools is the perceived disconnect between school science practices and practices in the home and community environments of non-mainstream students. Students are more likely to disengage from schooling if they do not see it as relevant and meaningful to their lives beyond school. Yet, students bring to the science classroom funds of knowledge from their homes and communities that can serve as resources for academic learning if teachers understand and find ways to activate this prior knowledge (González et al., 2005; Moll, 1992). Academic learning is built upon tasks and activities that occur in the social contexts of day-to-day living, whether the school chooses to recognize this or not. The small number of studies on connections between science learning and students' families and communities can be grouped into two areas: 1) studies of the influence of families and home environments on students' science learning and 2) studies of school science and community connections.

FAMILIES AND HOME ENVIRONMENTS

There is clear evidence that family support influences children's achievement, attitudes, and aspirations, even after student ability and family SES are taken into account (Epstein, 1987; Oakes, 1990). Traditionally, research on family and home environments using large data sets has focused on demographic variables, especially social class measured by parental education, resources available at home, and parental involvement in their children's academics at home.

Peng and Hill (1994) studied the influence of home, school, and student factors that differentiated high- and low-achieving non-mainstream students (i.e., African American, Hispanic, Native American, and Native Alaskan students) in science and mathematics. Certain factors correlated with science achievement, regardless of the students' racial, ethnic, or cultural background. In terms of home influences, high achievers were more likely to come from families with more available learning materials and resources. Their parents were more likely to be in highly skilled occupations that provided appropriate role models for science and mathematics learning. Their parents also had higher educational expectations for their children. These results suggest that the economic and educational marginalization associated with non-mainstream status negatively affects science achievement.

In a large-scale study of 17-year-old students based on NAEP results, Schibeci and Riley (1986) examined the influence of five background variables (race, gender, availability of educational materials in the home, amount of homework, and parents' education level) on science achievement and attitudes. The results indicated that availability of educational materials in the home, homework supervision, and parent's educational background had a substantial influence on students' science achievement, regardless of the student's race and gender.

In a study of tracking patterns in middle and high school mathematics and science courses, Spade, Columba, and Vanfossen (1997) compared course offerings and placement procedures in schools serving students coming from different SES backgrounds. Spade and colleagues found that in high- and middle-SES schools, parents played a much more active role in decisions about students' academic placement in advanced science and mathematics courses than did parents in the lower-SES schools. They concluded that schools did little to solicit parental involvement when it came to student course-taking. Parents in high- and middle-SES schools often took the initiative to become advocates in this decision-making process, whereas parents in low-SES schools generally did not.

Together these studies provide evidence that parental involvement makes a difference in student achievement. Schools need to develop strategies for supporting the ongoing educational involvement of parents and other community members, both at home and in school. Baker and Stevenson (1986) found that parents reported greater school involvement when they felt comfortable with the school, felt knowledgeable about classroom practices, received frequent reports of their child's progress and accomplishments, and felt like a partner in their child's learning. Schools should improve in each of these areas without a large expenditure of resources. This will take some rethinking in terms of the roles that parents (and especially non-mainstream parents) are generally asked to play in schools.

According to Calabrese Barton, Drake, Perez, St. Louis, and George (2004), the literature on parents' roles and involvement in schools has traditionally been understood in terms of what parents do and how that fits or does not fit with the needs of the child or the goals of the school. This approach implicitly relies on a deficit model, especially in discussions of parental involvement with non-mainstream students in urban communities. Parents are often positioned as subjects to be manipulated or as powerless to position themselves in ways they see fit (i.e., what good parents do for their children's education, as described in the studies above). Instead, recent literature describes non-mainstream parents as possessing agency and demonstrating the value of parental power and voice in the organization of school knowledge and practice. This literature challenges long-held assumptions about the boundaries of parental involvement, the potential benefits of parental involvement, and conflicts that can emerge when parents have power within traditional school structures. The studies described below highlight the resources that parents of non-mainstream students bring to their children's education in science-related settings.

Calabrese Barton et al. (2004) addressed parental participation, interactions, and relationships in schools in high-poverty urban settings. They proposed an *ecologies of parental engagement* framework to understand the interconnections between how and why parents engage in their children's education in urban schools and how this engagement relates to their experiences and actions both inside and outside of the school. Using this framework, they examined how parents in high-poverty urban schools negotiated common understandings about beliefs and practices and built sustaining relationships with each other and with other actors in the school. Particularly, they focused on what happened when parents' beliefs and practices differed from expectations held by school personnel. Although the study was originally designed to address science education, it expanded to include reading and mathematics, primarily because these two subjects were tested and test scores were used to determine student promotion, school funding, and school ratings.

In a similar vein, Siegel, Esterly, Callahan, Wright, and Navarro (2007) tested the idea that if parent-child everyday conversations are important sources of children's early science learning, then it would be useful to know whether children from different family backgrounds have different experiences talking about science in informal settings. The study examined the relationship between parents' schooling, their explanatory talk in science-related activities, and the styles of interaction they used with their children. The participants were Mexican-descent families from different schooling backgrounds. Forty families were observed in two science-related activities. In the sink-or-float activity, families were asked to predict which of a variety of objects would sink and which would float, and then to test their predictions in a tub of water. The second activity was an open-ended visit to a local children's museum. Results indicated that in the sink-or-float activity, regardless of their schooling, parents had similarly rich explanatory conversations with their children and were mostly directive. The interaction style, however, varied according to parents' schooling level across the two activities: parents with higher schooling were more directive and used school-like strategies for discussing science activities with their children than the parents with basic schooling. Siegel and colleagues conclude that research into parent-child conversations in science-related activities can bridge children's learning environments—home, school, and museum—and potentially foster children's science learning, particularly in those groups underrepresented in science.

In another study that provided families with out-of-school science experiences, Simpson and Parsons (2008) examined the perspectives of African American parents regarding a science enrichment program composed of a community-based science camp with 1-week summer academy and two full-day sessions during the academic year. This program had successfully recruited African American students from third through sixth grades. The academy staff during the summer and the elementary school teachers during the academic year were all African American. Of the 49 families with children enrolled in the program, the study involved 11 African American parents, most of whom were from middle-class backgrounds and lived in suburban areas. Simpson and Parsons reasoned that informal science experiences could offer an opportunity for African American students to learn science in a setting where the cultural expectations for students could be less rigid than formal classrooms. The study analyzed multiple sources of data based on a model of Black cultural ethos. Results indicated that most of the African American parents' desires and opinions aligned with multiple dimensions of Black cultural ethos. According to parents, this program fostered African American identities by providing African American peers with whom their children could interact, African American role models to show realized dreams in science, and African American history to reiterate the possibilities available to these students. The parents' opinions highlighted the potential impact of culture on parental choice to enroll their children in an informal science program.

While much of the focus of research on family engagement has been with parents of elementary-grade children when parents are more likely to participate in classroom activities, some studies have looked at the parents of older students. Smith and Hausafus (1998) examined the relationship between mothers' support for mathematics and science learning and eighth-grade students' scores on standardized tests in mathematics and science. The student sample included children participating in a special cooperative partnership program between a university and an urban community school district. The 80 students in the study included 32 recent immigrants from Southeast Asia, 28 African Americans, 17 Hispanics, and 3 Native Americans. The research considered ways that parents could be supportive of their children's mathematics and science learning, even though they might not be able to be active participants. Mothers of 80 students responded via telephone with regard to their own behavior, the physical environment of the home, and their attitudes toward science and mathematics. The results indicated that students had higher test scores when parents helped them see the importance of taking advanced science and mathematics courses, set limits on TV watching, and visited science and mathematics exhibits and fairs with their children. Smith and Hausafus note that these activities do not require parental knowledge of science and mathematics. Instead, parents can be supportive simply by communicating and enforcing high expectations for achievement with their children.

While the studies discussed so far have focused on the importance of parents becoming actively involved in their children's science learning at home and decision making in school, the studies in the next section focus on how the content of school science can be connected to activities and experiences in the community.

SCHOOL SCIENCE AND COMMUNITY CONNECTIONS

Several studies have investigated intervention programs to help non-mainstream students recognize the meaning and relevance of science and make connections between school science and experiences in their communities. Consistent with the recent literature on parents' roles and involvement that highlight their agency and voice, as described above, the studies on the connections between school science and communities have generally highlighted the funds of knowledge that non-mainstream students bring to science learning, as described below.

Rodriguez and Berryman (2002) worked with 38 10th-grade students in predominantly Latino and impoverished school settings in a U.S.-Mexican border city. The instructional approach in the study was guided by a *sociotransformative constructivism* that merged multicultural education with social constructivism. Using a curriculum unit on investigating water quality in their community, the students explored how this topic was socially relevant and connected to their everyday lives. Rodriguez and Berryman asked students to complete a concept map on the topic before and after instruction, and analyzed the maps for changes in the students' ideas. They found that the instructional approach enhanced not only students' enthusiasm for the science curriculum but also knowledge and understanding of the science content. They also found that the experience empowered and encouraged the students to take additional action such as testing water in their homes and investigating ways to improve water standards in their communities. Students quickly understood the precariousness of water availability in their desert region and informed their families of ways to conserve water at home. Having come to see science as relevant to their lives, students then saw scientific investigations as worthwhile. Rodriguez and Berryman conclude that their approach has the potential to open empowering spaces where students can engage with science curricula in socially relevant and transformative ways.

In a project that brought together multiple school and community stakeholders, Hammond (2001) described collaborative efforts in which pre-service teachers, mentor teachers, and teacher educators worked together with immigrant Mien and Hmong students and their families to explore options for elementary science and other subject areas. Through these efforts, children, parents, teachers, and student teachers gathered community funds of knowledge about the science topics to be studied, and then incorporated this knowledge into instruction by calling upon the parents as experts and creating *community books*. The community-generated materials paralleled and complemented standards-based curricula, although science topics that had natural significance in particular communities were used as a starting point. By describing the process of building a Mien-American house, the study illustrates how a new kind of *multiscience* can emerge by drawing on participants' funds of knowledge, and how such multiscience can both be made accessible to all collaborating members and be responsive to school standards.

In another variation of a funds of knowledge approach, Bouillion and Gomez (2001) explored a model of *connected science* as a way to provide all students with opportunities for meaningful and intellectually challenging science learning. In connected science, real-world problems that are current, unresolved, consequential, and school-community partnerships were used as the context for bridging students' community-based knowledge and school-based knowledge. This case study examined the potential value of using a connected science model with a team of elementary teachers at one elementary school. The study used the student-identified problem of pollution along a river near the students' predominantly Mexican-American neighborhood. The community partners included parents, scientists, and local community organizations. The study focused on how diverse forms of science knowledge and experience could be brought together to support student learning, particularly in settings in which students' home culture may differ from or even conflict with the culture of school science. Bouillion and Gomez concluded that the connected science model both supported project activities and enhanced students' science learning, interest, and efficacy.

In a project that connected community experience with science learning, Rahm (2002) described an inner-city youth gardening program and the kinds of science learning opportunities it supported. Participants were inner-city middle school students who had been identified as being at risk of dropping out of school. The research took place in a 4–H community youth program that ran through the summer, in which the students earned money by participating in gardening and then selling their produce at a community market. Particularly, the study examined the ways in which working together in the garden environment supported youth-initiated actions and talk, while also enabling connections to be made among science, community, and work. The study also emphasized the value of a science that emerged from participants' engagement in activities that they deemed valuable, meaningful, and authentic. Some students volunteered to continue their gardening projects after the summer program was over. Rahm concluded that the gardening program, though it did not have academic learning as its primary goal, provided valuable science and mathematics learning opportunities that were meaningful, relevant, and real to the students. The results also highlighted the educational value of opportunities for the integration of science, community, and work.

While some studies have created science-learning communities beyond the school walls, other studies have created spaces for community-building during the school day. Seiler (2001) described her work with eight African American male high school students who met for a science lunch group. She met with the students once each week to eat together, talk about their lives, and discuss science-related activities. These science activities started from students' own interests, prior knowledge, and lived experiences. Through participation over time in the science lunch group, students forged a learning community based on respect and caring that provided the opportunity to participate in science in new ways. Seiler concludes that the push for more rigorous standards in inner-city schools will do little to reduce achievement gaps because these standards fail to address the significance of students' social and cultural lives.

Many of the studies of community connections to school science are fundamentally about building and sustaining students' intellectual curiosity and motivation. Basu and Calabrese Barton (2007) examined the connections between the funds of knowledge that urban, high-poverty students brought to science learning and the development of a sustained interest in science. By sustained interest, Basu and Calabrese Barton mean that students complete more than the task at hand in a classroom. They considered that youth exhibit a sustained interest toward science if the youth pursue self-motivated science explorations outside of the classroom or use science in an ongoing way to improve, expand, or enhance an exploration or activity to which they are already deeply committed. Thus, the study addressed the extent to which using students' funds of knowledge could help to establish a sustained interest in science. The study participants consisted of primarily African American and Latino students attending a middle school located in a large urban center. The study was conducted in an after-school program focused on invention and exploration. The after-school program offered a learning environment in which youth's lives shaped the research agenda and day-to-day interactions, students had some control over their own work, and students were provided with a broad range of science learning contexts. The results indicated that youth developed a sustained interest in science when: 1) their science experiences connected with how they envisioned their own futures, including both personal and professional desires; 2) learning environments supported the kinds of social relationships that students valued; and 3) science activities supported students' views on the purpose of science. Basu and Calabrese Barton conclude that science curricula and classrooms that make space for students' funds of knowledge can exist alongside goals for science content and skills.

SUMMARY

There is a small but emerging body of literature on the connections between school science and students' home and community environments. Traditionally, research on home-school connections has looked at how the family and home environments of non-mainstream students measured up to the expectations and practices of the mainstream. The results were interpreted in terms of deficits in students' family and home environments, as compared to their mainstream counterparts. In contrast, more recent research has identified resources and strengths in the family and home environments of non-mainstream students (Calabrese Barton et al., 2004). Even parents with limited education or limited science knowledge can promote their children's science learning by communicating and enforcing high expectations for science achievement and by demonstrating agency, power, and voice. However, schools that serve predominantly non-mainstream students have been slow to take actions to involve and empower non-mainstream parents in ways that are likely to enhance their participation.

Another set of studies highlighted in this chapter focus on the connections that can be drawn between community science activities and school science. Some of these activities included parents and community members as well as students, while others focused only on students. The studies took place outside of the constraints of the regular science class. These studies provide detailed descriptions of students' engagement and learning as they participated in programs connecting school science with their community environments. The results consistently indicate that students gained a better understanding of science, recognized the relevance of science to their personal lives, and developed interest and agency in science as either a direct or indirect outcome of the interventions. These studies make a compelling case for the value of informal science experiences as critical to learning science. Some of the researchers argue that school science should be reconceptualized to give a more central role to students' lived experiences and identities. Furthermore, the studies highlight ways in which utilizing funds of knowledge can enhance science engagement and learning. When youth find science education to be empowering and transformative, they are likely to embrace and further investigate what they are learning, instead of being resistant to learning science.

ACTIVITIES FOR CHAPTER 9

1. It is critically important that teachers learn to work closely with parents, families, and community members who are representative of all the students in their classes and not just the communities that feel familiar and comfortable.
    A. Construct brief interviews with parents of your students or community members in your students' neighborhoods. Consider questions that help to elaborate community funds of knowledge connected to school science. Some questions to get you started include the following:
        i. What local sources of food are found in the community? What knowledge is needed to produce and/or prepare this food? How do young people gain this knowledge?
        ii. What arts and crafts are practiced in the community? What knowledge is needed to produce these arts and crafts? How do young people gain this knowledge?
        iii. What traditional cures, remedies, or medical practices are found in the community? What knowledge is needed to use these cures, remedies, or medical practices? How do young people gain this knowledge?
    B. See what additional questions you can develop that connect community funds of knowledge to science topics. Try out your interview with at least two parents or community members in your students' neighborhoods.
    C. What do you conclude about connecting school science to community knowledge?
2. An essential approach to understanding similarities and differences between the cultural practices of your students' homes and communities and the cultural practices of your school is to reflect on your own cultural experiences and expectations. In the table below, consider your own experiences of how different elements of culture have played out in your childhood home, in your own adult household, and in your classroom.

Cultural Element	My Childhood Household	My Adult Household	My Classroom
DISCIPLINE OF CHILDREN (Who? How?)			
CHILDREN'S HOMEWORK (Who is responsible? Who checks? Who helps?)			
WHO MAKES THE RULES? (How are they made clear? How are they enforced?)			
LANGUAGE (What language is spoken predominantly? What language(s) are encouraged? How is academic language learned?)			

Based on your responses, consider the following discussion questions. Talk them over with a classmate and be prepared to discuss similarities and differences with the whole class.

A. How similar or different is your classroom culture to your own household culture? How do you explain this?

B. Do you think there are some students in your class for whom elements of classroom culture might be uncomfortable? Explain your thinking.

C. What could you do to tap into the funds of knowledge that you uncovered in the interview in Activity 1 to counteract the feelings of discomfort mentioned in question (b) of Activity 2?

PART IV

Call for Action

In this book we have described research programs and studies that examine the relationship between students' science outcomes, broadly defined, and factors that may affect those outcomes. In particular, we have attempted to provide insights into why gaps in science outcomes among racial, ethnic, cultural, linguistic, and socioeconomic groups have persisted over the years, in the hope that a better understanding of these issues may point the way toward reducing or eliminating those gaps. We believe that a thoughtful consideration of the many factors that influence science teaching and learning, ranging from curriculum and instruction to policy issues and family involvement, is beneficial for the teaching of all students, not just for non-mainstream students. Thus, while the teaching of non-mainstream students is the focus throughout, the studies that have been described and the stories they tell should provide food for thought for any teacher of science, regardless of the context of teaching. The book is based primarily on scholarship that has been published in peer-reviewed journal articles and guided by other criteria to ensure the methodological rigor of research (Shavelson & Towne, 2002).

CHAPTER 10

Conclusions and Research Agenda

Based on the research that has been discussed in the previous chapters, we offer conclusions in three main areas: 1) key features of the literature with regard to theoretical and methodological perspectives, 2) key findings about factors related to science outcomes of non-mainstream students, and 3) proposals for an ongoing research agenda. Future research should address current limitations in theory and practice as well as build on those areas that demonstrate promising findings. New research should focus on improving science outcomes, narrowing gaps among diverse student groups, and addressing those areas or topics that have been largely ignored in the literature to date.

THEORETICAL AND METHODOLOGICAL
ISSUES IN THE LITERATURE

Research on diversity and equity in science education is still a young and emerging field. Most studies in the field have been published since the mid-1990s, perhaps brought about by the emphasis on the dual goals of excellence and equity laid out in *Science for All Americans* (AAAS, 1989) and *National Science Education Standards* (NRC, 1996).

The studies have been conducted from a wide range of theoretical and disciplinary perspectives, including psychological, cognitive science, cross-cultural, and sociopolitical. The researchers have used a variety of research methods, including experimental designs, surveys, case studies, and ethnographies. Overall, experimental studies are less common than studies using qualitative methods such as case studies. No meta-analysis of statistical research studies, a research approach common to more mature research fields, is found in the literature on diversity and equity in science education.

Because the research in the field is still developing, the relationships between non-mainstream students' science outcomes, such as achievement data, and the learning experiences and educational processes experienced by the students are tenuous in many of the studies. Studies focusing on educational processes often do not report student outcome data, and studies linking student outcomes to causal mechanisms are rare. Studies reporting on the impact of intervention programs on achievement gaps among racial, ethnic, cultural, linguistic, and socioeconomic groups are scarce. Because outcome measures are often developed independently by researchers for use in a specific study, it is difficult to compare outcomes across studies.

In this book we have attempted to consider the relationships of race, ethnicity, culture, language, and SES to science education in a broad sense. With some exceptions, the included studies have treated these variables separately and fail to examine the intersections among them. For example, studies focusing on poverty in urban education often do not consider students' language or culture, and studies focusing on language and culture in the classroom often fail to consider the broader social context in which classroom interactions are situated. At the same time, studies often fail to distinguish between variables that tend to occur together, such as race or ethnicity with culture, SES with prior science knowledge, or literacy with English proficiency. Rather than either combining these variables or treating them in isolation, future research should aim to examine their intersections more systematically.

In addition to the methodological shortcomings that are common to a young field of research, the theoretical frameworks that support this research are also somewhat uneven. Although some researchers have connected their work to important concepts and research findings from related fields like cognitive psychology, sociolinguistics, and cultural anthropology, other researchers have not tried to make these connections to more mature fields. This limited theoretical grounding can give rise to research designs that are flawed, and interpretations that are ethnocentric or underdeveloped.

We have paid special attention to the needs of ELL students in the science classroom. We have treated studies involving ELL students separately in many chapters, while also acknowledging that the challenges faced by ELL students overlap with the challenges faced by other non-mainstream students. ELL students often face an added layer of challenges, however, and research in this area remains scarce. Studies that report on student outcomes in both science and literacy are rare, and only a few studies have examined student achievement in both science and literacy for students at different levels of English proficiency (Amaral et al., 2002; Lee, Deaktor, et al., 2005, 2008; Lee, Maerten-Rivera, et al., 2008; Lee, Mahotiere, et al., 2009).

While most of the research that has been done on diversity and equity in science education has been small in scale, there is a growing trend toward implementing and testing educational interventions on a large scale at the district or state level (Blumenfeld et al., 2000; Gamoran et al., 2003; Kahle, 1998; Marx et al., 2004). This trend reflects the emphasis on systemic reform in mathematics and science education during the 1990s (primarily through the NSF support) and, more recently, on scaling up of educational innovations during the 2000s (primarily through the NCLB Act). These larger-scale studies face the cultural and linguistic complexities described above, plus the day-to-day challenges of working in large education systems. In addition, the current policy context of high-stakes assessment and accountability often limits implementation of ambitious projects, such as long-term and intensive teacher professional development. When high-stakes assessment emphasizes low-level knowledge and abilities, and when insufficient resources or instructional time are allocated for science instruction, some potentially effective interventions become impractical or do not produce sustainable change (Coburn, 2003; McDonald et al., 2006). Accountability policies have also limited implementation of some educational programs, such as bilingual education and performance assessments. Thus, the feasibility of research on diversity and equity in science education needs to be considered within the shifting policy context in which the research is conducted.

KEY FINDINGS IN THE LITERATURE

While science learning is demanding for all students, non-mainstream students often face additional challenges. Students from all racial, ethnic, cultural, linguistic, and socioeconomic backgrounds come to school with a wide range of prior knowledge, including their home language and cultural values, ideas about science, and ideas about schooling, acquired in their home and community environments. This prior knowledge serves as the framework for constructing new academic and social understandings (Warren, Ballenger, et al., 2001). However, some aspects of students' prior knowledge, beliefs, and experience may be discontinuous with the worldview and knowledge system of science as traditionally defined in Western modern science (Aikenhead & Jegede, 1999; Lee, 2002, 2003). Furthermore, even the experiences and prior knowledge that non-mainstream students bring to school that could potentially serve as intellectual resources for new learning in science classrooms are generally marginalized from school science. This is just one of many ways in which the education system often fails to provide equitable science learning opportunities for non-mainstream students.

Curriculum materials seldom incorporate cultural experiences, analogies, or artifacts representative of non-mainstream groups (Aikenhead, 2001b; Matthews & Smith, 1994; Stephens, 2000). Teachers are often underprepared to build on the cultural and linguistic influences that non-mainstream students value and depend upon. Many teachers do not consider teaching for diversity as their responsibility, purposefully overlook cultural and linguistic differences among their students, accept inequities as a given condition of schooling, and actively resist multicultural views of learning either in science or more generally (Bryan & Atwater, 2002). Assessment practices may provide poor measures of what non-mainstream students know and are able to do. ELL students are seldom assessed in their home language, low-income students often confront test items that have contexts completely unrelated to their lived experiences, and the academic language needed to decode and interpret test items is assumed more often than it is explicitly taught. All of these assessment practices may result in a major underestimation of non-mainstream students' science knowledge and skills because they confound science knowledge with other types of cultural and linguistic knowledge (Solano-Flores, 2008; Solano-Flores & Trumbull, 2003). In contrast, the cultural and linguistic knowledge and experiences of mainstream students tend to enhance their abilities to perform well on these assessments. Mainstream students are tested in their home language, the context of test items tends to reflect their lived experiences, and they are more likely to have been explicitly taught the academic language they need both inside and outside of the classroom setting.

Tracking or ability grouping also results in inequitable learning opportunities, as non-mainstream students are generally overrepresented in lower tracks where content is less challenging, science course offerings are less varied, and expectations of student achievement are lower (Gilbert & Yerrick, 2001; Lee & Smith, 1995; Lee, Smith, & Croninger, 1997). The consequences of tracking policies, as well as the assessment policies that are often responsible for the tracking, are especially critical in urban school districts where the majority of non-mainstream students are educated. Both the number and the scale of the challenges facing students in urban schools diminish the likelihood that non-mainstream students will receive equitable science learning opportunities when compared to their mainstream peers.

When non-mainstream students are provided with equitable learning opportunities in formal or informal learning environments, they demonstrate academic achievement, interest, and agency. When learning environments are created that present science content in ways that are aligned with non-mainstream students' cultural and linguistic practices, they capitalize on their intellectual resources and prior knowledge and embrace science learning. When non-mainstream students are provided with socially safe learning environments, they explore and construct academic and scientific identities. When educational policies and practices are put in place that set high expectations for advanced course-taking for all students, non-mainstream students succeed in challenging science courses. When science is presented as a way of talking, thinking, and problem solving in the world and when these practices are explicitly taught, non-mainstream students embrace the role of bicultural and bilingual border crossers between their own cultural and speech communities and the science learning community.

The literature on teaching science to non-mainstream students is consistent in some aspects and inconsistent in others. For example, it is widely accepted that connecting students' cultural and linguistic experiences to the practices of science is central to effective teaching and learning. However, the specific approaches to achieving this goal differ from one theoretical perspective to another. For example, from a cognitive science perspective, researchers have argued that there is a significant overlap between students' explorations of the natural world and the way science is practiced by scientists (e.g., Rosebery, Warren, & Conant, 1992; Warren et al., 2001). From this perspective, the focus for creating more equitable learning opportunities should be on helping teachers to understand the dynamics between scientific practices and students' everyday knowledge. Teachers need to learn to facilitate and guide students' investigations of their own questions as they learn to think and act as members of a science learning community.

In contrast, from a cross-cultural perspective, researchers have argued that because non-mainstream students are not from the "culture of power" (e.g., Western modern science), teachers need to make that culture's rules and norms explicit and visible for students (Aikenhead & Jegede, 1999; Lee, 2002, 2003). From this perspective, the focus for creating more equitable learning opportunities should be on teaching students those "rules of the game" and help them make smooth transitions between different cultural contexts. In addition, if students come from backgrounds in which questioning and inquiry are not encouraged or if they have limited formal science experience, teachers need to guide students progressively along the teacher-explicit to student-exploratory continuum, while students learn to take the initiative and assume responsibility for their own learning (Fradd & Lee, 1999; Lee, 2002).

From a sociopolitical perspective, researchers have argued that science education for non-mainstream students must shift from the traditional paradigm that locates science at the center as a target to be reached by students at the margins, to a decentered model in which students' experiences and identities remain in tension with scientific ways of studying the world (Calabrese Barton, 1998a, 2001). From this perspective, the focus for creating more equitable learning opportunities should be on validating students' experiences by taking those experiences as the starting point for explorations of the natural and social world. Teachers need to learn to help students arrive at more rigorous and powerful ways of critically exploring questions relevant to their lives.

Efforts to develop curriculum materials for non-mainstream student groups present particular challenges. The literature points to a deep concern over the fact that science curriculum materials tend to exclude the cultural and linguistic experiences of non-mainstream students. Despite this concern, actual curriculum development efforts to better meet the needs of non-mainstream student populations are few and far between. Even when culturally relevant materials have been developed (e.g., Aikenhead, 1997, 2001b; Matthews & Smith, 1994; Stephens, 2000), their effectiveness may be limited to the particular cultural or linguistic group for which they are designed. Conversely, when materials are developed for wide use and are implemented across a range of educational settings, local adaptations are essential to make the materials culturally and socially relevant. However, making these local adaptations requires expertise and training on the part of teachers (Blumenfeld et al., 2000; Fishman et al., 2004; Marx et al., 2004; Songer et al., 2002, 2003).

The issue of culturally and linguistically relevant materials has implications not only for curriculum, but also for assessment. Except for NAEP or TIMSS public release items, there are few widely used achievement tests in science. For this reason, research programs often develop their own assessment instruments, and many employ authentic or performance assessments. The resulting variability in assessment practices hinders the comparability of research findings. In addition, assessments designed for specific cultural and linguistic groups may not be valid or equitable for other groups (Solano-Flores, 2008; Solano-Flores & Trumbull, 2003). Efforts to develop either culturally neutral or culturally relevant assessments each present their own set of difficulties (Luykx et al., 2007). Thus, providing valid and equitable assessments is complicated because factors such as students' linguistic and cultural experiences confound the accurate measurement of scientific knowledge or inquiry.

Yet another obstacle to equitable science education of non-mainstream students is the current policy context of high-stakes assessment and accountability. Because science is currently not part of AYP calculations (although it is part of NCLB), it is usually given less importance than language arts and mathematics (Penfield & Lee, in press). Science gets squeezed out of the curriculum at the elementary school level. This is especially the case for non-mainstream students and others who are perceived to be at risk for low standardized test performance in language arts and mathematics. For these students, science class time is often reduced to prepare for tests in these other core subjects. This tendency is reinforced when school funding and resources for science instruction are overlooked in favor of resources to support language arts and mathematics.

Current science education research now has to take place within the context of policies that promote standards-based reform and accountability. This context severely limits the nature of educational interventions that can take place within the bounds of the normal school day and may particularly impact research efforts with non-mainstream students (Marx & Harris, 2006; Southerland, Smith, Sowell, & Kittleson, 2007). Despite research indicating that sensitivity to student diversity requires variations in educational processes to meet the needs of specific student groups or individuals, the policy context pushes research toward standardized solutions. As with other equity issues that have been discussed, these tensions are more acute in inner-city classrooms where educational resources and opportunities are more limited and where non-mainstream students are overrepresented.

RESEARCH AGENDA

Research on diversity and equity in science education is a relatively new field of study, and our understanding of many aspects is just beginning to take shape. Thus, future research can and must pursue a broad range of issues. Virtually all of the areas discussed in earlier chapters require further investigation. However, some priorities for future research need to be identified based on the likelihood that they can help create more equitable science learning opportunities for non-mainstream students.

Science Outcomes. One area ripe for further investigation involves conceptualizing and measuring science outcomes. Some research programs emphasize students' agency or engagement in science, rather than more commonly recognized outcome measures based on academic achievement. Conceptions of science outcomes vary widely from one research program to another. While teachers and researchers share the dual goals of improving science outcomes and eliminating gaps, many existing research programs do not pay sufficient attention to student achievement outcomes. For example, quantitative achievement data can provide an additional perspective that confirms or complicates narrative descriptions about other types of student outcomes, such as increased engagement or agency.

Other issues concerning science outcomes deserve special attention. First, more work is needed to make connections between students' learning processes and outcomes. Second, more research is needed to examine the effectiveness of educational interventions in reducing achievement gaps among demographic groups. Third, future research should consider new ways to disaggregate achievement results for the intersections of race, ethnicity, culture, language, and SES, as well as for subgroups within broader racial and ethnic categories. Fourth, longitudinal data of student achievement over the course of several grade levels is largely absent from the current literature. Fifth, a broader variety of outcome measures, such as agency and linguistic and cultural identity, should be included in studies of non-mainstream students. Finally literacy outcomes should be considered along with science outcomes in studies of ELL students.

Student Diversity. Although the studies discussed in this book were selected because of their focus on diversity and equity, many of them do not address these issues in sufficient depth or complexity (see the discussion about research methodology in Luykx & Lee, 2007). For example, studies focusing on students' race or ethnicity seldom consider SES within racial or ethnic groups, and studies on ELL students' science learning seldom consider its relationship to students' home language and culture. Future research needs to conceptualize the interrelated effects of race, ethnicity, culture, language, and SES on students' science learning in more nuanced ways (Lemke, 2001). For example, while the intersections that influence student identity formation are being studied in more sophisticated ways in sociology, anthropology, and social psychology, these perspectives have rarely been applied to research on school science learning. In studies involving ELL students, research should build upon new ideas coming out of research in language and literacy education when considering relationships among content learning, literacy development, and English proficiency.

There is a special need for studies that combine cognitive, cultural, sociolinguistic, and sociopolitical perspectives on science learning, rather than focusing on only one aspect to the exclusion of others. This will require multidisciplinary efforts to bring together research traditions that have generally been developed in isolation from one another.

Diversity of Student Experiences in Relation to Science Curriculum and Instruction.
Another area where further research is needed is a focus on the cultural and linguistic experiences that students from diverse backgrounds bring to the science classroom, and how these experiences can be connected to science learning (Lee & Fradd, 1998; Warren, Ballenger, et al., 2001). Researchers should work to clearly identify students' cultural and linguistic experiences that can serve as intellectual resources for science learning, as well as their beliefs and practices that may be discontinuous with the normal view of the science disciplines. This research requires a balanced view of non-mainstream students' intellectual resources as well as of the challenges they face in learning science. Ideologically driven research that focuses only on students' strengths or only on their weaknesses is less useful to teachers who are struggling to both engage students in meaningful learning and help them demonstrate that learning on standardized outcome measures.

Another area for future research concerns the demands involved in learning science through inquiry. Although current reforms in science education emphasize inquiry as the core of science teaching and learning (NRC, 1996, 2000), engaging in science inquiry presents challenges to many students (and many teachers as well) because it requires a range of skills including a critical stance, scientific skepticism, a tolerance for uncertainty and ambiguity, and patience. These challenges are greater for students coming from backgrounds that do not encourage inquiry practices (Aikenhead & Jegede, 1999), those who have limited experience with school science (Moje et al., 2001; Songer et al., 2003), and those who do not see the relevance of science to their daily lives or to their future (Gilbert & Yerrick, 2001). Research has emphasized the importance of role models, trust, and personal connections between teachers and non-mainstream students as the starting point for participation in science inquiry (Sconiers & Rosiek, 2000; Seiler, 2001; Tobin, 2000; Tobin, Seiler, & Walls, 1999). Future research may identify other essential aspects of inquiry-based teaching and learning, and how these can be identified, supported, and developed in the science learning experiences of non-mainstream students.

The use of computer technology in science curriculum and instruction has yet to play a major role in studies on creating more equitable science learning opportunities. The limited research on science instruction that employs interactive Web-based technology shows promising outcomes in urban schools (e.g., LeTUS and Kids as Global Scientists). Further research in this vein may provide more detailed descriptions of how computer technology in science classrooms can support science learning for non-mainstream students.

Teacher Education. The literature reported throughout this book is full of accounts of the difficulties that teachers experience in teaching science to non-mainstream students (Bryan & Atwater, 2002). While some teachers have low expectations of non-mainstream students and blame students, their families, or their cultural environments for academic failure, even teachers who hold empowering views of their non-mainstream students still face challenges related to student diversity in their teaching. These problems are likely to be exacerbated as diversity within the teaching population fails to keep pace with increasing diversity among the student population (Jorgenson, 2000).

Teachers do not need to share the same racial or ethnic background as their students in order to teach the students effectively (Ladson-Billings, 1994, 1995). However, effective teachers generally have an understanding of their students' language and culture and the ability to connect their students' experiences with science in ways that are meaningful and relevant as well as scientifically accurate. While many teachers may lack the cultural knowledge necessary to identify students' academic strengths and funds of knowledge, even teachers with the relevant cultural understandings may be unsure of how to relate their students' experiences to science learning (Lee, 2004). Teacher education programs need to incorporate more in-depth treatment of issues related to student diversity in science instruction.

Future research is needed to address how to design teacher education programs to better enable pre-service and in-service teachers to connect science content with students' cultural and linguistic practices. More research is also needed to examine how teachers' knowledge, beliefs, and practices evolve as they work to integrate the science, cultural, and linguistic domains. In addition, further research should examine the challenges involved in changing the beliefs and practices of teachers who ignore student diversity, resist multicultural views, or reproduce racism through their teaching practice (Ladson-Billings, 1999; Tate, 2001). Some educators (Delpit, 2003; Hilliard, 2003) have argued that an overemphasis on racial and ethnic minority students' academic failure in teacher education programs feeds stereotypes and lowers teachers' expectations of their students' future. From this perspective, research on preparation of pre-service K–12 science teachers should examine the relationship between the content of teacher preparation programs and teachers' subsequent notions of students' science knowledge and abilities.

Teacher professional development programs that have been the most successful in promoting fundamental changes in teachers' knowledge, beliefs, and practices with non-mainstream students have tended to involve small numbers of committed teachers over an extended period of time (Wilson & Berne, 1999). Effective teacher professional development to support more equitable science teaching of non-mainstream students requires time, resources, and personal commitment on the part of both teachers and teacher educators. Future research should examine what is involved in taking this sort of effective teacher education model to scale. Research is also needed to examine the relationship between resources required and the impact of an innovation in terms of both the number of teachers, schools, districts, or states affected and the sustainability of the impact (Coburn, 2003). Such research is likely to intersect with policies that guide decision making about teacher education at the state level—another topic that deserves further investigation (Cochran-Smith & Zeichner, 2005).

High-Stakes Assessment and Accountability Policy.
Current high-stakes assessment and accountability policies are particularly consequential for non-mainstream students (Abedi, 2004; Abedi et al., 2004). After a decade of high-stakes assessment in reading, writing, and mathematics, more states are now moving to incorporate science and social studies into their accountability policies.

Policy changes at the federal and state levels may bring about dramatic changes in science education. A culture of decision making based on high-stakes assessment already dominates the teaching landscape. For example, an emphasis on discrete facts and basic skills on high-stakes science assessments discourages many teachers from taking time to promote deeper understandings of big ideas or inquiry practices in science (Marx & Harris, 2006; Settlage & Meadows, 2002). Complex issues around high-stakes assessments abound, such as which students are to be included or excluded in accountability systems, what assessment accommodations are appropriate for students with special testing needs including ELL students, and how science content knowledge may be assessed separately from English proficiency or general literacy (Shaw, 1997; Siegel, 2007). A basic concern is that ELL students' science achievement is underestimated when they are not allowed to demonstrate their knowledge and abilities in their home language (Solano-Flores, 2008; Solano-Flores & Trumbull, 2003). Yet, if science instruction has been taught predominantly or exclusively in English, simply assessing ELL students in the home language will not guarantee an accurate picture of their science knowledge and abilities since they may not possess academic language or literacy skills in their home language (Kieffer et al., 2009).

Future research should examine the impact of policy changes on various aspects of science education, for example, to what degree does teaching for inquiry and reasoning also prepare students for high-stakes assessment (and vice versa), or what trade-offs occur during attempts to achieve both aims simultaneously. From an equity perspective, research may examine whether recent policy changes differentially affect students from different backgrounds and what institutional, social, and political factors lead to those policies.

School Science and Home/Community Connections. Students' early cultural and linguistic experiences occur in their homes and communities. If science education is to build on students' experiences, educators need a more complete knowledge base about the norms, practices, and expectations that exist in students' homes and communities. Unfortunately, research on the connection between school science and students' home and community environments is very limited. As a result, school science tends to be presented exclusively from the perspective of Western modern science, without adequate consideration of how science-related activities have been carried out in diverse cultures over time. Too often, the task of bridging the worlds of home and school falls almost exclusively to the students, with little support or guidance from either teachers (who may not understand the home culture) or parents (who may not understand the school culture). Thus students may be forced to choose one worldview at the cost of the other (Aikenhead & Jegede, 1999; Jegede & Aikenhead, 1999; Snively & Corsiglia, 2001). Given this dilemma, it is not surprising that non-mainstream students are often underrepresented and disenfranchised in science.

Future research on equitable science learning opportunities should give a high priority to examining the science-related funds of knowledge that exist in diverse contexts and communities (Basu & Calabrese Barton, 2007; Bouillion & Gomez, 2001; Rodriguez & Berryman, 2002). Given the strong emphasis on the experiences of non-mainstream students in urban centers in the literature, study of the funds of knowledge of non-mainstream students in rural communities, such as families of migrant agricultural workers, could be fruitful. Such research may focus on how parents and other community members can serve as resources for school-based science learning, or how community-based projects can help students recognize the meaning and relevance of science for their daily lives and for their future.

SUMMARY

The literature on the intersection of school science and student diversity is currently insufficient for the task of effectively explaining and addressing persistent gaps in science outcomes, but it does point in some promising directions. Deeper examination of the complex relationships among factors that influence science outcomes, combined with greater attention to the potential contributions of multiple theoretical perspectives and methodological approaches, should produce powerful additions to the existing knowledge in this emerging field. Just as non-mainstream students must become bicultural and bilingual border crossers in order to gain access to the discourse and practice of science, teachers must learn to cross cultural boundaries in order to make school science meaningful and relevant for all their students. Similarly, researchers must learn to cross borders between different theoretical and methodological traditions, if they are to disentangle the complex connections between student diversity and science education. Furthermore, policy makers must shape the policy contexts to allow a balance between the need for standards and accountability and an understanding of student diversity and teacher professionalism.

ACTIVITIES FOR CHAPTER 10

1. Think about your own teaching experiences to date in light of the conclusions drawn in this book. In what ways have you been successful in meeting the learning needs of your non-mainstream students? In what ways do you think you could improve in meeting the learning needs of your non-mainstream students?

   A. Create a personal action plan of two to three concrete areas where you would like to focus on better meeting the needs of your non-mainstream students in the coming year. For each area, consider the following questions:

      i. Describe the area of improvement as clearly and concretely as possible. What is the problem you want to address?

      ii. What would it look like if improvement is made? What would you see taking place in your classroom that would be different from what has taken place in the past? What would you be doing differently? What would your students be doing differently? What would parents be doing differently? And so forth.

      iii. What timeline is reasonable to see different aspects of these changes take place?

      iv. What specific and measurable outcomes would indicate success?

   B. For each area you wish to focus on, create a one-page document that spells out your action plan addressing items i through iv above.

   C. Share your action plan with at least one colleague, as well as your plan to meet with him or her periodically over the next school year to discuss your progress.

2. Researchers are sometimes guilty of not listening closely enough to the needs of teachers when designing and implementing their research projects. Based on your teaching experiences, what research questions do you think are most important for researchers to be asking in order to improve science education with non-mainstream students? Work with a partner to make a list of three questions and reasons for why you think knowing the answers to these questions would improve the educational experiences of non-mainstream students.

CHAPTER 11

Educational Practices and Policies

While researchers are engaged in the gradual work of trying to better understand the factors that influence effective science teaching and learning, educators and policy makers are faced with the imperative of providing effective instruction for all students, including those who have traditionally been underrepresented in the sciences and underserved in science education. While the U.S. student population grows increasingly more diverse, science achievement gaps among demographic groups persist. At the same time, non-mainstream students now count toward science accountability under NCLB (although not yet included in AYP), which is historically unprecedented.

To promote equitable science education in the midst of expanding student diversity, science educators must not only value and respect the experiences that non-mainstream students bring from their home and community environments, but learn to actively build upon them. Science educators must help students articulate their cultural and linguistic knowledge with the science disciplines, and offer the material and human resources needed to support their learning. Policies and practices at every level of the education system should be aligned to provide equitable learning opportunities for all students. The call for systemic reform in science education is now 2 decades old, but reforms to date have largely been piecemeal rather than integrated. When provided with appropriate opportunities, non-mainstream students are capable of demonstrating high science achievement, expressing agency in learning science, and developing positive science learner identities. The findings of the studies discussed in this book lead to the conclusion that many, if not most, of the academic difficulties faced by non-mainstream students in the science classroom are rooted in the education system serving them, rather than in the students, their families, or their communities.

EDUCATIONAL PRACTICES

The traditional approach to science education grounded in the assumption that science is universal and culture-free has often forced non-mainstream students to choose between maintaining their linguistic and cultural identities and adopting identities as science learners. By questioning the dominance of Western modern science, multicultural science educators place race, ethnicity, culture, language, and SES at the center of the science teaching and learning process. From the multicultural perspective, effective science education connects the specific demands of science disciplines with students' linguistic, cultural, and socioeconomic experiences.

Instruction. Students of all backgrounds should be provided with academically challenging learning opportunities that allow them to explore scientific phenomena and construct scientific meanings based on their own linguistic and cultural experiences. Too often, non-mainstream students have been taught through direct instruction of basic skills, placed in low-track classes with low academic expectations, and pulled out of science classrooms to receive instruction in basic literacy and numeracy. Such practices place non-mainstream students further and further behind in learning science.

To promote academically rigorous and culturally relevant science instruction, some students may need more explicit guidance to connect their cultural and linguistic experiences with scientific knowledge and practices. Teachers need to take students' differing needs into account when deciding how much explicit instruction to provide and to what degree students can assume responsibility for their own learning (Fradd & Lee, 1999; Lee, 2002). The proper balance of teacher-directed and student-initiated activities depends on the degree of continuity or discontinuity between science disciplines and students' backgrounds, the extent of students' prior experience with science investigations, and the level of cognitive difficulty of science tasks. Teachers need to decide when and how to provide explicit instruction and how to scaffold specific inquiry tasks appropriately for their students.

While hands-on, inquiry-based science provides essential opportunities for all students to engage in science practice and develop scientific understanding, these experiences are particularly important for non-mainstream students to support the integration of doing, knowing, and talking science. However, many teachers, particularly those without adequate science backgrounds themselves, consider hands-on to be synonymous with science inquiry. Teachers' use of hands-on activities without engaging in the discussions necessary to foster student thinking and reasoning can easily turn into activity mania. Students may enjoy participating in hands-on activities, but may gain little or no conceptual understanding that the activities are meant to develop. Furthermore, hands-on activities are often conducted using a cookbook approach that does not foster reasoning or understanding. Thus, it is critically important that teachers make the distinction between hands-on and minds-on science teaching to promote scientific inquiry and understanding (NRC, 2000).

In contrast to the common focus on the deficits and academic failures of non-mainstream students, other literature has also highlighted educational settings in which non-mainstream students achieve academic excellence (Hilliard, 2003;

Ladson-Billings, 1994). This work has not focused specifically on science education, but does make a compelling case for challenging the traditional explanations of achievement gaps. Science education researchers would benefit from examining science instruction in these academically high-achieving settings.

Curriculum. Science curriculum materials for non-mainstream students require attention at multiple levels if they are to be effective. All students need to be challenged by a rigorous science curriculum that is aligned with reform-oriented practices as outlined by national and state science content standards (Kesidou & Roseman, 2002; NSF, 1996). However, when teaching non-mainstream students, science curriculum materials need to take into account additional issues related to culture, language, worldview, and SES (NSF, 1998). There are some inherent tensions in attempts to design curriculum materials to best meet the needs of all students and those designed to target specific student groups. One possible approach could be to develop multiple versions of curriculum materials targeted for specific cultural groups by incorporating analogies, examples, and artifacts relevant to each group. Another approach could be to adapt curriculum materials for different language groups (not literal translation).

In the current context of high-stakes assessments and accountability, science curriculum materials need to be aligned with state content standards. On the one hand, although state assessments may not necessarily be good measures of science achievement, preparing all students to perform well on these assessments is an important equity issue. Curriculum materials that are standards-based have a better chance to convince teachers that all their students, regardless of background, can learn the science they need to perform well on high-stakes assessments. On the other hand, state science standards need to be thought of as the floor rather than the ceiling when it comes to science curriculum. Curriculum materials can and should focus on more than just standards. As many of the studies on science instruction (Chapter 4) and curriculum (Chapter 5) have pointed out, science must be made relevant and accessible to non-mainstream students before students are likely to be either willing or able to embrace standards-based curriculum. Thus, for non-mainstream students, curriculum materials need to be aligned with their lives as well as standards.

Assessment. Given the body of evidence that the validity and fairness of science assessments are jeopardized for non-mainstream students due to cultural and linguistic properties of the assessments, we need a clearer and more complete understanding of how to design science assessments for non-mainstream students. Assessment designers should take into account the components (e.g., content of items, tasks, item format, wording) that are differentially difficult for non-mainstream students. For example, the content of items and tasks should be relevant to students' experiences in school and/or at home.

In addition to understanding why and how linguistic and cultural factors can adversely impact the validity and fairness of test scores of non-mainstream students, it is important to develop assessments that are sensitive to linguistic and cultural differences among student groups. For example, accommodation strategies that reduce the linguistic complexity of science assessments may lessen the impact of bias, a result that has been demonstrated in mathematics assessment (Abedi & Lord, 2001). Similarly, science assessments conducted in English with ELL students are assessments of English proficiency as much as assessments of science knowledge. Testing accommodations should be provided to ELL students so that they can demonstrate their science knowledge separate from levels of English proficiency or general literacy. Such accommodations may include assessments conducted in ELL students' home language(s) in addition to English.

Standardized testing should be thought of as only one part of a classroom assessment program. Diagnostic assessments are needed to evaluate students' prior knowledge and to better target instruction to their learning needs. Ongoing, formative assessments (e.g., portfolios, student interviews, lab practicums, and group presentations) allow non-mainstream students to express what they have learned in different ways that may better highlight academic strengths. Teacher-created summative assessments, whether traditional tests or alternative assessments (e.g., exhibitions or concept maps), can be closely matched to the science content that was taught. Together, this range of assessments can paint a more accurate picture of what the students are learning than what standardized tests are likely to measure.

ELL Students. ELL students face a unique challenge of learning science in a second (or sometimes third) language that they are still in the process of acquiring. In many educational settings, beginning or emergent ELL students are initially given intensive language instruction through ESOL programs, often at the expense of content area instruction. English language and literacy development in such ESOL programs is rarely taught in the context of grade-appropriate academic learning. Instead, the language instruction tends to focus on basic interpersonal communication skills with much less emphasis on the academic language that is necessary for ELL students to succeed in school. As the studies described in this book have pointed out, this traditional approach is limiting to ELL students' opportunities to learn science.

Despite the additional challenges facing less English proficient students, these students should not be asked to wait to engage in rigorous academic learning until their English proficiency is determined to be at an acceptable level. Such practices are inequitable, not only because they force students to fall further behind their grade-level peers in academic learning, but also because the very same academic learning that they miss can promote further development of English language and literacy. For today's ELL students, an unforgiving clock is ticking that will determine their long-term academic success or failure. Current accountability policy demands high academic achievement from all students, with little delay granted for ESOL status. It is incumbent upon educators to help all students meet this challenge.

Coordination of curriculum and instruction across grade levels within schools should be fostered to provide ELL students with a sense of continuity and consistency as they gradually acquire English proficiency and academic content knowledge. While the learning needs of ELL students require these concerted and systemic efforts as an issue of equitable learning opportunity and educational accountability, the research outlined in this book also supports the claim, long made by ESOL educators, that effective teaching practices for ELL students are effective practices for all students. Thus, special efforts made on the part of ELL students are not detracting from the learning opportunities of non-ELL students in the same classrooms.

Professional Development. Teachers are the key to educational innovations and improvements, and the success of any professional development project relies on considering teachers' perspectives while enabling teachers to adopt reform-oriented practices. As our nation's schools become increasingly diverse, there is a growing awareness that today's teachers need a broader array of knowledge, skills, and dispositions to provide equitable learning opportunities for all students. Despite this trend, only limited progress has been made in addressing the professional development needs of teachers to better prepare them to succeed in today's culturally and linguistically diverse classrooms.

There are several reasons for these shortcomings in professional development, which are magnified in large urban school districts where non-mainstream students tend to be concentrated. First, professional development is often *strategy-focused* and rarely attempts to conceptualize or address the multiple challenges of promoting classroom practices that are both rigorous and equitable. Second, even when professional development efforts do address multiple classroom challenges simultaneously, an awareness of complexity does not necessarily translate into a workable model of professional development or classroom practice. For professional development to be both comprehensive and self-sustaining, it must be convincing to teachers and school administrators in terms of how it addresses both the learning needs of the students and the accountability needs of the school. This is especially true for professional development efforts in urban schools, where student diversity highlights the woes of educational inequity.

One approach to professional development that has guided some of the studies described in this book is to build on the strengths and limitations of teachers' knowledge and practices. Professional development in this vein helps teachers to recognize and capitalize on their strengths, while also identifying and building capacity in their areas of weakness. For example, elementary school teachers are generally more comfortable teaching language arts than science. When they have opportunities to become familiar with science teaching practices, they are more likely to recognize the benefits of integrating science with English literacy for ELL students. In contrast, secondary school science teachers generally feel more competent with their science knowledge, but often do not view the teaching of English literacy for ELL students as part of their responsibility. Secondary science teachers need professional development opportunities to integrate explicit literacy goals into their science teaching. Furthermore, teachers who share the language and culture of their students often have a greater understanding of linguistic and cultural resources that their students bring to the science classroom. Just as science teachers need to be sensitive to the linguistic, cultural, and socioeconomic experiences of diverse groups of students, professional development facilitators need to be sensitive to and build upon the strengths and limitations of diverse groups of teachers.

Another approach to professional development is to help teachers focus their instruction on promoting student reasoning and problem solving rather than limiting their focus to teaching facts and concepts. In other words, professional development can help teachers reconceptualize their goal from curriculum coverage to helping their students learn to think. When professional development makes use of reform-oriented curriculum materials, it should also provide the opportunity for teachers to fully realize the intentions of those curriculum materials. A hallmark of reform-oriented curriculum materials is that they use science content as a way to teach thinking processes, including science inquiry, reasoning, and the nature or science. Strategies for teaching these thinking processes need to be explicitly embedded in the curriculum, following the notion of *educative curriculum materials* (Davis & Krajcik, 2005).

Still another approach to professional development focuses on enabling teachers to recognize, value, and apply students' home language and culture in science instruction. By using specific examples that highlight students' funds of knowledge from their home and community, professional development of this type can help teachers understand how prior knowledge from outside the school setting can promote student learning of school science. Professional development can help teachers think about where students' ideas come from and how these ideas develop based on both formal and informal experiences. The latest synthesis of research on science learning by the National Research Council panel (including panel member Okhee Lee, the first author of the book) makes it clear that non-mainstream students bring rich science-related experiences from their home and community, and that these experiences should be used to support students' engagement in academically rigorous tasks in science classrooms (NRC, 2007).

The ultimate test of the effectiveness of professional development is sustainability of the intervention and long-term success in improving student learning. If professional development projects are truly effective in changing teachers' beliefs and practices regarding the teaching of science to non-mainstream students, then those changes will be sustained in classroom practices after the professional development project has concluded. Those new practices will become part of the teachers' permanent repertoire. Professional development projects bring benefits to teachers, such as stipends, graduate or recertification credits, curriculum materials, instructional supplies, classroom support, or enhanced status. When the professional development project ends, these benefits usually end as well, and teachers may return to former practices. If the new practices end when the intervention is over, the professional development efforts will not have a lasting impact for teachers or for students. This is especially true when there are policy pressures pushing teachers away from the goals of the professional development (such as a push for explicit test preparation in response to high-stakes testing and accountability measures). Given the multitude of challenges in teaching science to non-mainstream students, the question remains as to how professional development can create conditions whereby teachers are likely to sustain content-rich and reform-oriented practices in teaching science to non-mainstream students once they exit the professional development intervention.

EDUCATIONAL POLICIES

Because science has traditionally not been included in state accountability measures, science education has not received high priority compared to the core subjects of language arts and mathematics. Although NCLB began requiring science assessments in 2007, science is not yet part of AYP. Some states include science for state accountability, but, at present, no state includes science as an additional academic indicator for AYP. Science instruction for non-mainstream students needs to be considered in the context of standards-based instruction, high-stakes assessments, and accountability policies (Penfield & Lee, in press; Shaver et al., 2007). Special attention must be paid to urban schools, where non-mainstream students tend to be concentrated, and where sanctions against poor academic performance are disproportionately leveled (Settlage & Meadows, 2002). All students, especially those who have traditionally performed poorly in science, must be provided with equitable learning opportunities. States, districts, and schools should consider how they allocate material and human resources to support non-mainstream students in learning rigorous science standards and closing science achievement gaps.

Instruction. Effective instruction involves more than an understanding of best practices, but also requires concerted and systemic efforts, such as legislative support for educational policies and administrative support for classroom practices. First, at the elementary school level, instructional time for science should be ensured in low-performing urban schools, where science instruction is too often pushed aside due to the urgency of developing basic literacy and numeracy. This concern is more pronounced if science is not part of state accountability while reading, writing, and mathematics make up the bulk of instructional time during the school day.

Second, science instructional materials and supplies should be provided to support hands-on science. Hands-on science activities are particularly effective with ELL students and other non-mainstream students who have experienced only limited formal school science. In reality, many elementary schools lack appropriate science instructional materials and supplies, or the personnel and funding to keep the materials organized, consumables resupplied, and lab space set up to accommodate large class sizes. These science-specific supply problems are often exacerbated by a more generalized lack of resources and funding in urban schools.

Third, all of the lessons that have been learned about effective instructional practices for teaching science to non-mainstream students are irrelevant if school or district policies mandate that what limited science time is available must be spent for test preparation drills. The research evidence presented in this book is clear—non-mainstream students need opportunities to engage in hands-on, inquiry-based science that connects new learning to prior knowledge from home, community, and former schooling. If policies prevent or severely curtail these opportunities, there is little hope of reducing achievement gaps.

Curriculum. While science curriculum for student diversity often focuses on developing materials for specific student groups, standardized science curriculum is intended for large-scale implementation across a wide range of student groups or educational settings. The competing goals of localization using culturally relevant curriculum, on one hand, and large-scale implementation using standardized curriculum, on the other hand, present unique challenges. The demand for localized knowledge in culturally relevant curriculum reduces its applicability to student groups other than those originally intended, whereas large-scale implementation of standardized curriculum requires adaptations and modifications to account for local educational settings. The tensions between these two competing goals have grown more serious in the context of high-stakes science assessment and accountability policies for all students. School-level decision making has become increasingly driven by triage calculations in which groups of students who may be able to increase their test scores enough to push school grades to the next achievement level are given extra attention. Other students are correspondingly given less attention, an ironic perversion of "no child left behind." When curriculum decisions are driven by the impact of students' test scores on school grades, rather than by student learning goals, the challenge of innovative curriculum development efforts is to ensure equitable learning opportunities for non-mainstream students.

Educational policies should support the efforts of curriculum developers and teachers to develop, adapt, and modify curriculum materials so that they can incorporate non-mainstream students' linguistic and cultural experiences. Educational policies should acknowledge that curriculum materials are not meant to be used in a one-size-fits-all manner, but rather as flexible guidelines that need to be adapted and modified in response to the needs of particular student groups and local settings.

Assessment. The current policies of high-stakes assessments and accountability are the driving force behind most current educational decision making at the school, district, and state levels. This applies to subject areas that are not tested as well as those that are tested. These high-stakes assessments are meant to drive reforms in curriculum and instruction, following the old adage that what gets tested is what gets taught. Thus, the goals that an education system has for student learning in a given content area should be visible in the assessments that are used. If the education system wants science teaching that is based on inquiry and problem solving, then assessment items need to test these abilities. If high-stakes assessments focus on factual recall, then curriculum and instruction will adopt that focus. Currently, there is a disconnect in many states between the stated goals of science content standards and the nature of science assessments. In the case of such discrepancies, it is the assessments rather than the standards that will shape instructional practices.

High-stakes assessments that are large-scale also face enormous pragmatic challenges, such as how much content can be covered within a limited number of test items, how much it costs to test all students, how often students should be tested, how tests will be scored, how test results will be reported, and so forth. With non-mainstream students, there are fundamental issues of validity and fairness of testing. Again, there is an inherent tension between standardization of test content and administration, and accommodations for the needs of specific student groups.

Given these complex trade-offs, decisions are sometimes made to maximize the validity and fairness for all students, at the expense of supporting the unique needs of specific student groups or individual students. For example, although performance assessments to demonstrate students' abilities to engage in hands-on inquiry tasks may be cost prohibitive or not feasible for large-scale testing, test items can attempt to capture students' understanding of hands-on inquiry using written forms and graphic representations. Considering the limited English proficiency of ELL students as well as other students with limited literacy, their written responses could be scored for the accuracy of content in multiple formats (written, graphic, pictorial, and so forth), separate from the quality of their writing. Although it may not be feasible to design test items without bias against any groups of students, test developers can go a long way toward avoiding blatant biases based on racial, ethnic, cultural, linguistic, and socioeconomic groups. In short, large-scale assessment policy should consider these variables throughout the process to establish the validity and fairness for all students, especially non-mainstream students.

Once achievement data become available, these data should be disaggregated in multiple ways to identify gaps among demographic subgroups. Ongoing examination of disaggregated student outcomes can alert school, district, and state leaders and policy makers as to how to reallocate and redistribute resources.

ELL Students. With more and more states adopting English-only policies, ELL students have less access to academic content presented in their home language. This puts an enormous burden on ELL students to acquire English proficiency and learn academic content with little or no instructional support in their home language. However, even in English-only policy contexts where formal home language instruction is prohibited, educational policies should encourage ELL students and their teachers to use the students' home language as instructional support to promote science learning (Goldenberg, 2008). For example, in small group settings where students engage in hands-on inquiry, code-switching is a common phenomenon as students conceptualize and verbalize their developing understandings of science content in their home language. These conversations should be encouraged, even when the teacher does not speak students' home language. In addition, the language of science derives from Romance languages rooted in Latin, and cognates help ELL students understand science vocabulary in their home language.

English-only policies apply beyond classroom instruction to all other areas of science education as well. Science curriculum materials in languages other than English have always been difficult to find. Existing curriculum materials often place inappropriate language demands on ELL students. Assessments are rarely conducted in students' home languages, and existing assessment instruments are not sensitive to language demands on ELL students. In short, even in the context of the English-only policy, home language supports can and should be provided in all aspects of science education with ELL students, including curriculum materials and assessment instruments in students' home languages or bilingual paraprofessionals to help ELL students learn and demonstrate science content knowledge.

Professional Development. Teachers require extensive support to teach reform-oriented science to all students. They need to be knowledgeable of science content standards and be comfortable engaging in inquiry-based science themselves. In addition, they need the knowledge and abilities to articulate the specific demands of science learning with students' linguistic and cultural experiences. Teachers who voluntarily seek out professional development opportunities are already attuned to the need to improve their knowledge and practices. A challenge in developing policy to support effective professional development involves reaching those teachers who are less open to reform-oriented practices or less willing to improve their teaching practices. The need is urgent in urban schools where the preparation of the teaching force tends to be low, with large numbers of beginning teachers or those without certification in their fields.

Educational policies should provide opportunities for schoolwide professional development and should include teachers who normally do not volunteer for such opportunities. In addition, collective participation of teachers from the same school, department, or grade level can promote strategic allocation of material resources and human and social capital within the school. Such endeavors require extensive financial and human resources, however, which are not possible without supportive policies in place.

Urban schools face unique challenges for teacher professional development, including high rates of student and teacher mobility. Not only does mobility impede student achievement, but it also impedes researchers' ability to identify which interventions are most effective for enhancing achievement. First, teacher and student mobility may compromise the *fidelity of implementation* of an intervention, since the impact of any intervention may depend on exposure. Second, mobility raises an important issue in conducting evaluation of the *efficacy* of an intervention, or how well the intervention works under optimal or extremely favorable conditions. Third, mobility raises an important issue in conducting evaluations of the *effectiveness* of an intervention, or how well the intervention works under resource constraints in typical settings. Finally, mobility underestimates *student achievement*, which, in turn, underestimates the potential (true) effect of the intervention. Educational researchers, curriculum developers, and policy makers alike must consider teacher and student mobility issues in designing, implementing, and evaluating educational interventions in urban settings in order to reach those students who need such interventions the most.

SUMMARY

Education practices and policies need to work in unison to support teacher effectiveness and improve student learning. This is true for all content areas and for all students. It is even more true when either the content area or the students in question is marginalized. In the case of teaching science to non-mainstream students, the marginalization both of content and of students runs deep. Non-mainstream students rarely receive the variety of high-quality, inquiry-based science learning opportunities that are typically available to White, middle-class, suburban youth.

The research studies described in this book go a long way toward pointing out both the challenges and the opportunities that arise when considering how to improve the science education of non-mainstream students. There are many hurdles, but many benefits as well. Much more research is needed to fully understand the best ways to move forward. Yet, much is already known that can guide educational practice and policy. It is our hope that by pulling together and synthesizing what is known, we can provide a road map for teachers, administrators, teacher educators, researchers, and policy makers who are interested in making a difference in improving science education for non-mainstream students. It will take a concerted effort by all the stakeholders, but this work is essential to create more equitable learning opportunities for all students. There has been much rhetoric about educational policies that are meant to leave no child behind. A great deal of work remains to be done before such claim can be taken seriously.

ACTIVITIES FOR CHAPTER 11

1. This book has addressed a wide range of practices that research has shown can improve science learning with non-mainstream students. Some of these practices are related to instruction, some to curriculum, some to assessment, some to professional development, and some to school organization. The need to consider and juggle all of these features is a major challenge for teachers. It is at least as challenging for school administrators. Imagine that you are the principal of your school (or another hypothetical school if you prefer).
   A. Briefly describe your school.
   B. Make an outline of the part of your school improvement plan that deals with science education. Consider the following questions:
      i. Think about the lessons learned from research that have been described in this book. How should these lessons influence your school improvement plan?
      ii. What would you focus on?
      iii. What choices would you have to make?
      iv. How would you organize students? Teachers?
      v. What features would you look for in instructional practices?
      vi. What features would you look for in curriculum materials?
      vii. What features would you look for in assessments?
      viii. What kinds of professional development would you seek for your staff?
      ix. How would you allocate material and human resources?
   C. Be prepared to discuss your plan with other members of your class.
2. The book has also addressed a wide range of educational policies that research has shown can improve science learning with non-mainstream students. Policy makers need to make difficult decisions based on budget, the perceived desires of constituents, and their own understanding of the issues. Imagine that you are a state legislator who is serving on the education subcommittee for your state. You are asked to make a prioritized list of potential policies that could serve to improve science education for the students in your state.

A. Use what you have learned in this book to generate your list of at least five policy measures, paying particular attention to issues of equity and the learning needs of non-mainstream students. For each policy, consider the following:
   i. What would the policy entail? Be as specific as you can.
   ii. How should the policy be implemented?
   iii. What types of rewards should be attached to the policy?
   iv. What types of sanctions should be attached to the policy?
   v. What material resources would be needed to carry out the policy?
   vi. What human resources would be needed to carry out the policy?

References

Abedi, J. (2004). The No Child Left Behind *Act* and English language learners: Assessment and accountability issues. *Educational Researcher, 33*(1), 4–14.

Abedi, J., Hofstetter, C. H., & Lord, C. (2004). Assessment accommodations for English language learners: Implications for policy-based empirical research. *Review of Educational Research, 74*(1), 1–28.

Abedi, J., & Lord, C. (2001). The language factor in mathematics tests. *Applied Measurement in Education, 14*, 219–234.

Agar, M. (1996). *Language shock: Understanding the culture of conversation.* New York: William Morrow.

Aikenhead, G. S. (1997). Toward a First Nations cross-cultural science and technology curriculum. *Science Education, 81*(2), 217–238.

Aikenhead, G. S. (2001a). Students' ease in crossing cultural borders into school science. *Science Education, 85*(2), 180–188.

Aikenhead, G. S. (2001b). Integrating Western and aboriginal sciences: Cross-cultural science teaching. *Research in Science Education, 31*(3), 337–355.

Aikenhead, G. S., & Jegede, O. J. (1999). Cross-cultural science education: A cognitive explanation of a cultural phenomenon. *Journal of Research in Science Teaching, 36*(3), 269–287.

Akatugba, A. H., & Wallace, J. (1999). Sociocultural influences on physics students' use of proportional reasoning in a non-Western country. *Journal of Research in Science Teaching, 36*(3), 305–320.

Allen, N. J., & Crawley, F. E. (1998). Voices from the bridge: Worldview conflicts of Kickapoo students of science. *Journal of Research in Science Teaching, 35*(2), 111–132.

Amaral, O. M., Garrison, L., & Klentschy, M. (2002). Helping English learners increase achievement through inquiry-based science instruction. *Bilingual Research Journal, 26*(2), 213–239.

American Anthropological Association. (1998). *Statement on "race."* Available online, retrieved October 26, 2009, from www.aaanet.org/stmts/racepp.htm

American Association for the Advancement of Science. (1989). *Science for all Americans.* New York: Oxford University Press.

American Association for the Advancement of Science. (1993). *Benchmarks for science literacy.* New York: Oxford University Press.

Amrein, A. L., & Berliner, D. C. (2002). High-stakes testing, uncertainty, and student learning. *Education Policy Analysis Archives, 10*(18). Retrieved February 5, 2009, from http://epaa.asu.edu/epaa/v10n18/

Arellano, E. L., Barcenal, T., Bilbao, P. P., Castellano, M. A., Nichols, S., & Tippins, D. J. (2001). Case-based pedagogy as a context for collaborative inquiry in the Philippines. *Journal of Research in Science Teaching, 38*(5), 502–528.

Atwater, M. M. (1993). Multicultural science education: Perspectives, definitions, and research agenda. *Science Education, 77*(6), 661–668.

Atwater, M. M. (1994). Research on cultural diversity in the classroom. In D. L. Gabel (Ed.), *Handbook of research on science teaching and learning* (pp. 558–576). New York: Macmillan.

Atwater, M. M. (1996). Social constructivism: Infusion into the multicultural science education research agenda. *Journal of Research in Science Teaching, 33*(8), 821–837.

Atwater, M. M. (2000). Equity for Black Americans in precollege science. *Science Education, 84*(2), 154–179.

Atwater, M. M., & Riley, J. P. (1993). Multicultural science education: Perspectives, definitions, and research agenda. *Science Education, 77,* 661–668.

Au, K. H. (1980). Participation structures in a reading lesson with Hawaiian children: Analysis of a culturally appropriate instructional event. *Anthropology and Education Quarterly, 11*(2), 91–115.

Au, K. H. (1998). Social constructivism and the school literacy learning of students of diverse backgrounds. *Journal of Literacy Research, 30*(2), 297–319.

August, D., & Hakuta, K. (Eds.). (1997). *Improving schooling for language-minority children: A research agenda.* Washington, DC: National Academy Press.

August, D., & Shanahan, T. (Eds.). (2006). *Developing literacy in second-language learners: Report of the national literacy panel on language minority children and youth.* Mahwah, NJ: Lawrence Erlbaum Associates.

Baker, D. P., & Stevenson, D. L. (1986). Mothers' strategies for children's achievement: Managing the transition to high school. *Sociology of Education, 59,* 156–166.

Ball, D. L., & Cohen, D. K. (1996). Reform by the book: What is—or might be—the role of curriculum materials in teacher learning and instructional reform? *Educational Researcher, 25,* 6–8.

Ballenger, C. (1992). Because you like us: The language of control. *Harvard Educational Review, 62*(2), 199–208.

Ballenger, C. (1997). Social identities, moral narratives, scientific argumentation: Science talk in a bilingual classroom. *Language and Education, 11*(1), 1–14.

Banks, J. A. (1993a). Canon debate, knowledge construction, and multicultural education. *Educational Researcher, 22*(5), 4–14.

Banks, J. A. (1993b). Multicultural education: Historical development, dimensions and practice. In L. Darling-Hammond (Ed.), *Review of Research in Education: Vol. 19* (pp. 3–49). Washington, DC: American Educational Research Association.

Banks, J., & McGee Banks, C. A. (1995). Equity pedagogy: An essential component of multicultural education. *Theory into Practice, 34*(3), 152–158.

Barba, R. H. (1993). A study of culturally syntonic variables in the bilingual/bicultural science classroom. *Journal of Research in Science Teaching, 30,* 1053–1071.

Basu, S. J. (2008a). Powerful learners and critical agents: The goals of five urban Caribbean youth in a conceptual physics classroom. *Science Education, 92,* 252–277.

Basu, S. J. (2008b). How students design and enact physics lessons: Five immigrant Caribbean youth and the use of cultivation of student voice. *Journal of Research in Science Teaching, 45*(8), 881–899.

Basu, S. J., & Calabrese Barton, A. (2007). Developing a sustained interest in science among urban minority youth. *Journal of Research in Science Teaching, 44*(3), 466–489.

Bianchini, J. A., & Cavazos, L. M. (2007). Learning from students, inquiry into practice, and participation in professional communities: Beginning teachers' uneven progress toward equitable science teaching. *Journal of Research in Science Teaching, 44*(4), 586–612.

Bianchini, J. A., Cavazos, L. M., & Rivas, M. (2003). At the intersection of the social studies of science and issues of equity and diversity: Student teachers' conceptions of, rationales, and instructional practices. *Journal of Science Teacher Education, 14,* 259–290.

Bianchini, J. A., Johnston, C. C., Oram, S. Y., & Cavazos, L. M. (2003). Learning to teach science in contemporary and equitable ways: The successes and struggles of first-year science teachers. *Science Education, 87*(3), 419–443.

Bianchini, J. A., & Solomon, E. M. (2003). Constructing views of science tied to issues of equity and diversity: A study of beginning science teachers. *Journal of Research in Science Teaching, 40*(1), 53–76.

Bloome, D., Katz, L., Solsken, J., Willett, J., & Wilson-Keenan, J. (2000). Interpellations of family/community and classroom literacy practices. *Journal of Educational Research, 93*(3), 155–63.

Blumenfeld, P., Fishman, B. J., Krajcik, J., & Marx, R. W. (2000). Creating usable innovations in systemic reform: Scaling-up technology embedded project-based science in urban schools. *Educational Psychologist, 26*(3&4), 369–398.

Boone, W. J., & Kahle, J. B. (1998). Student perceptions of instruction, peer interest, and adult support for middle school science: Differences by race and gender. *Journal of Women and Minorities in Science and Engineering, 4*(4), 333–340.

Bouillion, L. M., & Gomez, L. M. (2001). Connecting school and community with science learning: Real world problems and school-community partnerships as contextual scaffolds. *Journal of Research in Science Teaching, 38*(8), 878–898.

Bourdieu, P. (1984). *Distinction: A social critique of the judgment of taste.* London: Routledge.

Boykin, A., & Allen, B. (1988). Rhythmic-movement facilitation of learning in working-class Afro-American children. *Journal of Genetic Psychology, 149,* 333–348.

Boykin, A., & Allen, B. (1999). Enhancing African American children's learning and motivation: Evolution of the verve and movement expressiveness paradigms. In R. Jones (Ed.), *African American children, youth and parenting* (pp. 115–152). Hampton, VA: Cobb & Henry Publishers.

Brand, B. R., & Glasson, G. E. (2004). Crossing cultural borders into science teaching: Early life experiences, racial and ethnic identities, and beliefs about diversity. *Journal of Research in Science Teaching, 41*(2), 119–142.

Brenner, M. E. (1998). Adding cognition to the formula for culturally relevant instruction in mathematics. *Anthropology and Education Quarterly, 29*(2), 213–244.

Brickhouse, N. W. (1994). Bringing in the outsiders: Reshaping the sciences of the future. *Curriculum Studies, 26,* 401–416.

Brickhouse, N. W. (2006). Celebrating 90 years of science education: Reflections on the gold standard and ways of promoting good research. *Science Education, 90,* 1–7.

Brown, A. L. (1992). Design experiments: Theoretical and methodological challenges in creating complex interventions in classroom settings. *The Journal of the Learning Sciences, 2,* 141–178.

Brown, A. L. (1994). The advancement of learning. *Educational Researcher, 23*(8), 4–12.

Brown, B. A. (2004). Discursive identity: Assimilation into the culture of science and its implications for minority students. *Journal of Research in Science Teaching, 41*(8), 810–834.

Brown, B. A. (2006). "It isn't slang that can be said about this stuff": Language, identity, and appropriating science discourse. *Journal of Research in Science Teaching, 43*(1), 96–126.

Brown, B. A., Reveles, J. M., & Kelly, G. J. (2005). Scientific literacy and discursive identity: A theoretical framework for understanding science learning. *Science Education, 89*, 779–802.

Brown, B. A., & Ryoo, K. (2008). Teaching science as a language: A "content-first" approach to science teaching. *Journal of Research in Science Teaching, 45*(5), 529–553.

Brown, B. A., & Spang, E. (2008). Double talk: Synthesizing everyday and science language in the classroom. *Science Education, 92*, 708–732.

Bruna, K. R., & Gomez, K. (Eds.). (2008). *Talking science, writing science: The work of language in multicultural classrooms.* Mahwah, NJ: Taylor and Francis.

Bryan, L. A., & Atwater, M. M. (2002). Teacher beliefs and cultural models: A challenge for science teacher preparation programs. *Science Education, 86*(6), 821–839.

Buck, G. A., & Cordes, J. G. (2005). An action research project on preparing teachers to meet the needs of underserved student populations. *Journal of Science Teacher Education, 16*, 43–64.

Buck, G. A., Mast, C., Ehlers, N., & Franklin, E. (2005). Preparing teachers to create a mainstream science classroom conducive to the needs of English language learners: A feminist action research project. *Journal of Research in Science Teaching, 42*(9), 1013–1031.

Bullock, L. D. (1997). Efficacy of gender and ethnic equity in science education curriculum for preservice teachers. *Journal of Research in Science Teaching, 34*(10), 1019–1038.

Buxton, C. (1998). Improving science education of English language learners: Capitalizing on educational reform. *Journal of Women and Minorities in Science and Engineering, 4*(4), 341–369.

Buxton, C. (2001a). Modeling science teaching on science practice? Painting a more accurate picture through an ethnographic lab study. *Journal of Research in Science Teaching, 38*(4), 387–407.

Buxton, C. (2001b). Feminist science in the case of a reform-minded biology department. *Journal of Women and Minorities in Science and Engineering, 7*(3), 173–199.

Buxton, C. (2005). Creating a culture of academic success in an urban science and math magnet high school. *Science Education, 89*(3), 392–417.

Buxton, C. (2006). Creating contextually authentic science in a "low-performing" urban elementary school. *Journal of Research in Science Teaching, 43*(7), 695–721.

Buxton, C., Carlone, H., & Carlone, D. (2005). Boundary spanners as bridges of student and school discourses in an urban science and math high school. *School Science and Mathematics, 105*(6), 302–312.

Buxton, C., Lee, O., & Santau, A. (2008). Promoting science among English language learners: Professional development for today's culturally and linguistically diverse classrooms. *Journal of Science Teacher Education, 19*(5), 495–511.

Calabrese Barton, A. (1998a). Reframing "science for all" through the politics of poverty. *Educational Policy, 12*, 525–541.

Calabrese Barton, A. (1998b). Teaching science with homeless children: Pedagogy, representation, and identity. *Journal of Research in Science Teaching, 35*(4), 379–394.

Calabrese Barton, A. (1998c). Examining the social and scientific roles of invention in science education. *Research in Science Education, 28*(1), 133–151.

Calabrese Barton, A. (2001). Science education in urban settings: Seeking new ways of praxis through critical ethnography. *Journal of Research in Science Teaching, 38*(8), 899–917.

Calabrese Barton, A., Drake, C., Perez, J. G., St. Louis, K., & George, M. (2004). Ecologies of parental engagement in urban education. *Educational Researcher, 33*(4), 3–12.

Calabrese Barton, A. C., Koch, P., Contento, I., & Hagiwara, S. (2005). From global sustainability to inclusive education: Understanding urban children's ideas about the food system. *International Journal of Science Education, 27*(10), 1163–1186.

Calabrese Barton, A., & Tan, E. (2009). Funds of knowledge and discourses and hybrid space. *Journal of Research in Science Teaching, 46*(1), 50–73.

Calabrese Barton, A., Tan, E., & Rivet, A. (2008). Creating hybrid spaces for engaging school science among urban middle school girls. *American Educational Research Journal, 45*(1), 68–103.

Campbell, J. R., Hombo, C. M., & Mazzeo, J. (2000). *NAEP 1999 trends in academic progress: Three decades of student performance (NCES 2000–469)*. Washington, DC: U.S. Department of Education, National Center for Education Statistics.

Carey, S. (1987). *Conceptual change in childhood* [1st MIT Press ed.]. Cambridge, MA: MIT Press.

Carr, J., Sexton, U., & Lagunoff, R. (2006). *Making science accessible to English learners: A guidebook for teachers*. San Francisco: WestEd.

Carter, L. (2004). Thinking differently about cultural diversity: Using postcolonial theory to (re)read science education. *Science Education, 88*(6), 819–836.

Casteel, C. P., & Isom, B. A. (1994). Reciprocal processes in science and literacy learning. *The Reading Teacher, 47*, 538–545.

Cervetti, G. N., Pearson, P. D., Bravo, M. A., & Barber, J. (2006). Reading and writing in the service of inquiry-based science. In R. Douglas, M. P. Klentschy, K. Worth, & W. Binder (Eds.), *Linking science and literacy in the K–8 classroom* (pp. 221–244). Arlington, VA: National Science Teachers Association.

Champagne, A. (2006). Then and now: Science assessment 1996–2006. *School Science and Mathematics, 106*, 113–123.

Chinn, P. (2007). Decolonizing methodologies and indigenous knowledge: The role of culture, place and personal experience in professional development. *Journal of Research in Science Teaching, 44*(9), 1247–1268.

Chipman, S. F., & Thomas, V. G. (1987). The participation of women and minorities in mathematical, scientific, and technical fields. In E. Z. Rothkopf (Ed.), *Review of Research in Education, Vol. 14* (pp. 387–430). Washington, DC: American Educational Research Association.

Cobern, W. W. (1991*). Worldview theory and science education research (NARST Monograph, No. 3)*. Kansas State University, KS: The National Association for Research in Science Teaching.

Cobern, W. W. (1996). Worldview theory and conceptual change in science education. *Science Education, 80*(5), 579–610.

Cobern, W. W., & Aikenhead, G. S. (1998). Cultural aspects of learning science. In B. Fraser & K. Tobin (Eds.), *International handbook of science education. Part 1* (pp. 39–52). Dordrecht, the Netherlands: Kluwer Academic Publishers.

Coburn, C. E. (2003). Rethinking scale: Moving beyond numbers to deep and lasting change. *Educational Researcher, 32*(6), 3–12.

Cochran-Smith, M. (1995a). Color blindness and basket making are not the answers: Confronting the dilemmas of race, culture, and language diversity in teacher education. *American Educational Research Journal, 32*, 493–522.

Cochran-Smith, M. (1995b). Uncertain allies: Understanding the boundaries of race and teaching. *Harvard Educational Review, 65*, 541–570.

Cochran-Smith, M., & Zeichner, K. M. (2005). Executive summary: The report of the AERA panel on research and teacher education. In M. Cochran-Smith & K. M. Zeichner (Eds.), *Studying teacher education: The report of the AERA panel on research and teacher education* (pp. 1–36). Mahwah, NJ: Lawrence Erlbaum Associates.

Cohen, C., Deterding, N., & Clewell, B. (2005). *Who's left behind?* Baltimore, MD: Urban Institute Press.

Cohen, D. K., & Hill, H. C. (2000). Instructional policy and classroom performance: The mathematics reform in California. *Teachers College Record, 102*(2), 294–343.

Costa, V. B. (1995). When science is "another world": Relationships between worlds of family, friends, school, and science. *Science Education, 79*, 313–333.

Cuevas, P., Lee, O., Hart, J., & Deaktor, R. (2005). Improving science inquiry with elementary students of diverse backgrounds. *Journal of Research in Science Teaching, 42*(3), 337–357.

Damnjanovic, A. (1998). Ohio Statewide Systemic Initiative (SSI) factors associated with urban middle school science achievement: Differences by student sex and race. *Journal of Women and Minorities in Science and Engineering, 4*(2&3), 217–233.

Dane, A. V., & Schneider, B. H. (1998). Program integrity in primary and early secondary prevention: Are implementation effects out of control? *Clinical Psychology Review, 18*(1), 23–45.

Darling-Hammond, L. (1994). Performance-based assessment and educational equity. *Harvard Educational Review, 64*, 5–30.

Darling-Hammond, L. (1996). The right to learn and the advancement of teaching: Research, policy, and practice for democratic education. *Educational Researcher, 25*(6), 5–17.

Davis, E., & Krajcik, J. (2005). Designing educative curriculum materials to promote teacher learning. *Educational Researcher, 34*(3), 3–14.

Deboer, G. E. (2002). Student-centered teaching in a standards-based world: Finding a sensible balance. *Science and Education, 11*(4), 405–417.

Delpit, L. (1988). The silenced dialogue: Power and pedagogy in educating other people's children. *Harvard Educational Review, 58*, 280–298.

Delpit, L. (1995). *Other people's children: Cultural conflict in the classroom*. New York: W. W. Norton.

Delpit, L. (2003). Educators as "seed people" growing a new future. *Educational Researcher, 32*(7), 14–21.

Desimone, L. M., Porter, A. C., Garet, M. S., Yoon, K. S., & Birman, B. F. (2002). Effects of professional development on teachers' instruction: Results from a three-year longitudinal study. *Educational Evaluation & Policy Analysis, 24*(2), 81–112.

Desimone, L. M., Smith, T. M., & Phillips, K. J. R. (2007). Does policy influence mathematics and science teachers' participation in professional development? *Teachers College Record, 109*, 1086–1122.

Deyhle, D., & Swisher, K. (1997). Research in American Indian and Alaska Native education: From assimilation to self-determination. In M. W. Apple (Ed.), *Review of Research in Education: Vol. 22* (pp. 113–194). Washington, DC: American Educational Research Association.

Diamond, J. B., & Spillane, J. P. (2004). High-stakes accountability in urban elementary schools: Challenging or reproducing inequality? *Teachers College Record, 106*(6), 1145–1176.

diSessa, A. & Sherin, B. (1998). What changes in conceptual change? *International Journal of Science Education, 20*(10), 1155–1191.

Domestic Policy Council, Office of Science and Technology Policy. (2006). *American competitiveness initiative: Leading the world in innovation.* Retrieved August 11, 2008, from www.nist.gov/director/reports/ACIBooklet.pdf

Douglas, R., Klentschy, M. P., Worth, K., & Binder, W. (Eds.). (2006). *Linking science and literacy in the K–8 classroom.* Arlington, VA: National Science Teachers Association.

Driver, R., Asoko, H., Leach, J., Mortimer, E., & Scott, P. (1994). Constructing scientific knowledge in the classroom. *Educational Researcher, 23*, 5–12.

Dusenbury, L., Brannigan, R., Falco, M., & Hansen, W. B. (2003). A review of research on fidelity of implementation: Implications for drug abuse prevention in school settings. *Health Education Research, 18*(2), 237–256.

Edmin, C. (2008). The three C's for urban science education. *Phi Delta Kappan, 89*(10), 772–775.

Eisenhart, M., Finkel, E., & Marion, S. F. (1996). Creating the conditions for scientific literacy: A re-examination. *American Educational Research Journal, 33*, 261–295.

Elmesky, R., & Tobin, K. (2005). Expanding our understandings of urban science education by expanding the roles of students as researchers. *Journal of Research in Science Teaching, 42*(7), 807–828.

Elmore, R. (1996). Getting to scale with good educational practice. *Harvard Educational Review, 66*(1), 1–26.

Engec, N. (2006). Relationship between mobility and student performance and behavior. *Journal of Educational Research, 99*(3), 167–178.

Epstein, J. (1987). Parent involvement: What research says to administrators. *Education and Urban Society, 19*, 119–136.

Fathman, A. K., & Crowther, D. T. (Eds.). (2006). *Science for English language learners: K–12 classroom strategies.* Arlington, VA: National Science Teachers Association.

Ferguson, R. (2008). If multicultural science education standards existed, what would they look like? *Journal of Science Teacher Education, 19*(6), 547–564.

Fishman, B., Marx, R. W., Blumenfeld, P., Krajcik, J., & Soloway, E. (2004). Creating a framework for research on systemic technology innovations. *Journal of the Learning Sciences, 13*(1), 43–76.

Fox Keller, E. (1985). *Reflections on gender and science.* New Haven, CT: Yale University Press.

Fradd, S. H., & Lee, O. (1999). Teachers' roles in promoting science inquiry with students from diverse language backgrounds. *Educational Researcher, 28*(6), 4–20, 42.

Fradd, S. H., Lee, O., Sutman, F. X., & Saxton, M. K. (2002). Materials development promoting science inquiry with English language learners: A case study. *Bilingual Research Journal, 25*(4), 479–501.

Furman, M., & Calabrese Barton, B. (2006). Capturing urban student voices in the creation of a science mini-documentary. *Journal of Research in Science Teaching, 43*(7), 667–694.

Fusco, D. (2001). Creating relevant science through urban planning and gardening. *Journal of Research in Science Teaching, 38*(8), 860–877.

Fusco, D., & Calabrese Barton, A. (2001). Representing student achievement in science. *Journal of Research in Science Teaching, 38*(3), 337–354.

Gamoran, A., Anderson, C. W., Quiroz, P. A., Secada, W. G., Williams, T., & Ashmann, S. (2003). *Transforming teaching in math and science: How schools and districts can support change.* New York: Teachers College Press.

Garaway, G. B. (1994). Language, culture, and attitude in mathematics and science learning: A review of the literature. *Journal of Research and Development in Education, 27*(2), 102–111.

Garcia, E. E. (1999). *Student cultural diversity: Understanding and meeting the challenge* (2nd ed.). Boston, MA: Houghton Mifflin Company.

Garcia, E. E., & Curry Rodríguez, J. (2000). The education of limited English proficient students in California schools. *Bilingual Research Journal, 24*(1–3), 15–35.

García, G. E., & Pearson, D. P. (1994). Assessment and diversity. In L. Darling-Hammond (Vol. Ed.), *Review of research in education: Vol. 20* (pp. 337–391). Washington, DC: American Educational Research Association.

Garet, M. S., Porter, A. C., Desimone, L., Birman, B. F., & Yoon, K. S. (2001). What makes professional development effective? Results from a national sample of teachers. *American Educational Research Journal, 38*(4), 915–945.

Gay, G. (2002). Preparing for culturally responsive teaching. *Journal of Teacher Education, 53*(2), 106–116.

Gee, J. (2002). Identity as an analytic lens for research in education. In W. G. Secada (Ed.), *Review of research in education: Vol. 26* (pp. 99–125). Washington, DC: American Educational Research Association.

Geier, R., Blumenfeld, P. C., Marx, R. W., Krajcik, J. S., Fishman, B., Soloway, E., & Clay-Chambers, J. (2008). Standardized test outcomes for students engaged in inquiry-based science curricula in the context of urban reform. *Journal of Research in Science Teaching, 45*, 922–939.

Gilbert, A., & Yerrick, R. (2001). Same school, separate worlds: A sociocultural study of identity, resistance, and negotiation in a rural, lower track science classroom. *Journal of Research in Science Teaching, 38*(5), 574–598.

Giroux, H. (1992). *Border crossings: Cultural workers and the politics of education.* New York: Routledge.

Goldenberg, C. (2008). Teaching English language learners: What the research does—and does not—say. *American Educator, 32*(2), 42–44.

González, N., Moll, L. C., & Amanti, C. (2005). Funds of knowledge: *Theorizing practices in households, communities, and classrooms.* Mahwah, NJ: Erlbaum Associates.

Grandy, J. (1998). Persistence in science of high-ability minority students: Results of a longitudinal study. *Journal of Higher Education, 69*(6), 589–620.

Gutiérrez, K. D., Asato, J., Pacheco, M., Moll, L. C., Olson, K., Horng, E. L., Ruiz, R., García, E., & McCarty, T. (2002). "Sounding American": The consequences of new reforms on English language learners. *Reading Research Quarterly, 37*(3), 328–343.

Gutiérrez, K.D., & Rogoff, B. (2003). Cultural ways of learning: Individual traits or repertoires of practice. *Educational Researcher, 32*(5), 19–25.

Haberman, M. (1988). Proposals for recruiting minority teachers: Promising practices and attractive detours. *Journal of Teacher Education, 33*(4), 38–44.

Hamilton, J. S., Nussbaum, E. M., Kupermintz, H., Kerkhoven, J. I. M., & Snow, R. E. (1995). Enhancing the validity and usefulness of large-scale educational assessments: II. NELS: 88 science achievement. *American Educational Research Journal, 32*(3), 555–581.

Hamilton, L. S. (1998). Gender differences on high school science achievement tests: Do format and content matter? *Educational Evaluation and Policy Analysis, 20*(3), 179–195.

Hammond, L. (2001). An anthropological approach to urban science education for language minority families. *Journal of Research in Science Teaching, 38*(9), 983–999.

Hampton, E., & Rodriguez, R. (2001). Inquiry science in bilingual classrooms. *Bilingual Research Journal, 25*(4), 461–478.

Haraway, D. J. (1990). *Primate visions: Gender, race and nature in the world of modern science*. New York: Routledge.

Haraway, D. J. (1991). *Simians, cyborgs, and women: The reinvention of nature*. New York: Routledge.

Harding, S. (1991). *Whose science? Whose knowledge? Thinking from women's lives*. Ithaca, NY: Cornell University Press.

Hart, J. E., & Lee, O. (2003). Teacher professional development to improve science and literacy achievement of English language learners. *Bilingual Research Journal, 27*(3), 475–501.

Hayes, M. T., & Deyhle, D. (2001). Constructing difference: A comparative study of elementary science curriculum differentiation. *Science Education, 85*(3), 239–262.

Heath, S. B. (1983). *Ways with words: Language, life, and work in communities and classroom*. New York: Cambridge University Press.

Hewson, P. W., Kahle, J. B., Scantlebury, K., & Davies, D. (2001). Equitable science education in urban middle schools: Do reform efforts make a difference? *Journal of Research in Science Teaching, 38*(10), 1130–1144.

Hill, O. W., Pettus, C., & Hedin, B. A. (1990). Three studies of factors affecting the attitudes of blacks and females toward the pursuit. *Journal of Research in Science Teaching, 27*(4), 289–314.

Hilliard, A. G. (2003). No mystery: Closing the achievement gap between Africans and excellence. In T. Perry, C. Steele, & A. G. Hilliard (Eds.), *Young, gifted, and Black: Promoting high achievement among African American students* (pp. 131–165). Boston: Beacon Press.

Hodson, D. (1993). In search of a rationale for multicultural science education. *Science Education, 77*(6), 685–711.

Hodson, D. (1999). Going beyond cultural pluralism: Science education for sociopolitical action. *Science Education, 83*(6), 775–796.

Hodson, D., & Dennick, R. (1994). Antiracist education: A special role for the history of science and technology. *School Science and Mathematics, 94*(5), 255–262.

Howes, E. V. (2002). Learning to teach science for all in the elementary grades: What do prospective teachers bring? *Journal of Research in Science Teaching, 39*(9), 845–869.

Hudicourt-Barnes, J. (2003). The use of argumentation in Haitian Creole science classrooms. *Harvard Educational Review, 73*(10), 73–93.

Inhelder, B., & Piaget, J. (1964). *The early growth of logic in the child, classification and seriation*. New York: Harper & Row.

Irzik, G., & Irzik, S. (2002). Which multiculturalism? *Science and Education, 11*(4), 393–403.

Jegede, O. J., & Aikenhead, G. S. (1999). Transcending cultural borders: Implications for science teaching. *Research in Science and Technology Education, 17*(1), 45–66.

Jegede, O. J., & Okebukola, P. A. (1991a). The effect of instruction on socio-cultural beliefs hindering the learning of science. *Journal of Research in Science Teaching, 28*(3), 275–285.

Jegede, O. J., & Okebukola, P. A. (1991b). The relationship between African traditional cosmology and students' acquisition of a science process skill. *International Journal of Science Education, 13*(1), 37–47.

Jegede, O. J., & Okebukola, P. A. (1992). Differences in sociocultural environment perceptions associated with gender in science classrooms. *Journal of Research in Science Teaching, 29*, 637–647.

Jiménez, R. T., & Gersten, R. (1999). Lessons and dilemmas derived from the literacy instruction of two Latina/o teachers. *American Educational Research Journal, 36*(2), 265–301.

Jorgenson, O. (2000). The need for more ethnic teachers: Addressing the critical shortage in American public schools. *Teachers College Record*. On-line format only. Date published: September 13, 2000. http://www.tcrecord.org ID Number: 10551.

Kahle, J. B. (1998). Equitable systemic reform in science and mathematics: Assessing progress. *Journal of Women and Minorities in Science and Engineering, 4*, 91–112.

Kahle, J. B., & Kelly, M. K. (2001). Equity in reform: Case studies of five middle schools involved in systemic reform. *Journal of Women and Minorities in Science and Engineering, 7*, 79–96.

Kahle, J. B., Meece, J., & Scantlebury, K. (2000). Urban African-American middle school science students: Does standards-based teaching make a difference? *Journal of Research in Science Teaching, 37*(9), 1019–1041.

Kawagley, A. O., Norris-Tull, D., & Norris-Tull, R. A. (1998). The indigenous worldview of Yupiaq culture: Its scientific nature and relevance to the practice and teaching of science. *Journal of Research in Science Teaching, 35*(2), 133–144.

Kawasaki, K. (1996). The concepts of science in Japanese and Western education. *Science & Education, 5*(1), 1–20.

Keil, F. C., & Wilson, R. A. (2000). *Explanation and cognition*. Cambridge, MA: MIT Press.

Kelly, G. J., & Breton, T. (2001). Framing science as disciplinary inquiry in bilingual classrooms. *Electronic Journal of Science and Literacy, 1*(1). Available online, accessed October 26, 2009, from http://www2.sjsa.edu/elementaryed/ejlts/

Kennedy, M. M. (1998). Education reform and subject matter knowledge. *Journal of Research and Science Teaching, 35*(3), 249–263.

Kerbow, D. (1996). Patterns of urban student mobility and local school reform. *Journal of Education for Students Placed At Risk, 1*, 147–169.

Kesidou, S., & Roseman, J. E. (2002). How well do middle school science programs measure up? Findings from Project 2061's curriculum review. *Journal of Research in Science Teaching, 39*(6), 522–549.

Kieffer, M. J., Lesaux, N. K., Rivera, M., & Francis, D. J. (2009). Accommodations for English language learners on large-scale assessments: A meta-analysis on effectiveness and validity. *Review of Educational Research, 79*(3), 1168–1201.

Klahr, D. (2000). *Exploring science: The cognition and development of discovery processes.* Cambridge, MA: MIT Press.

Klein, S. P., Jovanovic, J., Stecher, B. M., McCaffrey, D., Shavelson, R. J., Haertel, E., Solano-Flores, G., & Comfort, K. (1997). Gender and racial/ethnic differences on performance assessment in science. *Educational Evaluation and Policy Analysis, 19*(2), 83–97.

Knapp, M. S. (1997). Between systemic reforms and the mathematics and science classroom: The dynamics of innovation, implementation, and professional learning. *Review of Educational Research, 67*, 227–266.

Knapp, M. S., & Plecki, M. L. (2001). Investing in the renewal of urban science teaching. *Journal of Research in Science Teaching, 38*(10), 1089–1100.

Krajcik, J., Blumenfeld, P. C., Marx, R. W., Bass, K. M., & Fredricks, J. (1998). Inquiry in project-based science classrooms: Initial attempts by middle school students. *Journal of the Learning Sciences, 7*, 313–350.

Krajcik, J., Blumenfeld, P. C., Marx, R., & Solloway, E. (1994). A collaborative model for helping middle grade teachers learn project-based instruction. *The Elementary School Journal, 94*, 483–498.

Krashen, S. (1981). *Second language acquisition and second language learning.* New York: Pergamon Press.

Krugly-Smolska, E. (1996). Scientific culture, multiculturalism and the science classroom. *Science and Education, 5*(1), 21–29.

Kuhn, D. (1991). *The skills of argument.* Cambridge: Cambridge University Press.

Kuhn, D., White, S. H., Klahr, D., & Carver, S. M. (1995). *Strategies of knowledge acquisition.* Chicago, IL: University of Chicago Press.

Labov, W. (1966). *The social stratification of English in New York City.* Washington, DC: Center for Applied Linguistics.

Lacelle-Peterson, M. W., & Rivera, C. (1994). Is it real for all kids? A framework for equitable assessment policies for English language learners. *Harvard Educational Review, 64*, 55–75.

Ladson-Billings, G. (1994). *The dreamkeepers: Successful teachers of African American children.* San Francisco, CA: Jossey-Bass Publishers.

Ladson-Billings, G. (1995). Toward a theory of culturally relevant pedagogy. *American Educational Research Journal, 32*(3), 465–491.

Ladson-Billings, G. (1999). Preparing teachers for diverse student populations: A critical race theory perspective. *Review of Research in Education: Vol. 24* (pp. 211–248). Washington, DC: American Educational Research Association.

Latour, B., & Woolgar, S. (1986). *Laboratory life: The social construction of scientific facts.* Princeton, NJ: Princeton University Press.

Lave, J., & Wenger, E. (1991). *Situated learning: Legitimate peripheral participation.* New York: Cambridge University Press.

Lawrenz, F., Huffman, D., & Welch, W. (2001). The science achievement of various subgroups of alternative assessment formats. *Science Education, 85*(3), 279–290.

Lee, C. D. (2001). Is October Brown Chinese? A cultural modeling activity system for underachieving students. *American Educational Research Journal, 38*(1), 97–141.

Lee, H. S., & Songer, N. B. (2003). Making authentic science accessible to students. *International Journal of Science Education, 25*(1), 1–26.

Lee, J. S., & Anderson, K. T. (2009). Negotiating linguistic and cultural identities: Theorizing and constructing opportunities and risks in education. In V. L. Gadsden, J. E. Davis, & A. J. Artiles (Eds.), *Review of research in education: Vol. 33* (pp. 181–211). Washington, DC: American Educational Research Association.

Lee, O. (1996). Diversity and equity for Asian American students in science education. *Science Education, 81*, 107–122.

Lee, O. (1999a). Equity implications based on the conceptions of science achievement in major reform documents. *Review of Educational Research, 69*(1), 83–115.

Lee, O. (1999b). Science knowledge, worldviews, and information sources in social and cultural contexts: Making sense after a natural disaster. *American Educational Research Journal, 36*(2), 187–219.

Lee, O. (2002). Science inquiry for elementary students from diverse backgrounds. In W. G. Secada (Ed.), *Review of research in education: Vol. 26* (pp. 23–69). Washington, DC: American Educational Research Association.

Lee, O. (2003). Equity for culturally and linguistically diverse students in science education: A research agenda. *Teachers College Record, 105*(3), 465–489.

Lee, O. (2004). Teacher change in beliefs and practices in science and literacy instruction with English language learners. *Journal of Research in Science Teaching, 41*(1), 65–93.

Lee, O. (2005). Science education and English language learners: Synthesis and research agenda. *Review of Educational Research, 75*(4), 491–530.

Lee, O., & Buxton, C. A. (2008). Science curriculum and student diversity: Culture, language, and socioeconomic status. *The Elementary School Journal, 109*(2), 123–137.

Lee, O., Buxton, C. A., Lewis, S., & LeRoy, K. (2006). Science inquiry and student diversity: Enhanced abilities and continuing difficulties after an instructional intervention. *Journal of Research in Science Teaching, 43*(7), 607–636.

Lee, O., Deaktor, R., Enders, C., & Lambert, J. (2008). Impact of a multi-year professional development intervention on science achievement of culturally and linguistically diverse elementary students. *Journal of Research in Science Teaching, 45*(6), 726–747.

Lee, O., Deaktor, R. A., Hart, J. E., Cuevas, P., & Enders, C. (2005). An instructional intervention's impact on the science and literacy achievement of culturally and linguistically diverse elementary students. *Journal of Research in Science Teaching, 42*(8), 857–887.

Lee, O., & Fradd, S. H. (1996a). Literacy skills in science performance among culturally and linguistically diverse students. *Science Education, 80*(6), 651–671.

Lee, O., & Fradd, S. H. (1996b). Interactional patterns of linguistically diverse students and teachers: Insights for promoting science learning. *Linguistics and Education: An International Research Journal, 8*, 269–297.

Lee, O., & Fradd, S. H. (1998). Science for all, including students from non-English language backgrounds. *Educational Researcher, 27*(3), 12–21.

Lee, O., Fradd, S. H., & Sutman, F. X. (1995). Science knowledge and cognitive strategy use among culturally and linguistically diverse students. *Journal of Research in Science Teaching, 32*, 797–816.

Lee, O., Hart, J., Cuevas, P., & Enders, C. (2004). Professional development in inquiry-based science for elementary teachers of diverse students. *Journal of Research in Science Teaching, 41*(10), 1021–1043.

Lee, O., LeRoy, K., Thornton, C., Adamson, K., Maerten-Rivera, J., & Lewis, S. (2008). Teachers' perspectives on a professional development intervention to improve science instruction among English language learners. *Journal of Science Teacher Education, 19*, 41–67.

Lee, O., Lewis, S., Adamson, K., Maerten-Rivera, J., & Secada, W. G. (2008). Urban elementary school teachers' knowledge and practices in teaching science to English language learners. *Science Education, 92*(4), 733–758.

Lee, O., & Luykx, A. (2005). Dilemmas in scaling up educational innovations with non-mainstream students in elementary school science. *American Educational Research Journal, 43*, 411–438.

Lee, O., Luykx, A., Buxton, C. A., & Shaver, A. (2007). The challenge of altering elementary school teachers' beliefs and practices regarding linguistic and cultural diversity in science instruction. *Journal of Research in Science Teaching, 44*(9), 1269–1291.

Lee, O., Maerten-Rivera, J., Penfield, R. D., LeRoy, K., & Secada, W. G. (2008). Science achievement of English language learners in urban elementary schools: Results of a first-year professional development intervention. *Journal of Research in Science Teaching, 45*, 31–52.

Lee, O., Mahotiere, M., Salinas, A., Penfield, R. D., & Maerten-Rivera, J. (2009). Science writing achievement among English language learners: Results of three-year intervention in urban elementary schools. *Bilingual Research Journal, 32*(2), 153–167.

Lee, O., & Paik, S. (2000). Conceptions of science achievement in major reform documents. *School Science and Mathematics, 100*(1), 16–26.

Lee, O., Penfield, R. D., & Maerten-Rivera, J. (2009). Effects of fidelity of implementation on science achievement gains among English language learners. *Journal of Research in Science Teaching, 46*(7), 836–859.

Lee, V., & Smith, J. B. (1993). Effects of school restructuring on the achievement and engagement of middle grade students. *Sociology of Education, 66*, 164–187.

Lee, V., & Smith, J. B. (1995). Effects of high school restructuring and size on gains in achievement and engagement for early secondary school students. *Sociology of Education, 68*, 241–247.

Lee, V., Smith, J., Croninger, J. B., & Robert, G. (1997). How high school organization influences the equitable distribution of learning in mathematics and science. *Sociology of Education, 70*, 128–150.

Lehrer, R., & Schauble, L. (2000). Modeling in mathematics and science. In R. Glaser (Ed.), *Advances in instructional psychology: Vol. 5* (pp. 101–159). Mahwah, NJ: Lawrence Erlbaum Associates.

Lemke, J. L. (1990). *Talking science: Language, learning and values.* Norwood, NJ: Ablex.

Lemke, J. L. (2001). Articulating communities: Sociocultural perspectives on science education. *Journal of Research in Science Teaching, 38*(3), 296–316.

Lipka, J. (1998). *Transforming the culture of schools: Yup'ik Eskimo examples.* Mahwah, NJ: Erlbaum.

Loeb, S., Darling-Hammond, L., & Luczak, J. (2005). How teaching conditions predict teacher turnover in California schools. *Peabody Journal of Education, 80*(3), 44–70.

Longino, H. (1990). *Science as social knowledge: Values and objectivity in scientific inquiry.* Princeton, NJ: Princeton University Press.

Loucks-Horsley, S., Hewson, P. W., Love, N., & Stiles, K. E. (1998*). Designing professional development for teachers of science and mathematics.* Thousand Oaks, CA: Corwin Press.

Loving, C. C. (1997). From the summit of truth to its slippery slopes: Science education's journey through positivist-postmodern territory. *American Educational Research Journal, 34*, 421–452.

Loving, C. C. (1998). Cortes' multicultural empowerment model and generative teaching and learning in science. *Science & Education, 7*, 533–552.

Lubienski, S. (2003). Celebrating diversity and denying disparities: A critical assessment. *Educational Researcher, 32*(8), 30–38.

Luft, J. A. (1999). The border crossings of a multicultural science education enthusiast. *School Science and Mathematics, 99*(7), 380–388.

Luft, J. A., Bragg, J., & Peters, C. (1999). Learning to teach in a diverse setting: A case study of a multicultural science education enthusiast. *Science Education, 83*(5), 527–543.

Luykx, A., & Lee, O. (2007). Measuring instructional congruence in elementary science classrooms: Pedagogical and methodological components of a theoretical framework. *Journal of Research in Science Teaching, 44*(3), 424–447.

Luykx, A., Lee, O., & Edwards, U. (2008). Lost in translation: Negotiating meaning in a beginning ESOL science classroom. *Educational Policy, 22*(5), 640–674.

Luykx, A., Lee, O., Mahotiere, M., Lester, B., Hart, J., & Deaktor, R. (2007). Cultural and home language influence in elementary students' constructed responses on science assessments. *Teachers College Record, 109*(4), 897–926.

Lynch, M. (1985). *Art and artifact in laboratory science: A study of shop work and shop talk in a research laboratory*. Boston: Routledge and Kegan Paul.

Lynch, S. (2000). *Equity and science education reform*. Mahwah, NJ: Erlbaum Associates.

Lynch, S., Kuipers, J., Pyke, C., & Szesze, M. (2005). Examining the effects of a highly rated science curriculum unit on diverse populations: Results from a planning grant. *Journal of Research in Science Teaching, 42*(8), 912–946.

Maple, S., & Stage, F. (1991). Influences on the choice of math/science major by gender and ethnicity. *American Educational Research Journal, 28*, 37–60.

Marx, R. W., Blumenfeld, P. C., Krajcik, J. S., Fishman, B., Soloway, E., Geier, R., & Tal, R. T. (2004). Inquiry-based science in the middle grades: Assessment of learning in urban systemic reform. *Journal of Research in Science Teaching, 41*(10), 1063–1080.

Marx, R. W., & Harris, C. J. (2006). No Child Left Behind and science education: Opportunities, challenges, and risks. *The Elementary School Journal, 106*(5), 467–477.

Matthews, C. E., & Smith, W. S. (1994). Native American related materials in elementary science instruction. *Journal of Research in Science Teaching, 31*(4), 363–380.

Matthews, M. R. (1998). The nature of science and science teaching. In B. Fraser & K. Tobin (Eds.), *International handbook of science education: Part 2* (pp. 981–1000). Dordrecht, the Netherlands: Kluwer Academic Publishers.

McCarty, T. L., Lynch, R. H., Wallace, S., & Benally, A. (1991). Classroom inquiry and Navajo learning styles: A call for reassessment. *Anthropology and Education Quarterly, 22*(1), 42–59.

McDonald, S-K., Keesler, V. A., Kauffman, N. J., & Schneider, B. (2006). Scaling-up exemplary interventions. *Educational Researcher, 35*(3), 15–24.

McKinley, E. (2004). Locating the global: Culture, language and science education for indigenous students. *International Journal of Science Education, 27*(2), 227–241.

McKinley, E. (2005). Locating the global: Culture, language and science education for indigenous students. *International Journal of Science Education, 27*(2), 227–241.

McKinley, E. (2007). Postcolonialism, indigenous students, and science education. In S. K. Abell & N. G. Lederman (Eds.), *Handbook of research in science education* (2nd ed., pp. 199–226). Mahwah, NJ: Lawrence Erlbaum Associates.

McKinley, E., Waiti, P. M., & Bell, B. (1992). Language, culture and science education. *International Journal of Science Education, 14*(5), 579–595.

McLaughlin, M. W., Shepard, L. A., & O'Day, J. A. (1995). *Improving education through standards-based reform: A report by the national academy of education panel on standards-based education reform.* Stanford, CA: Stanford University, National Academy of Education.

McNeil, L. M. (2000). Creating new inequalities: Contradictions of reform. *Phi Delta Kappan, 81*(10), 729–734.

Mehana, M., & Reynolds, A. (2004). School mobility and achievement: A meta-analysis. *Children and Youth Services Review, 26*, 93–119.

Merino, B., & Hammond, L. (2001). How do teachers facilitate writing for bilingual learners in "sheltered constructivist" science? *Electronic Journal in Science and Literacy, 1*(1). Available online, retrieved October 26, 2009, from http://www2.sjsu.edu/elementaryed/ejlts/

Metz, K. E. (1991). Development of explanation: Incremental and fundamental change in children's physics knowledge. *Journal of Research in Science Teaching, 28*(9), 785–797.

Moje, E., Collazo, T., Carillo, R., & Marx, R. W. (2001). "Maestro, what is quality?": Examining competing discourses in project-based science. *Journal of Research in Science Teaching, 38*(4), 469–495.

Moje, E. B., Ciechanowski, K. M., Kramer, K., Ellis, L., Carrillo, R., & Collazo, T. (2004). Working toward third space in content area literacy: An examination of everyday funds of knowledge and discourse. *Reading Research Quarterly, 39*(1), 38–70.

Moll, L. C. (1992). Bilingual classroom studies and community analysis: Some recent trends. *Educational Researcher, 21*(2), 20–24.

Moore, F. M. (2007a). Preparing elementary preservice teachers for urban elementary science classrooms: Challenging cultural biases toward diverse students. *Journal of Science Teacher Education, 19*(1), 85–109.

Moore, F. M. (2007b). Teachers' coping strategies for teaching science in a "low performing" school district. *Journal of Science Teacher Education, 18*(5), 773–794.

Moore, F. M. (2007c). Language in science education as a gatekeeper to learning, teaching, and professional development. *Journal of Science Teacher Education, 18*(2), 319–343.

Moore, F. M. (2008a). The role of the elementary science teacher and linguistic diversity. *Journal of Elementary Science Education, 20*(3), 49–61.

Moore, F. M. (2008b). Agency, identity, and social justice education: Preservice teachers' thoughts on becoming agents of change in urban elementary science classrooms. *Research in Science Education, 38*, 589–610.

Moore, F. M. (2008c). Positional identity and science teacher professional development. *Journal of Research in Science Teaching, 45*(6), 684–710.

Moore, F. M. (in press). Confronting assumptions, biases, and stereotypes in preservice teachers' conceptualizations of science teaching through the use of book clubs. *Journal of Research in Science Teaching.*

Mowbray, C. T., Holter, M. C., Teague, G. B., & Bybee, D. (2003). Fidelity criteria: Development, measurement, and validation. *American Journal of Evaluation, 24*(3), 315–340.

Muller, P. A., Stage, F. K., & Kinzie, J. (2001). Science achievement growth trajectories: Understanding factors related to gender and racial-ethnic differences in precollege science achievement. *American Educational Research Journal, 38*(4), 981–1012.

National Center for Education and the Economy. (2006). *Tough choices or tough times: The Report of the New Commission on the Skills of the American Workforce.* New York: Jossey-Bass.

National Center for Education Statistics. (1996). *Pursuing excellence: A study of U.S. eighth-grade mathematics and science teaching, learning, curriculum, and achievement in international context.* Washington, DC: U.S. Department of Education, Office of Educational Research and Improvement.

National Center for Education Statistics. (1999). *Teacher quality: A report on the preparation and qualifications of public school teachers.* Washington, DC: U. S. Department of Education, Office of Educational Research and Improvement.

National Center for Education Statistics. (2000). *Highlights from the trends in international mathematics and science study (TIMSS) 1999.* Washington, DC: U.S. Department of Education.

National Center for Education Statistics. (2004). *Highlights from the trends in international mathematics and science study (TIMSS) 2003.* Washington, DC: U.S. Department of Education.

National Center for Education Statistics. (2005). *The nation's report card: Science 2005.* Washington, DC: U.S. Department of Education.

National Center for Education Statistics. (2006a). *The condition of education, 2006.* Washington, DC: U.S. Department of Education.

National Center for Education Statistics. (2006b). *U.S. student and adult performance on international assessments of education achievement.* Washington, DC: U.S. Department of Education.

National Center for Education Statistics. (2008). *The condition of education, 2008.* Washington, DC: U.S. Department of Education.

National Clearinghouse for English Language Acquisition. (2007). *The growing numbers of limited English proficient students: 1996–2006.* Washington, DC: NCELA.

National Council of La Raza. (2008). *NCLR 2008 annual report.* Washington, DC: NCLR.

National Institute of Child Health and Human Development—Early Child Care Research Network. (2005). A day in third grade: A large-scale study of classroom quality and teacher and student behavior. *The Elementary School Journal, 105,* 305–323.

National Research Council. (1996). *National science education standards.* Washington, DC: National Academy Press.

National Research Council. (2000). *Inquiry and the national science education standards: A guide for teaching and learning.* Washington, DC: National Academy Press.

National Research Council. (2007). *Taking science to school: Learning and teaching science in grades K–8.* Washington, DC: National Academy Press.

National Science Foundation. (1996). *Review of instructional materials for middle school science.* Washington, DC: Author.

National Science Foundation. (1998). *Infusing equity in systemic reform: An implementation scheme.* Washington, DC: Author.

National Science Foundation. (2002). *Women, minorities, and persons with disabilities in science and engineering.* Arlington, VA: Author.

National Science Foundation. (2009). *Women, minorities, and persons with disabilities in science and engineering.* Arlington, VA: Author.

Nelson-Barber, S., & Estrin, E. T. (1995). Bringing Native American perspectives to mathematics and science teaching. *Theory into Practice, 34*(3), 174–185.

Nelson-Barber, S., & Estrin, E. T. (1996). *Culturally responsive mathematics and science education for native students.* San Francisco, CA: Far West Laboratory for Educational Research and Development.

Ninnes, P. (1994). Toward a functional learning system for Solomon Island secondary science classrooms. *International Journal of Science Education, 16*(6), 677–688.

Ninnes, P. (1995). Informal learning contexts in Solomon Islands and their implications for the cross-cultural classroom. *International Journal of Educational Development, 15*(1), 15–26.

Ninnes, P. (2000). Representations of indigenous knowledges in secondary school science textbooks in Australia and Canada. *International Journal of Science Education, 22*(6), 603–617.

No Child Left Behind Act (2002). Public Law No. 107–110, 115 Stat. 1425.

Norman, O. (1998). Marginalized discourses and scientific literacy. *Journal of Research in Science Teaching, 35*(4), 365–374.

Norman, O., Ault, C. R., Bentz, B., & Meskimen, L. (2001). The Black-White "achievement gap" as a perennial challenge of urban science education: A sociocultural and historical overview with implications for research and practice. *Journal of Research in Science Teaching, 38*(10), 1101–1114.

Nussbaum, E. M., Hamilton, L. S., & Snow, R. E. (1997). Enhancing the validity and usefulness of large-scale educational assessments: IV. NELS: 88 science achievement to 12th grade. *American Educational Research Journal, 34*(1), 151–173.

Oakes, J. (1990). Opportunities, achievement, and choice: Women and minority students in science and mathematics. In C. B. Cazden (Ed.), *Review of research in education: Vol. 16* (pp. 153–221). Washington, DC: American Educational Research Association.

O'Donnell, C. (2008). Defining, conceptualizing, and measuring fidelity of implementation and its relationship to outcomes in K–12 curriculum intervention research. *Review of Educational Research, 78*(1), 33–84.

Ogawa, M. (1995). Science education in a multiscience perspective. *Science Education, 79*(5), 583–593.

Ogunniyi, M. B. (2007a). Teachers' stances and practical arguments regarding a science-indigenous knowledge curriculum: Part I. *International Journal of Science Education, 29*(8), 963–986.

Ogunniyi, M. B. (2007b). Teachers' stances and practical arguments regarding a science-indigenous knowledge curriculum: Part II: *International Journal of Science Education, 29*(10), 1189–1207.

Okebukola, P. A., & Jegede, O. J. (1990). Eco-cultural influences upon students' concept attainment in science. *Journal of Research in Science Teaching, 27*(7), 651–660.

O'Loughlin, M. (1992). Rethinking science education: Beyond Piagetian constructivism toward a sociocultural model of teaching and learning. *Journal of Research in Science Teaching, 29*, 791–820.

Orfield, M. (2002). *American metropolitics: The new suburban reality.* Washington, DC: Brookings Institution Press.

Osborne, A. B. (1996). Practice into theory into practice: Culturally relevant pedagogy for students we have marginalized and normalized. *Anthropology and Education Quarterly, 27*(3), 285–314.

Osborne, J., Erduran, S., & Simon, S. (2004). Enhancing the quality of argument in school science. *Journal of Research in Science Teaching, 41*(10), 994–1020.

O'Sullivan, C. Y., Lauko, M. A., Grigg, W. S., Qian, J., & Zhang, J. (2003). *The nation's report card: Science 2000.* Washington, DC: U.S. Department of Education, Institute of Education Sciences.

Palincsar, A. S., & Magnusson, S. J. (2001). The interplay of firsthand and text-based investigations to model and support the development of scientific knowledge and reasoning. In S. Carver & D. Klahr (Eds.), *Cognition and instruction: Twenty-five years of progress* (pp. 151–194). Mahwah, NJ: Lawrence Erlbaum.

Parsons, E. C. (2000). Culturalizing science instruction: What is it, what does it look like and why do we need it? *Journal of Science Teacher Education, 11*(3), 207–219.

Parsons, E. C. (2008). Learning contexts, Black cultural ethos, and the science achievement of African American students in an urban middle school. *Journal of Research in Science Teaching, 45*(6), 665–683.

Parsons, E. C., Foster, S., Travis, C., & Simpson, J. (2007). Diversity knowledge in science teacher education—translating concept to instruction: An example specific to African Americans. *Journal of Science Teacher Education, 19*(1), 69–83.

Penfield, R. D., & Lee, O. (in press). Test-based accountability: Potential benefits and pitfalls of science assessment with student diversity. *Journal of Research in Science Teaching.*

Peng, S., & Hill, S. (1994). Characteristics and educational experiences of high-achieving minority secondary students in science and mathematics. *Journal of Women and Minorities in Science and Engineering, 1*, 137–152.

Piaget, J. (1973). *The child and reality: Problems of genetic psychology.* New York: Grossman Publishers.

Porter, A. C. (1995). The uses and misuses of opportunity-to-learn standards. *Educational Researcher, 24*, 21–27.

Prophet, R. B. (1990). Rhetoric and reality in science curriculum development in Botswana. *International Journal of Science Education, 12*(1), 13–23.

Prophet, R. B., & Rowell, P. M. (1993). Coping and control: Science teaching strategies in Botswana. *Qualitative Studies in Education, 6*, 197–209.

Rahm, J. (2002). Emergent learning opportunities in an inner-city youth gardening program. *Journal of Research in Science Teaching, 39*(2), 164–184.

Raizen, S. (1998). Standards for science education. *Teachers College Record, 100*, 66–121.

Rakow, S. J., & Bermudez, A. B. (1993). Science is "ciencia": Meeting the needs of Hispanic American students. *Science Education, 77*, 547–560.

Raudenbush, S. W. (2007). Designing field trials of educational innovations. In B. Schneider & S. McDonald (Eds.), *Scale up in education: Vol. 2. Practice* (pp. 23–40). Lanham, MD: Rowman & Littlefield.

Remillard, J. T. (2005). Examining key concepts in research on teachers' use of mathematics curricula. *Review of Educational Research, 75*(2), 211–246.

Reveles, J. M., & Brown, B. A. (2008). Contextual shifting: Teachers emphasizing students' academic identity to promote scientific literacy. *Science Education, 92*, 1015–1041.

Reyes, M. (1992). Challenging venerable assumptions: Literacy instruction for linguistically diverse students. *Harvard Educational Review, 62*(4), 427–446.

Richardson, V., & Placier, P. (2001). Teacher change. In D. V. Richardson (Ed.), *Handbook of research on teaching* (4th ed., pp. 905–950). Washington, DC: American Educational Research Association.

Riggs, E. M. (2005). Field-based education and indigenous knowledge: Essential components of geoscience education for Native American communities. *Science Education, 89*, 296–313.

Rivet, A. E., & Krajcik, J. S. (2004). Achieving standards in urban systemic reform: An example of a sixth grade project-based science curriculum. *Journal of Research in Science Teaching, 41*(7), 669–693.

Rodriguez, A. (1997). The dangerous discourse of invisibility: A critique of the NRC's National Science Education Standards. *Journal of Research in Science Teaching, 34*, 19–37.

Rodriguez, A. (1998a). Busting open the meritocracy myth: Rethinking equity and student achievement in science education. *Journal of Women and Minorities in Science and Engineering, 4*(2, 3), 195–216.

Rodriguez, A. (1998b). Strategies for counter-resistance: Toward sociotransformative constructivism and learning to teach science for diversity and for understanding. *Journal of Research in Science Teaching, 35*(6), 589–622.

Rodriguez, A. J. (2001a). Courage and the researcher's gaze: (Re)defining our roles as cultural warriors for social change. *Journal of Science Teacher Education, 12*(3), 277–294.

Rodriguez, A. J. (2001b). From gap gazing to promising cases: Moving toward equity in urban education reform. *Journal of Research in Science Teaching, 38*(10), 1115–1129.

Rodriguez, A. J., & Berryman, C. (2002). Using sociotransformative constructivism to teach for understanding in diverse classrooms: A beginning teacher's journey. *American Educational Research Journal, 39*(4), 1017–1045.

Rodríguez, A., & Kitchen, R. S. (Eds.) (2005). *Preparing prospective mathematics and science teachers to teach for diversity: Promising strategies for transformative action.* Mahwah, NJ: Erlbaum Associates.

Romberg, T. A., Carpenter, T., & Dremock, F. (Eds.). (2005). *Understanding mathematics and science matters.* Mahwah, NJ: Lawrence Erlbaum Associates.

Rosebery, A. S., & Warren, B. (Eds.). (2008). *Teaching science to English language learners: Building on students' strengths.* Arlington, VA: National Science Teachers Association.

Rosebery, A. S., Warren, B., & Conant, F. R. (1992). Appropriating scientific discourse: Findings from language minority classrooms. *The Journal of the Learning Sciences, 21*, 61–94.

Roth, W-M., Tobin, K., Carambo, C., & Dalland, C. (2004). Coteaching: Creating resources for learning and learning to teach chemistry in urban high schools. *Journal of Research in Science Teaching, 41*(9), 882–904.

Ruby, A. (2006). Improving science achievement at high-poverty urban middle schools. *Science Education, 90*, 1005–1027.

Rudolph, J. (2002). *Scientists in the classroom: The Cold War reconstruction of American science education.* New York: Palgrave.

Ruiz-Primo, M. A., & Shavelson, R. J. (1996). Rhetoric and reality in science performance assessments: An update. *Journal of Research in Science Teaching, 33*(10), 1045–1063.

Rumberger, R. (2003). The causes and consequences of student mobility. *The Journal of Negro Education, 72,* 6–21.

Schauble, L. (1996). The development of reasoning in knowledge-rich contexts. *Developmental Psychology, 32*(1), 102–119.

Schibeci, R. A., & Riley, J. P. (1986). Influence of students' background and perceptions of science attitudes and achievement. *Journal of Research in Science Teaching, 23*(3), 177–187.

Schmidt, W. H., McKnight, C. C., & Raizen, S. A. (1997). *A splintered vision: An investigation of U.S. science and mathematics education.* Dordrecht, the Netherlands: Kluwer Academic Publishers.

Schneider, B., & McDonald, S. (2007a). (Eds.). *Scale up in education: Vol. 2. Ideas in principle.* Lanham, MD: Rowman & Littlefield.

Schneider, B., & McDonald, S. (2007b). (Eds.). *Scale up in education: Vol. 2. Practice.* Lanham, MD: Rowman & Littlefield.

Sconiers, Z. D., & Rosiek, J. L. (2000). Historical perspective as an important element of teachers' knowledge: A sonata-form case study of equity issues in a chemistry classroom: Voices inside schools. *Harvard Educational Review, 70*(3), 370–404.

Seiler, G. (2001). Reversing the "standard" direction: Science emerging from the lives of African American students. *Journal of Research in Science Teaching, 38*(9), 1000–1014.

Seiler, G., & Elmesky, R. (2007). The role of communal practices in the generation of capital and emotional energy among urban African American students in science classrooms. *Teachers College Record, 109*(2), 391–419.

Seiler, G., Tobin, K., & Sokolic, J. (2001). Design, technology, and science: Sites for learning, resistance, and social reproduction in urban schools. *Journal of Research in Science Teaching, 38,* 746–767.

Settlage, J., & Meadows, L. (2002). Standards-based reform and its unintended consequences: Implications for science education within America's urban schools. *Journal of Research in Science Teaching, 39*(2), 114–127.

Settlage, J., Southerland, S. A., Smith, L. K., & Ceglie, R. (2009). Constructing a doubt-free teaching self: Self-efficacy, teacher identity, and science instruction within diverse settings. *Journal of Research in Science Teaching, 46*(1), 102–125.

Shavelson, R. J., Baxter, G. P., & Pine, J. (1992). Performance assessments: Political rhetoric and measurement reality. *Educational Researcher, 24*(4), 22–27.

Shavelson, R. J., & Towne, L. (Eds.). (2002). *Scientific research in education.* Washington, DC: National Academy Press

Shaver, A., Cuevas, P., Lee, O., & Avalos, M. (2007). Teachers' perceptions of policy influences on science instruction with culturally and linguistically diverse elementary students. *Journal of Research in Science Teaching, 44*(5), 725–746.

Shaw, J. M. (1997). Threats to the validity of science performance assessments for English language learners. *Journal of Research in Science Teaching, 34*(7), 721–743.

Shumba, O. (1999). Relationship between secondary science teachers' orientation to traditional culture and beliefs concerning science instructional ideology. *Journal of Research in Science Teaching, 36*(3), 333–355.

Siegel, D. R., Esterly, J., Callahan, M. A., Wright, R., & Navarro, R. (2007). Conversations about science across activities in Mexican-descent families. *International Journal of Science Education, 29*(12), 1447–1466.

Siegel, H. (1997). Science education: Multicultural and universal. *Interchange, 28*(2), 97–108.

Siegel, H. (2002). Multiculturalism, universalism, and science education: In search of common ground. *Science Education, 86*(6), 803–820.

Siegel, M. A. (2007). Striving for equitable classroom assessments for linguistic minorities: Strategies for and effects of revising life science items. *Journal of Research in Science Teaching, 44*, 864–881.

Simpson, J. S., & Parsons, E. C. (2008). African American perspectives and informal science educational experiences. *Science Education, 93*, 293–321.

Smith, C. L., Maclin, D., Houghton, C., & Hennessey, M. G. (2000). Sixth-grade students' epistemologies of science: The impact of school science experiences on epistemological development. *Cognition and Instruction, 18*(3), 349–422.

Smith, F. M., & Hausafus, C. O. (1998). Relationship of family support and ethnic minority students' achievement in science and mathematics. *Science Education, 82*(1), 111–125.

Smith, M. S., & O'Day, J. (1991). Systemic school reform. In S. H. Fuhrman & B. Malen (Eds.), *The politics of curriculum and testing: The 1990 yearbook of the politics of education association* (pp. 233–268). Briston, PA: The Falmer Press.

Snively, G. (1990). Traditional native Indian beliefs, cultural values, and science instruction. *Canadian Journal of Native Education, 17*, 44–59.

Snively, G., & Corsiglia, J. (2001). Discovering indigenous science: Implications for science education. *Science Education, 85*(1), 6–34.

Solano-Flores, G. (2006). Language, dialect, and register: Sociolinguistics and the estimation of measurement error in the testing of English language learners. *Teachers College Record, 108*, 2354–2379.

Solano-Flores, G. (2008). Who is given tests in what language by whom, when, and where? The need for probabalistic views of language in the testing of English language learners. *Educational Researcher, 37*(4), 189–199.

Solano-Flores, G., Lara, J., Sexton, U., & Navarrete, C. (2001). *Testing English language learners: A sampler of student responses to science and mathematics test items.* Washington, DC: Council of Chief State School Officers.

Solano-Flores, G., & Nelson-Barber, S. (2001). On the cultural validity of science assessments. *Journal of Research in Science Teaching, 38*(5), 553–573.

Solano-Flores, G., & Trumbull, E. (2003). Examining language in context: The need for new research and practice paradigms in the testing of English-language learners. *Educational Researcher, 32*(2), 3–13.

Songer, N. B., Lee, H-S., & Kam, R. (2002). Technology-rich inquiry science in urban classrooms: What are the barriers to inquiry pedagogy? *Journal of Research in Science Teaching, 39*(2), 128–150.

Songer, N. B., Lee, H-S., & McDonald, S. (2003). Research towards an expanded understanding of inquiry science beyond one idealized standard. *Science Education, 87*(4), 490–516.

Southerland, S. A. (2000). Epistemic universalism and the shortcomings of curricular multicultural science education. *Science & Education, 9*, 289–307.

Southerland, S., & Gess-Newsome, J. (1999). Preservice teachers' views of inclusive science teaching as shaped by images of teaching, learning, and knowing. *Science Education, 83*(2), 131–150.

Southerland, S., Kittleson, J., Settlage, J., & Lanier, K. (2005). Individual and group mean-ing-making in an urban third grade classroom: Red fog, cold cans, and seeping vapor. *Journal of Research in Science Teaching, 42*(9), 1032–1061.

Southerland, S., Smith, L. K., Sowell, S. P., & Kittleson, J. M. (2007). Resisting unlearn-ing: Understanding science education's response to the United States' national ac-countability movement. In L. Parker (Ed.), *Review of research in education: Vol. 31* (pp. 45–77). Washington, DC: American Educational Research Association.

Spade, J., Columba, L., & Vanfossen, B. (1997). Tracking in mathematics and science courses and course-selection procedures. *Sociology of Education, 70*, 108–127.

Spillane, J. P., Diamond, J. B., Walker, L. J., Halverson, R., & Jita, L. (2001). Urban school leadership for elementary science instruction: Identifying and activating resources in an undervalued school subject. *Journal of Research in Science Teaching, 38*(8), 918–940.

Stanley, W. B., & Brickhouse, N. (1994). Multiculturalism, universalism, and science educa-tion. *Science Education, 78*(4), 387–398.

Stanley, W., & Brickhouse, N. (2001). Teaching sciences: The multicultural question revised. *Science Education, 85*(1), 35–49.

Stecher, B. M., & Klein, S. P. (1997). The cost of performance assessments in large-scale test-ing programs. *Educational Evaluation and Policy Analysis, 19*, 1–4.

Stephens, S. (2000). *Handbook for culturally responsive science curriculum.* Fairbanks, AK: Alaska Science Consortium and the Alaska Rural Systemic Initiative.

Stoddart, T., Pinal, A., Latzke, M., & Canaday, D. (2002). Integrating inquiry science and language development for English language learners. *Journal of Research in Science Teaching, 39*(8), 664–687.

Tal, T., Krajcik, J., & Blumenfeld, P. C. (2006). Urban schools' teachers enacting project-based science. *Journal of Research in Science Teaching, 43*(7), 722–745.

Tan, E., & Calabrese Barton, A. (2007). From peripheral to central, the story of Mela-nie's metamorphosis in an urban middle school science class. *Science Education, 92*, 567–590.

Tate, W. F. (2001). Science education as civil right: Urban schools and opportunity-to-learn considerations. *Journal of Research in Science Teaching, 38*(9), 1015–1028.

Teachers of English to Speakers of Other Languages. (1997). *ESL standards for pre-K–12 students.* Alexandria, VA: Author.

Teachers of English to Speakers of Other Languages. (2006). *Pre-K–12 English language proficiency standards.* Alexandra, VA: Author.

Temple, J., & Reynolds, A. (1999). School mobility and achievement: Longitudinal findings from an urban cohort. *Journal of School Psychology, 37*, 355–377.

Teresi, D. (2003). *Lost discoveries: The ancient roots of modern science: From the Babylonians to the Maya.* New York: Simon and Schuster.

Tharp, R., & Gallimore, R. (1988). *Rousing minds to life: Teaching, learning, and schooling in social context.* Cambridge, England: Cambridge University Press.

Tobin, K. (2000). Becoming an urban science educator. *Research in Science Education, 30*(1), 89–106.

Tobin, K., Roth, W., & Zimmerman, A. (2001). Learning to teach science in urban schools. *Journal of Research in Science Teaching, 38*(8), 941–964.

Tobin, K., Seiler, G., & Smith, M. W. (1999). Educating science teachers for the sociocultural diversity of urban schools. *Research in Science Education, 29*(1), 69–88.

Tobin, K., Seiler, G., & Walls, E. (1999). Reproduction of social class in the teaching and learning of science in urban high schools. *Research in Science Education, 29*(2), 171–187.

Toulmin, S. E. (1958). *The uses of argument*. Cambridge: Cambridge University Press.

Tuerk, P. W. (2005). Research in the high-stakes era: Achievement, resources, and No Child Left Behind. *Psychological Science, 16*, 419–425.

Upadhyay, B. R. (2006).Using students' lived experiences in an urban science classroom: An elementary school teacher's thinking. *Science Education, 90*, 94–110.

U.S. Census Bureau. (2005). *2005 American community survey*. Washington, DC: U.S. Department of Education.

U.S. Department of Education. (2007). *Participation in education: Elementary and secondary education*. Washington, DC: U.S. Department of Education.

Valeras, M., Becker, J., Luster, B., & Wenzel, S. (2002). When genres meet: Inquiry into a sixth-grade urban science class. *Journal of Research in Science Teaching, 39*(7), 579–605.

Valli, L. (1995). The dilemma of race: Learning to be color blind and color conscious. *Journal of Teacher Education, 46*(2), 120–129.

Van Eijck, M., & Roth, W-M. (2007). Keeping the local local: Recalibrating the status of science and traditional ecological knowledge (TEK) in education. *Science Education, 91*, 926–947.

Villegas, A. M., & Lucas, T. (2002). Preparing culturally responsive teachers: Rethinking the curriculum. *Journal of Teacher Education, 53*(1), 20–32.

Waldrip, B. G., & Taylor, P. C. (1999a). Standards for cultural contextualization of interpretive research: A Melanesian case. *International Journal of Science Education, 21*(3), 249–260.

Waldrip, B. G., & Taylor, P. C. (1999b). Permeability of students' worldviews to their school views in a non-Western developing country. *Journal of Research in Science Teaching, 36*(3), 289–303.

Warren, B., Ballenger, C., Ogonowski, M., Rosebery, A., & Hudicourt-Barnes, J. (2001). Rethinking diversity in learning science: The logic of everyday language. *Journal of Research in Science Teaching, 38*(5), 529–552.

Warren, B., & Rosebery, A. S. (1995). Equity in the future tense: Redefining relationships among teachers, students, and science in linguistic minority classroom. In W. G. Secada, E. Fennema, & L. B. Adajian (Eds.), *New directions for equity in mathematics education* (pp. 298–328). New York: Cambridge University Press.

Warren, B., & Rosebery, A. S., (1996). "This question is just too, too easy!" Students' perspectives on accountability in science. In L. Schauble & R. Glaser (Eds.), *Innovations in learning new environments for education* (pp. 97–125). Mahwah, NJ: Lawrence Erlbaum Associates.

Warren, B., Rosebery, A. S., & Conant, F. (1994). Discourse and social practice: Learning science in language minority classrooms. In D. Spencer (Ed.), *Adult biliteracy in the United States* (pp. 191–210). Washington, DC: Center for Applied Linguistics and Delta Systems Co.

Wideen, M. F., O'Shea, T., Pye, I., & Ivany, G. (1997). High-stakes testing and the teaching of science. *Canadian Journal of Education, 22*(4), 428–44.

Wiley, T. G., & Wright, W. E. (2004). Against the undertow: Language-minority education policy and politics in the "age of accountability." *Educational Policy, 18*(1), 142–168.

Wilson, S. M., & Berne, J. (1999). Teacher learning and the acquisition of professional knowledge: An examination of research on contemporary professional development. In A. Iran-Nejad & P. D. Pearson (Eds.), *Review of Research in Education* (pp. 173–209). Washington, DC: American Educational Research Association.

Wong-Fillmore, L., & Snow, C. (2002). *What teachers need to know about language.* Washington DC: Center for Applied Linguistics.

Yerrick, R. K., & Hoving, T. J. (2003). One foot on the dock and one foot on the boat: Differences among preservice science teachers' interpretations of field-based science methods in culturally diverse contexts. *Science Education, 87*(3), 390–418.

Zimmerman, C. (2000). The development of reasoning skills. *Developmental Review, 20*(1), 99–149.

Index

About the Authors

Okhee Lee is a professor at the School of Education, University of Miami, Florida. Her research areas include science education, language and culture, and teacher education. She was awarded a 1993–1995 National Academy of Education Spencer Post-Doctoral Fellowship. She was a 1996–1997 fellow at the National Institute for Science Education, Wisconsin Center for Education Research, University of Wisconsin–Madison. She received the Distinguished Career Award from the American Educational Research Association (AERA) Standing Committee for Scholars of Color in Education in 2003. She has directed research and teacher enhancement projects funded by the National Science Foundation, U.S. Department of Education, Spencer Foundation, and Florida Department of Education. Her current research projects implement and examine instructional interventions to promote science learning and English language development for elementary students from diverse language and cultural groups within a high-stakes testing policy context.

Cory A. Buxton is an associate professor at the College of Education at the University of Georgia. His research interests include the teaching and learning of science in multilingual and multicultural contexts. His past research has focused on using anthropological frameworks to explore and promote authentic science learning environments that build on students' funds of knowledge and promote social action. His current research focuses on using the context of science to create discursive spaces for students, parents, and teachers to come together to co-construct educational contexts that support academic rigor and cultural accommodation. His research has been funded by the National Science Foundation and by several private foundations. He serves as an associate editor of the *Journal of Research in Science Teaching* and as a reviewer for numerous other journals of educational research. Buxton has co-authored two books published by Sage Publishing.